Christmas 1995

"I love you, dad"

———————

Tigger

Parson Jack Russell Terriers

PARSON JACK RUSSELL TERRIERS
AN OWNER'S COMPANION

Jean and Frank Jackson

The Crowood Press

First published in 1990 by
The Crowood Press Ltd
Ramsbury, Marlborough
Wiltshire SN8 2HR

This impression 1994

British Library Cataloguing in Publication Data

Jackson, Jean *1935–*
    Parson Jack Russell terriers.
    1. Jack Russell terriers
    I. Title   II. Jackson, Frank *1933–*
    636.7'55

    ISBN 1 85223 392 3

Line-drawings by Aileen Hanson

Typeset by Avonset, Midsomer Norton, Bath
Printed by Redwood Books, Trowbridge, Wiltshire

Contents

Introduction

True terriers they were, but differing from the present show
dogs as the wild eglantine differs from a garden rose.

The Reverend John Russell

What are generally claimed to be Jack Russell Terriers probably
outnumber every other breed not just in Britain but in many other
countries throughout the world. Sadly, what are claimed to be Jack
Russell Terriers may often have little or no right to be called terriers
let alone Jack Russell Terriers. They exploit the name of a famous
breeder of Fox Terriers who died over 100 years ago.

Yet terriers of which the Parson might have been very proud and
which certainly would not have looked out of place in his kennel still
exist and still have their band of devoted admirers. These terriers
have recently been officially recognised by the Kennel Club in Britain
and are on the verge of official recognition in other parts of the world.
Recognition will enable their supporters to make use of all the
services provided by the Kennel Club as well as to take part in all the
activities which take place under Kennel Club Rules, while leaving
them free to continue to enjoy all the traditional activities in which
they have been involved for many years.

Our increasingly urbanised lives make it less easy for us fully to
understand what the Parson bred his terriers for and what characteristics he regarded as important. In addition, what appear to be
growing threats to the existence of the field sports which gave rise to
all our sporting breeds of terriers, hounds and gundogs, introduce
the possibility that at some time in the future it may no longer be
possible for many of these breeds to follow their traditional occupations. Recognition might, therefore, by offering alternative activities be regarded as an insurance against the possibility that these
breeds might disappear along with their traditional activities (the
most recent example being Otterhounds, whose traditional occu-

pations have already been lost). Also, official recognition provides a framework of authority, access to reliable services, a means to national and international influence, and opportunity to become involved as equals with other recognised breeds, which can only be of benefit.

This book represents an attempt to chronicle something of the origins, history, purpose and development of the Parson Jack Russell Terrier. We examine the struggle for recognition and its likely consequences and presume to offer advice to established breed enthusiasts for whom recognition will open doors to new activities, as well as to those whose admiration for the breed is of more recent origin.

The extent to which recognition of an old-fashioned type of dog distinct from its modern counterpart (and with the precedent of the Cavalier King Charles Spaniel also in mind) might signal the beginning of a growing appreciation of native British breeds in their old form, is a matter for conjecture and, perhaps, hope. Too often the desire to 'improve' has led to breeds developing into grotesque caricatures of their former selves. Certainly many breeders and exhibitors are becoming increasingly conscious of the importance of the origins, history and purpose of their breeds. We hope that this book will interest those who regard such matters as important to the Parson Jack Russell Terrier.

In writing this book we have received generous and invaluable assistance from a number of people. We are especially grateful to Ruth Hussey-Wilford and Sheila Atter, respectively Secretary and Registrar of the Parson Jack Russell Terrier Club; to Vernon Bartlett who, throughout a long life has remained true to the old type of terrier and who has provided valuable material; to John McDougall and Martin Sinnatt, respectively Chairman and Secretary of the Kennel Club, for co-operation and assistance; to Christies and Faber and Faber for permission to include material in their copyright and to Sheila Atter, Anne Roslin Williams and Ken Thomas who have provided most of the photographs. We must also express our thanks to Sam Dart without whose assistance, over long hours and at all hours of the day and night, we could not have hoped to come even close to a very tight schedule.

We hope that with this help we have managed to convey some degree of our high regard for a very fine British breed and by so doing will encourage others to share this regard.

1

Arrival of a Breed

When, on 28 April 1883, Parson Jack Russell died he had, during a long career as a breeder, produced a strain of rough coated Fox Terriers which were sufficiently distinctive to be regarded as a breed separate from the Wirehaired Fox Terriers then slowly beginning to find favour in the show ring. Smooth Fox Terriers had already become the most popular breed of any show dog and much of the refinement on which success in the show ring was based had already taken place. For the Wirehaired Fox Terriers this development still lay in the future.

During his long career the Parson had remained faithful to the older type of Fox Terrier. This dog was capable of running with hounds, intelligent and amicable, and a superlative worker to fox but lacking the elegance and refinement which the prevailing fashion both in the show ring and the hunting field demanded. Parson Jack Russell's only concession to fashion – though already a well-established fashion when he bought his first terrier – was a preference for white or predominantly white terriers. For the rest, though he refined, improved and made his terriers consistent in type, he remained faithful to the old type of working terrier he had admired during his student days in the early years of the century.

The Parson's later career as a breeder coincided with a time during which the Fox Terrier, particularly the Smooth Fox Terrier, was undergoing tremendous changes. He expressed strong feelings about these changes but was not so opposed to them that he could not find show terriers which he admired, and right up to the end of his life he remained prepared to judge Fox Terriers at shows. While criticising the general trend, he expressed admiration for the best show terriers and was prepared to make use of them in order to improve the quality of his own strain. That he chose not to follow the prevailing fashion need not imply that he was blind to the merits of what many of his fellow breeders were producing. Equally, present-day admiration for the modern Smooth Fox Terrier, the modern Wire

Fox Terrier, the Parson Jack Russell Terrier or the ubiquitous Jack Russell Terrier need not and should not imply an antipathy towards any of the others. It would be a pointless exercise, which could only be conducted on the basis of entirely spurious arguments, to make any attempt to say which of these four closely related breeds is the best. Each has its own history, its own strengths and weaknesses and each has and deserves its own place in the catalogue of breeds which satisfy modern tastes and needs.

The basis for Parson Jack Russell's strain was a bitch, Trump, which he had bought in 1819 while still a student at Oxford. After he graduated and had been ordained he returned to his native Devon to take up his vocation in the church. He would never again live outside Devon and, for the next sixty-four years, would develop his strain of terriers by making skilful use of the white terriers which were to be found in the Devonshire hunt kennels, in the hunt kennels which he would visit in order to assuage his thirst for hunting and in the kennels of other Fox Terrier breeders. By developing a strain of working terrier to suit his own particular purpose he was doing precisely what others were doing in different parts of the country. In Oxfordshire, John Cowley was producing a breed of short-legged terriers to work to fox. In Havorfordwest, Captain John Edwards was developing the Sealyham Terrier; in East Anglia, around the turn of the century, Frank Jones was developing what would first be known as the Trumpington Terrier and later as the Norfolk and Norwich Terriers; in Poltalloch, Colonel Malcolm was working on the West Highland White Terrier; the Robsons and Dodds were refining the native terriers of Northumberland to produce the Border Terrier; and in the Lake District, Lord Lonsdale was carefully breeding his own strain of white terriers which he would eventually claim were Border Terriers but which he happily showed as Wire Haired Fox Terriers. In later years Sir Jocelyn Lucas would develop the Lucas Terrier. Sealyham Terriers, West Highland White Terriers, Border Terriers and Norfolk and Norwich Terriers all achieved the distinction of Kennel Club recognition. The Cowley Terrier and the Lucas Terrier, in spite of determined efforts, failed to do so. The Cowley Terrier has disappeared but there has recently been a belated revival of interest in saving the Lucas Terrier from extinction. Lord Lonsdale's white terriers became absorbed by the stock of Lakeland and Fell Terriers but even today their influence is seen in the occasional appearance of white puppies to the surprise and sometimes even the consternation of their breeders.

It is to Cruft's credit that he was always prepared to help those who feared that a successful career in the show ring might divert their breed into a line of development which might take it away from its working ancestry. He is said to have chosen the February date for his show in order that working gundogs would have finished their season and be available for other, less serious, activities. He also went out of his way to provide classes for gamekeepers and the sort of entertainment which would attract them to his show. Indeed, it was only when the gamekeepers themselves ceased to support these classes, during the 1950s, that they were discontinued. Unfortunately, but not surprisingly, the classes for working terriers were never well supported. Working gundogs may well be free of other tasks by mid-February but the same cannot be said of working terriers or their owners. The hunting season was still in full swing and working terriers were needed elsewhere.

Predictably, Heinemann was not very much impressed by what he saw in the working terrier classes at Cruft's. He wrote that it was:

> impossible to judge by appearances, for a dead-game dog may bear a scar, while a more useful and cautious one with a tongue may not. I once judged a working-class, of course two ladies were among the competitors, for they dearly love dog shows, and like the late Lord Granville Gordon, I was tempted to give the first prize to the best-looking lady; but being out for business, I asked what each terrier had done. Well, one of them had killed twenty moles in one night, and the other was made to sit up and beg, when I discovered he was one I had bred and drafted as the ugly duckling of my litter! In this class the terrier I gave first prize to was utterly useless next week to badger, while an unplaced one was the best a man could wish to work. All of which shows I am a very bad judge; if not, what a farce it all is.

It is quite likely that Heinemann was a bad judge. Even on this small amount of evidence he manages to contradict himself by arguing that 'it is impossible to judge by appearance', yet, at the same time, admitting to having drafted a terrier because it was 'the ugly duckling of my litter'. More importantly, Heinemann totally misses the point of working terrier classes which are not to find good working terriers but to encourage the breeding of the sort of terriers which, given the opportunity, might make good workers.

Having dismissed appearance as being of no consequence Heinemann then describes in great detail the appearance of what he regards as the ideal working terrier:

Breeders of show terriers are never tired of dinning into one's ears that their dogs are workers as well, and bred on the right lines for make and shape, but they lose sight of the fact that while they have been breeding them for straightness, they have acquired a giraffe-like length of leg, . . . they have lost all their individuality, intelligence and stamina. . . . The long-punishing jaw one hears so much of is gained at the expense of a brain-pan, and is itself a misnomer. Turn to Nature's handiwork, and you will find the badger and otter with their short, puggy jaws give more punishing bites than the longer-jawed fox, whose brain-pan behind it is larger than a modern show terrier's.

Then as to coat; buy a show terrier, and do nothing to his coat, and in six months time you will think your kennel-man dishonest, for in the Teddy Bear he leads out for your inspection you will fail to recognise the pin-wire coated champion of Cruft's or the Crystal Palace. . . . Natural coats, hard as bristles on a dandy brush, with plenty of undercoat, are what you want and can get, too, if you have the right blood, and, generally speaking, a rough-coated terrier is more likely to turn a worker than a smooth one. . . . In fox hunting a smaller terrier is necessary, especially in drains, but you want one (at least in moorland countries) who can keep up with hounds all day, and run the line, casting up some few minutes after hounds have marked their fox to ground. To do this he must have a certain length of leg and be built on galloping lines.

What Heinemann wrote advances a reasonably coherent argument but it would be quite wrong to accept his argument without first listening to what the opposing side had to say. Fortunately this is possible because in 1915 Francis Redmond, the doyen of show Fox Terrier breeders, wrote an article for the Wire Fox Terrier Association's *Year Book* which faced many of the accusations which Heinemann had made.

Redmond was asked, 'Are the fox-terriers of today as good as those of forty or more years ago?'

His answer was predictable. He said that, 'In working instincts, gameness, and endurance they are quite up to the standard of their ancestors.'

'But they were smaller and more cobby in those days?'

'That is true, but in those days, as now, they varied in size. There were the good 'little 'uns' and the good 'big 'uns' which are recalled as memories of Old Jock, Tartar, Hornet, Trimmer, Trap, Tyrant, Sam, Spot, Belvoir Joe, Rattler, Vandal Tyke, Old Foiler. . . . But then, as now, with huntsmen and MFHs the small ones were most in favour; and it was a decade or more later, in the 1880s and 1890s when the bigger and heavier Terriers seemed to get more recognition, until at last we had among our champions dogs weighing twenty pounds and over. . . . when MFHs and huntsmen by the ringside of some of our largest and most representative shows saw prizes awarded to dogs of twenty pounds upwards, they began to think of some other Terrier for work with their hounds. . . . Above all, let their constructive points include sound, strong and compact feet and legs, hard, neat bone, muscular neck, well-laid shoulders, fair spring of ribs, strong back, loin, and hindquarters, standing rather low than high on the leg, and not too short in body, at the same time by no means long, which means weakness. They should closely follow their ally in sport, the Foxhound, which is perhaps the most symmetrical of all animals.'

Redmond went on to praise two 'small dogs at sixteen to seventeen pounds', which he had, during the last month, seen kill their fox. Francis Redmond's idea of what constituted a good working terrier was not the same as Jack Russell's. In his terms Fox Terriers were better, far better, than they had been when the Parson was alive. Heinemann thought they had changed for the worse. In the context of our present concern, the important thing is that they both agreed the breed had changed.

In 1926 concern about the working qualities of Fox Terriers provoked the formation of the Working Pedigree Fox-terrier Association. Its founder, C. Chester Master, explained in the Fox Terrier Club's *Year Book* that its aims were to:

> improve the quality of the Working Fox-terrier by proving the working quality of the pedigree fox-terrier; of bringing the pedigree, or show type, of fox-terrier more prominently into the foreground, to promote its working capabilities, to live down the too common prejudice that it is useless for work, and to increase the number and improve the quality and type of working pedigree fox-terriers.

There can be no doubt but that concern existed and was growing about the way in which Fox Terriers were becoming divorced from their working origins. That concern was every bit as much alive among those who had given their allegiance to the show Fox Terriers as it was among those who continued to support what had already come to be regarded as the old-fashioned working type.

Heinemann died, aged 59, in 1930 and his kennel of terriers went to his kennel maid Annie Harris (a relation of Will Rawle who had

25

been the Parson's kennel man from about the mid-1840s). Annie Harris then became housekeeper to Henry Williamson and must have found her situation very different there. Heinemann had spent his life hunting otters. Williamson wrote a telling tale, *Tarka the Otter*, in which his opposition to hunting, particularly of otters, seems very apparent. In fact, Henry Williamson was very far from being the opponent of field sports which he is often nowadays presented. When he came out of the forces in 1919 he went to live in Devon and was sometimes to be seen riding to hounds. He even spent at least one day, 14 February 1922, out with Heinemann's badger digging club, though the whole thing was not to his taste.

Down one field, moving slowly in the distance, was a trickle of black specks and tinier white specks – the men and terriers of the Badger Digging Club walking down the hillside. . . . When they came near I saw that some of the men carried picks and shovels; one, with a nose once broken and re-set irregularly, carried a large basket of sandwiches and a gallon earthenware jar of whiskey. About twelve terriers, some of the rough-haired kind, were trotting on single and double leashes. In front walked a tall man in old fawn riding breeches, cloth leggings, a red waistcoat, tweed coat, white stock fastened by a pin made from a badger's penis bone. It resembled a two-inch length of quill. He wore a grey bowler hat. He was, as I soon learned, the Master of the Club. . . . Just before the brake the master and huntsman stopped. The innkeeper who carried the food and drink put the basket on the grass and removed his cap to scratch his head. Terriers strained at the leash, yapping and howling. Some were shivering. The others walked up the hill, and stopped: a farmer and two labourers with digging tools; three small boys; an adolescent schoolgirl with flaxen hair, ruddy face, always smiling; her father a small, nattily-dressed, red-faced, long-nosed man who reminded me, vaguely, of a badger; and his wife, a brown-faced woman in tweeds. The master and huntsman, in their red waistcoats, scrambled up a mossy bank, and examined the entrance holes to the badger's home.
    . . . A terrier was slipped from leash, and crept down the pipe. On his knees the master kneeled and listened. He drew a copper horn from between the second and third button of his red waistcoat, pressed it against the side of his mouth, and blew three faint toots. He heard a terrier snarl come from the darkness, and the thud of feet. Tally ho!
    . . . A ragged hairy man seized a pick and drove it into the turf. The master commanded everyone to get back as he lit a cigarette, and with three toots of the copper horn encouraged a second terrier to enter the hole. . . . The terriers tied to various trees continued to howl into the

cold wind, and men began to swing their arms to get warmth into them. A terrier bitch was sent down, and the digging went on. . . . Soon the badger dig took on a jovial aspect . . . the master came for a drink; he told me with rage that someone recently shot a badger near Lynton. Such a thing, he declared, was monstrous, when a postcard would have brought himself and terriers and diggers. He insisted, and he was sincere, that badgers would soon be exterminated were it not for the clubs. . . . Also, declared the master, badger-digging improved the strain of terriers; the bravest dogs were sought after for breeding. Feeling the kick of the whiskey, I asked him if it improved the strain of badgers. He stared at me, and left me.

Williamson goes on to describe, in sickening detail, all the sadistic ritual of the badger dig. It was not an experience he enjoyed and it may well have killed any interest he might have had in terriers. Perhaps it is not surprising that he found no interest in the papers, from Russell and Heinemann, which Mrs Harris brought with her when she became his housekeeper. Possibly the papers are now irretrievably lost, though it is equally possible that they are tucked away in some neglected corner.

Williamson's lack of interest in terriers did not prevent Mrs Harris from continuing to breed them. By using the often iniquitous system of letting bitches out on breeding terms she was able to produce a great many so-called Jack Russell Terriers whose popularity spread far beyond Devon. They were to be found throughout Britain and were exported all over the world. Nowadays Mrs Harris would probably be regarded as a puppy farmer.

In 1931, Sir Jocelyn Lucas produced his *Hunt and Working Terriers.* The breeds suitable for employment were carefully described and it was the Jack Russell Terrier to which Lucas devoted most attention, more even than to his own Sealyhams. It is interesting to look back at the breeds which he regarded as being useful in the field. There was the Old English Black and Tan Terrier, the Border Terrier, the Fox Terrier, the Lakeland, Fell or Patterdale Terrier, the Norwich or Trumpington Terrier, the Sealyham Terrier and the Scotch Terrier which, as far as Lucas was concerned, included all the Scottish Terrier breeds. Throughout the book it is apparent that he regarded Jack Russell Terriers not merely as a strain, no matter how distinctive, of Fox Terriers but as a separate breed. He was also careful to differentiate between Jack Russells and 'non-pedigree Jack Russells' because 'in North Devon nowadays every terrier is called a Jack Russell by its proud owner'. In an appendix he listed the sort of

27

Ch Dandy Back and Ch St Brides Demon, two show and working Sealyhams owned by Lord Kensington, shortly after the breed achieved official recognition in 1900. Sir Jocelyn Lucas described Demon as 'an ideal working type'.

terriers being used by a number of packs during the 1929–30 hunting season. One pack was using Welsh Terriers, another was using Cairns and another Devonshire Terriers, and how fascinating it would be to learn more about these particular Devonshire Terriers. Four were using Lakeland Terriers, six were using Sealyhams, fourteen had no preference as to breed and nineteen were using Border Terriers. Twenty-two were using cross-bred terriers, twenty-three were using Jack Russell Terriers and forty-six were using Fox Terriers, though most Masters in their replies to Lucas made it clear that they were not using show Fox Terriers.

In 1932 Theo Marples published an extensive revision to Sidney Castle's *Monograph on the Fox Terrier*, itself published in 1912. It lists the twenty-eight clubs and associations which were then affiliated to the Fox Terrier Club. These included the Working Pedigree Foxterrier Association and the Parson Jack Russell Terrier Club, the first intended to try to restore the show Fox Terrier as a working breed and the second to perpetuate the old fashioned type of terrier bred by the Parson. The Parson Jack Russell Terrier Club was, in fact, Heinemann's old Devon and Somerset Badger Club masquerading under a new name and, perhaps, with somewhat different aims, but nevertheless still going strong over forty years after its foundation. Its association with the Fox Terrier Club appears to suggest that the Club was itself at least sympathetic to efforts to preserve the type of Fox Terrier bred by the Parson though it would be quite untrue to suggest that this in its turn implied any dissatisfaction with the modern Fox Terrier or the route which it was travelling. At that time, the Fox Terrier Club probably recognised the validity of both types and was prepared to make room for both. Perhaps, in the wider interests of Fox Terriers, that sort of understanding and co-operation will soon return.

Concern about the alleged split between show and working types and the very closely related efforts to perpetuate the type of terrier bred by the Parson had not subsided, though in future both concerns would be less closely associated with the Fox Terrier Club itself. It is apparent, however, that though committed to evolution the Club did not stand in the way of those among their members who wished to preserve the sort of terrier bred by Parson Jack Russell and even went so far as to offer them the help which affiliation to the Club provided. The support given to the preservationists was far sighted. We have only recently come to realise that the preservation of old breeds of farm and other animals whose economic usefulness may seem to have long passed or which have been bypassed by fashion, may well enable us to preserve genes, and characteristics produced by those genes, which may be of great value in the future. It is impossible to say precisely when the terriers bred by the Parson became sufficiently distinctive as to be regarded as a breed in their own right. We would suggest that there is sufficient evidence to show that this took place during the Parson's lifetime, but it doesn't much matter if others would prefer a later date. What is important is that the Parson's terriers did form a distinct type and this type is now so different from both Smooth and Wire Fox Terriers and from the terriers of the type developed by Heinemann and his successors, which are often referred to as Jack Russells, that it is worth recognising and, more importantly, preserving as a breed in its own right.

2

White Fox Terriers

Although the development of agricultural skills relieved man of the need to hunt in order to survive, he was not released from a desire to hunt. That desire remains, though it often goes unrecognised, is stifled or perverted. The desire has been satisfied in many ways but for at least the last five hundred years has, in Britain, been most widely satisfied by hunting the fox. The tradition of fox-hunting is uniquely British and so, since terriers are an important, and in some cases vital, part of fox-hunting it is no accident that the majority of the world's terrier breeds have their origins in the British Isles.

The fox began its unsought-for climb to popularity as a quarry at the start of the thirteenth century. Prior to this time it was despised as a cowardly creature, unworthy of the attention of any self-respecting huntsman. However, those who would search for the roots from which British terrier breeds have sprung must begin their search well before the advent of fox-hunting. Indeed, it is probably necessary to begin the search even before the word terrier came into use. Terriers appear in the Bayeaux Tapestry in which King Harold is seen using them in order to drive birds out of coverts to be taken by hawks. Terriers were also used to disturb deer so that they could be coursed by hounds. Since animals which were likely to seek refuge below ground were not among the most popular quarry, it follows that terriers were not then primarily intended to eject animals from underground refuges. It was not until the end of the thirteenth century that the fox achieved the status of a worthy quarry for hounds. William d'Blathwyck is described as 'huntsman to the King's foxhounds' in a cash account produced by the comptroller of the wardrobe of King Edward I in 1299. Even then there appears to have been no realisation that dogs small enough, brave enough and forceful enough to follow foxes below ground would materially assist in their capture.

It was not, as far as we have been able to ascertain, until 1359 that the word 'terrier' first appeared in print, though it is likely to have been common currency for a long time before this. It appears first in 'Poeme sur las Chasse' by Gace de la Vigne.

> Le va querir dedans terre
> Avec ses bons chiens terriers
> Que on met dedans les terriers.

Vigne's poetic effort makes it clear that, by the middle of the fourteenth century, terriers were being used to drive their quarry from underground retreats. The link between the word 'terre' and the word 'terriers' is here established in a way which appears to make the derivation of the word obvious; but what is obvious may not always be true.

In 1486, when the *Boke of St Albans*, ostensibly written by Dame Juliana Berners, Abbess of Sopewell Priory, was published, the name again appears in a slightly different form – 'teroures':

> This be the names of houndes, First ther is a Greyhound, a Bastard, a Mongrell, a Mastyffe, a Lemor, a Spanyell, Rachys, Kenettys, Teroures, Bochers hounds, Myddyng hounds, Tyndel-tayles, and Shepherd curris, and small ladies poppis that bere away the fleas.

Obviously the list includes a number of breeds – mastiffs, mongrels, spaniels and shepherd dogs – which we would no longer classify as hounds, but Dame Juliana was using the word 'hound' in much the same sense as similar words are still used by many European languages to refer to all dogs. The word 'hound' had not yet migrated to its current narrower meaning as a word which, in English, refers only to dogs of the chase. Her reference to 'teroures' was, almost certainly, a reference to a type of dog used to drive deer and birds out of places in which they had taken refuge, and not to a dog which was called upon to work underground.

In 1570 the Bishop of Bath, Dr Still, went so far as to pen a prayer which still echoes the sentiments of many terrier owners, and once more a spelling very similar to that employed by Dame Juliana was used.

> Body and limb go cold, go cold,
> Both foot and hand go bare;
> God send terroures so bold, so bold,
> Heart will harbour no care.

Dame Juliana's spelling of the word 'teroures' and Dr Still's 'terroures' offer some, if slight, suggestion that the word might well have its roots in a word of similar spelling. This, coupled with the use to which terriers had been put prior to the elevation of the fox to the status of a worthy beast of the chase, gives rise to an etymological puzzle. Most authorities accept that the word 'terrier' is derived from the Latin 'terra' and is a reference to the dog's subterranean occupations. A few, however, argue that, given the type's occupation when the word was first used, to frighten quarry which did not venture below ground, and given the spelling employed by both Dame Juliana and Dr Still, the word is more likely to be derived from the Latin 'terror', to frighten. Further support is given to this suggestion by the fact that a number of breeds which cannot be regarded as other than terriers have never been used to work below ground.

What, then, did these early terriers look like? The question is not one which is easy to answer. Those which appear on the Bayeaux Tapestry were long legged, long backed, long tailed and were either black or red. Perhaps all terriers looked like that. Certainly there is no proof of the existence of white terriers until, if Rawdon Lee's tentative evidence is to be accepted, the reign of King James I. Lee refers to an unnamed painting which contained four white terriers, or what might have been white terriers, though they might have been Beagles. If Lee is right, and he is usually reliable, white terriers existed at the beginning of the seventeenth century. For more substantial evidence it is necessary to wait until 1790 when an engraving by Walter Scott of a painting by Sawrey Gilpin of Colonel Thornton's Pitch was published. Then, in 1796, John Sartorious produced a painting of Viper, a hound marked terrier, of what Lady Bracknell might have described as 'singularly repellant aspect'. Other, later, paintings by Sartorious also illustrate white terriers, and within a very few years a number of other paintings and engravings which show white or predominantly white terriers were produced. It seems that by the end of the eighteenth century white and pied terriers were not uncommon.

Support for this suggestion is to be found in *The Sportsman's Cabinet* for 1803 which relates that:

> Terriers of the best blood and most determined ferocity are now by the prevalence of fashion, bred of all colours; red, black (with tanned faces, flanks, feet, and legs), and brindled sandy; some few brown, pied, and pure white; as well as one sort rough and wire-haired; the

other, soft, smooth, and delicate, the latter not much inferior in courage to the former, but the rough wire-haired breed is the most severe biter of the two. And this breed has been so enlarged and repeatedly crossed in and in with the bull-dog, for the favourite sport of badger-baiting, with the lower classes, that they are increased in size, strength, and stimulus for the particular purpose, since the more inhuman practice of bull-baiting has been on the decline.

The genuine and lesser breed of terrier is still preserved uncontaminate amongst the superior order of sportsmen, and constantly employed in a business to which his name, his size, his fortitude, persevering strength, and invincible ardour all become so characteristically and truly subservient, that he may justly be said to 'labour cheerfully in his vocation', this is in his tremulous and exulting attendance upon foxhounds, where like the most dignified and distinguished personage in a public procession, though last, he is not the least in consequence. Since the truly ecstatic and exhilarating sport of fox-hunting is so deservedly and universally popular in every county where it can be enjoyed, these sagacious, faithful, courageous little animals have become so high in estimation, that few stables of the independent are to be seen without them.

So *The Sportsman's Cabinet* confirms that white or largely white terriers, some with rough coats, some with smooth, existed at the start of the nineteenth century. It does not, however, give much clue as to what these terriers looked like. Fortunately, within a few years of this report being published, *The Sporting Magazine* published a picture of Vixen, a pied terrier, and Vixen is exactly the sort which was later to captivate the Parson. Her head is short and powerful with a broad skull, moderate stop and a wedge-shaped muzzle. Her expression is keen and intelligent; her ears are cropped after the fashion of the day and so their natural shape is obscured. Her neck is strong and her shoulders well laid, with a long upper arm. Her brisket is not over deep but her ribs are carried well back. Her loin is both long and strong, with more than just a hint of corpulence; her quarters are strong and well muscled. Her tail, which is docked, is carried gaily and she stands on well-boned legs of a length which would enable her to gallop across country with hounds. Her feet appear to be rather large and open. Her colour is fascinating in that it displays precisely the same markings which were later to be seen on Trump, which the Parson appears to have regarded as more than enough colour, and which is to be seen in very many specimens of the present day Parson Jack Russell Terrier. She has coloured ears

Vixen was described as a 'pied terrier' when she appeared in The
Sporting Magazine *in 1818. The similarity between her and*
Trump and Hannah of Clystlands demonstrates the existence of a
uniform type of terrier which spans over 170 years. No other terrier
breed could make such a claim.

with the colour running onto her skull and cheeks and, at the roots
of her tail and running into her croup, she has another patch of
colour; apart from that she is entirely white. Vixen could take her
place among any gathering of modern Parson Jack Russell Terriers
and would be indistinguishable from them.

By this time fox-hunting had become a popular sport and without
terriers would have been almost untenable. It is likely that the emer-
gence of wealthy and fashion-conscious Masters of Hounds gave rise
to the fashion for white terriers. These well-educated old Masters
were very conscious of appearance. They went to enormous lengths
and expense to ensure that their homes and all they contained, their
carriages, their own dress and everything about them presented a
pleasing and elegant picture. In order to enhance the picture they
presented in the hunting field, they even went so far as to adopt
pink, or even less likely colours, in preference to the older and more
serviceable green as the colour of their hunt uniforms. They took
pains to ensure that their hounds were well matched in size and
shape for functional reasons and in colour and voice for aesthetic
reasons. Colonel Thornton even went so far as to match the colour of
his own and his huntsman's mounts with that of his hounds and, of

course, his terriers were required to fit into the same colour scheme. The rise to popularity of white terriers was originally probably no more than a response to fashion, though it has since been justified on functional grounds.

It is true that a white terrier would have been less easy for the 'awkward people', to whom Peter Beckford refers to in his *Thoughts on Foxhunting*, to confuse with the fox. In this collection of letters to a young sportsman, Beckford expresses his personal preference for a 'black or a white terrier' and so ends any possible doubts that by 1781, when the book was first published, white terriers were to be found in hunt kennels. Hunts may nowadays be somewhat less concerned about appearances than were the fashion-conscious eighteenth-century Masters, and since few packs run terriers with hounds, their colour is of less importance either to the overall picture or to avoid causing confusion among the 'awkward people' whose numbers have probably multiplied since Beckford's day.

So which hunt kennels were using these white terriers? Obviously, the pack hunted by Colonel Thomas Thornton was one. Thornton was a Yorkshireman born in 1757 who, while still a young boy, inherited an enormous fortune. He served under the Duke of Cumberland at Culloden and Falkirk before returning to Yorkshire to concentrate on field sports. Thornton has been described as 'a poseur and a braggart no doubt, and a genius at exaggeration if not an accomplished liar', though it might be thought that a man who walked four miles in 32 minutes, could jump his own height, had jumped six five-barred gates in 6 minutes, whose stables contained racehorses by the mighty Eclipse and whose kennels contained coursing Greyhounds, spaniels, Pointers, Beagles, Foxhounds and, of course, terriers might have no need to exaggerate. Thornton, however, appears to have had full measure of the very Yorkshire desire to impress his superiority on all he met. He was not well liked and after his death it was said that 'no man who knew him ever spoke well of him'. Thornton lived at a time when speed was becoming an integral part of fox-hunting, and speed was something which suited him. He backed his terrier, Pitch, to beat any other over a fixed distance but there were no takers, just as there were no takers for a similar wager on Merkin, a favourite Foxhound. Even Thornton's own wife was heavily backed in a race against one of the country's leading jockeys. She lost only as a result of her saddle slipping, and the unfortunate jockey was left to savour the unpopularity which resulted from an undeserved win. The engraving of Pitch, who lived during the penultimate decade of the eighteenth century, contains the inscription that 'it would be necessary to notice Colonel Thornton's terriers if it were only on account of his justly celebrated Pitch, from whom are descended most of the white terriers in the kingdom'.

If this statement is to be taken at face value it might be said that white terriers largely owe their existence to the talents of an unlikable Yorkshireman, but Thornton's influence was not confined to Yorkshire. In 1805 he sold his palatial home, Thornville Royal, and a few years later also sold Falconers Hall, his lodge near Scarborough, and in 1808 moved to Wiltshire, having taken Spye Park. He arrived at his new home with a typical show of ostentation which included a dog cart containing all his terriers, each of the terriers wearing a jacket on which was embroidered the history of its exploits. Thornton did not stay at Spye Park long and in 1817 went to live in France where he died in 1823. However, he had been at Spye Hall for nine years, ample time to introduce white terriers to the hunts in the area. It is entirely possible that in Trump's veins ran Pitch's blood.

In his article on Fox Terriers, published in the first, 1903, edition of Drury's *British Dogs*, Scott complains that:

> Among all those who have written on Fox Terriers of late years, none appears to have been inclined to go to the root of the matter, and tell us anything of the origin and early history of the breed. A general idea seems to prevail that Fox Terriers are a production of modern times, and this idea has, no doubt, been fostered by the way in which spurious imitations of them have been from time to time manufactured, and by the ignorance of judges who have permitted various and very opposite types to find favour. The Fox Terrier proper is not a modern breed, and perhaps there was as good dogs fifty years ago as there are now.

Scott's reference to 'spurious imitations' and the 'ignorance of judges who have permitted various and very opposite types to find favour' need to be borne in mind. What could possibly have happened to justify such comments? *The Sportsman's Cabinet* suggested one answer when it mentioned 'the prevalence of fashion' which resulted in a litter of puppies being sold from the Running Horse livery stables for 'one-and-twenty-guineas'. It is difficult to assess just how much justification and how much prejudice lies behind Scott's outburst. Certainly he was not alone in complaining about the effects of fashion, not just on Fox Terriers but on many breeds, including Foxhounds. But what could have influenced fashion during the 1850s? Dog shows cannot reasonably be expected to shoulder the blame because they only began to develop as national events with a potential to influence the national development of a breed after the century had passed its mid-point. Agricultural and associated hound shows had begun some years earlier but is it possible that Scott was suggesting that the Master of Hounds had ruined Fox Terriers? The accusation might not be wide of the mark: their desire for speed had produced a very different type of hound than had previously existed and, in the case of Pitch, a very different terrier. Fashion had become important to Thornton and like-minded Masters. The influence of fashion in the early history of fox-hunting should not be underestimated; it resulted in a great many changes, some of which changed hounds themselves and, at times, brought them very close to ruin.

If we can, as we surely must, accept that white terriers found favour partly because of the fashion-conscious Masters of Hounds and, probably only incidentally, to avoid the difficulties which 'awkward people' might create, we must next ask how these white terriers were produced. The terriers which existed up to the end of the eighteenth century were black or red; nowhere is there any mention of terriers which were white or predominantly white. White is a very rare colour in the animal kingdom. There are no white wild dogs and very few white animals of any other species. There are, however, a number of old-established white breeds of domestic dogs. These include Greyhounds, Pointers and Foxhounds, all of which were in Thornton's kennels. He could easily have mated an old-fashioned coloured terrier to any one of these in the hope of producing white or white-marked terriers. In fact, if we look closely at Pitch and remember Thornton's desire for speed, it seems most likely that he made use of Greyhound blood. Other Masters, however, probably had recourse to Foxhound blood.

The fashion for white terriers did not, however, become universal among Foxhound packs in Britain. The North Country packs continued to use and still do use their traditional, stalwart, coloured terriers, the forerunners of our modern Border and Lakeland Terriers, and it appears that other packs, perhaps equally uninterested in keeping up with the current fashion, for a while at least remained true to their old terriers. Perhaps they were less troubled by awkward people or were better able to control them than were the more fashionable hunting countries. William Youatt, writing in 1845, described what he regarded as the typical terrier as being 'usually of a deep-black colour, with a yellow spot over the eyes'. No mention is made of white terriers. Those who read only Youatt, and some authorities appear to have looked no further, might conclude that white terriers did not exist, yet by this time, as we have seen, they had been in existence for at least half a century. It is our belief that the breed described by Youatt survives in its purest form in the Fell Terrier of the Cumberland, Lancashire and Yorkshire uplands.

In spite of rigorous culling over many generations, these and the working Lakeland Terrier still occasionally produce pure white puppies which may well have their origins in the white strain of terriers which Lord Lonsdale maintained at Lowther Castle from the early years of the eighteenth century. They worked both with the Lakeland hunts and with the Cottesmore. Nowadays these white throwbacks are much in demand to improve the quality, conformation and soundness of some of the short-legged Jack Russell strains. It is not unknown for owners to ignore their terriers' real parentage and to enter them in Jack Russell classes at hunt terrier shows where their quality ensures that they are often among the winners.

Classes for working terriers were provided among the few classes for dogs which were available at the early shows put on by agricultural societies from about 1780. Jack Russell was closely associated with some of the West Country societies and is known to have judged at their shows well before dog shows became popular. Fox Terriers probably also appeared at the first Cleveland Hound Show, in 1859 which, after moving to a number of different Yorkshire venues, was to become the Royal Hound Show, now held in conjunction with the East of England Agricultural Society Show at Peterborough. Classes for hounds, Beagles, Bassets and, of course, Foxhounds, continue to attract visitors from all over the world but, sadly, the terrier classes, once such an important feature of this event, have long since been discontinued. In 1860, the First Exhibition of Sporting and other Dogs took place. This now exists as the National Dog Show Society Show, held in Birmingham. It provided classes for terriers which included 'Black-and-tan Terriers, White and other English terriers, Scotch Terriers and Toy Terriers under 5lb'. Such a generous and diverse terrier classification makes it apparent not only that terriers were already a popular type of dog among the sporting dog owners who were largely responsible for the early development of dog shows, but also that a number of different breeds were already in existence.

Perhaps, before we take the tale any further, we should halt to take a closer look at the terrier classification at the Birmingham show. Black-and-tan Terriers would include both the old breed from which Fox Terriers had been developed and the smooth coated type employed in the urban rat pits and which now exist as the Manchester Terrier. Toy Terriers, now known as English Toy Terriers (Black and Tan) were the Miniature version of this breed. Scotch Terriers included the prototypes for all the Scottish breeds known today, with Skye Terriers at that time being the most popular, as well as Yorkshire Terriers which were known by a variety of names. White Terriers were not the white terriers which have been the subject of our discussion thus far, but the white version, now extinct, of the Black-and-Tan Terrier. Fox Terriers would be included, along with a number of other breeds, under the general heading of 'other English terriers'. Neveretheless, Fox Terriers were undoubtedly represented at this show and during the next couple of years what, according to Rawdon Lee, was regarded as the 'so-called new variety', quickly began to dominate the prize lists.

In 1861 three Fox Terriers appeared among the 'White and Other English Terriers except Black and Tan' at the Birmingham show. One of these terriers, Boosy by Billy, was the property of the Pytchley Hunt and was for sale at 10 guineas. It was not, however, until the Second International Show, held at the Agricultural Hall, Islington in May 1864 that classes were provided for 'Kennel- or Fox-terriers'. Thomas Wootton of Nottingham was first with Jock and second with Venom. H. J. Davenport's Tartar was third.

It was not long before Fox Terriers, particularly Smooth Fox Terriers, became very popular. Show specimens changed hands for what, even today, would be regarded as large prices and the breed became firmly established as the most popular in Britain, a position it was not to lose until well into the twentieth century. Of course, such great popularity over such a long period did have an effect: the somewhat rough, workaday terrier of the early years became more refined, not always with the approval of its old supporters. Its career in the show ring slowly became divorced from its role as a working terrier. Even though many of the breed's staunchest supporters seem to have divided their time between the show ring and the hunting field – indeed, many were Masters of Hounds – the refined lines of the show dog were less and less seen in the hunting field. Here the older type continued to earn its keep and the respect of those who had an eye for a good working terrier.

3

A Sporting Parson

John Russell was born in Dartmouth, Devon, on 12 December 1795. His father, the Reverend John Russell, was a cleric and schoolmaster whose twin passions were classical learning and hunting. He came of an old Devonshire family which could trace its lineage back to the John Russell who was sent to Devon by the Lord Protector and Duke of Somerset, Edward Seymour, to quell the riots with which the predominantly Catholic West Country folk welcomed Cranmer's English Prayer Book. Another illustrious member of the family was Admiral Russell, the victor of the Battle of La Hague which, in 1692, saved Britain from the threat of a French invasion. By the end of the eighteenth century the family, though not by any means rich, was well respected throughout Devon as well as further afield, which was to stand John in good stead in later years.

At the time of John's birth his father was Rector of Iddlesleigh in North Devon but when he was fourteen months old his father was appointed Rector of South Hill, near Callingham, in Cornwall. John grew up in Cornwall until he returned to Devon to study at the old Plympton Grammar School, where Sir Joshua Reynolds had been a pupil. When he was fourteen he left Plympton to further his studies in Tiverton and it was here that his father's love of hunting, though not his love of classical learning showed itself in the son.

This love of hunting was not one which was universal in the West Country. The Parson himself on one occasion had to dissuade some of his parishioners from shooting foxes and even official reports were less than understanding. Charles Vancouver surveyed the county, in 1808, for the Board of Agriculture and reported that:

> The furze-brakes, copses, and particularly the holes and cavities in the rocks and cliffs along the sea-coast, are found favourable to the escape and ultimate preservation of the breed of foxes. These places are regarded by sportsmen as valuable sanctuaries, from their being likely to conduce to the permanent amusements of the field. It is, however,

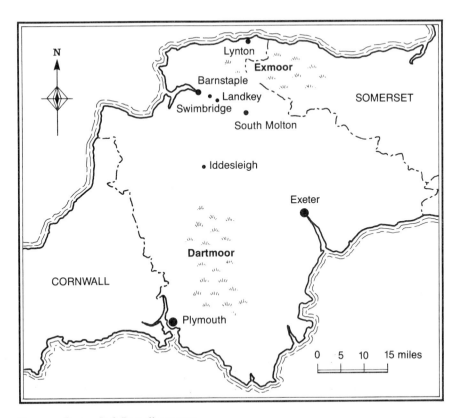

Devon – Parson Jack Russell country.

regarded far otherwise by those who derive their subsistence from the employments of the country.

It was entirely typical of Vancouver that, having dismissed hunting as a pastime which provided no service to the countryside, he should then consign all the moors and commons, including Dartmoor itself, all the bogs, fens and salt-marshes and forests of Devon to a short chapter entitled 'Wastes'.

With the willing assistance of Robert Bovey, a fellow pupil at Tiverton, a small scratch pack of hounds were gathered together. They were kennelled in a shed behind the village smithy and, with the sixteen-year-old John carrying the whip, quickly developed a local reputation as a sure source of sport. Such a reputation could not be kept from Dr Richards, the school's very strict Headmaster. Bovey

Parson Jack Russell was a tall, athletic man whose incredible stamina and enthusiasm survived up to within a few months of his death in his eighty-eighth year.

was expelled but Russell, who strongly, if not truthfully, denied any close involvement with the pack, was allowed to remain at the school after having received the sort of thrashing to which his hide, after a number of escapades, was doubtless becoming impervious.

He remained at Tiverton for two more years before, in 1814, being admitted to Exeter College, Oxford as a commoner. For the first two years John seems to have made little effort to improve his meagre stock of learning. He was far more interested in sport, whether it was boxing, wrestling or hunting, a passion which would continue for the rest of his long life. His time was largely spent hunting with the local packs, to which his lineage and easy manner made him a welcome guest. For someone who was to spend much of the next sixty-four years in the hunting field, John Russell could not have gone to a better university or at a better time. Oxford was then, as now, surrounded by packs of the highest class. What is now the Heythrop country, in the north-west, was hunted by the sixth Duke of Beaufort who had Philip Payne as his huntsman and Will Long as his first whip. The country to the north, now hunted by the Bicester and Warden Hill, had only recently lost John Warde, who many regard as the father of fox-hunting, and was then being hunted by Sir Thomas Mostyn whose huntsman was Stephen Goodall. In the south-west, what is now the Old Berkshire country was hunted by John Codrington's and the Vale of White Horse Hunts. John Russell could hunt four or even five days a week and seems to have done so, whenever his finances would allow, to the point at which he placed his degree in jeopardy. Later in life the Parson would enjoy ascribing Oxford's reputation as a repository for learning to the fact that 'men brought up a fair stock of school learning, but carried little away with them'.

The story of how Russell came to own his first terrier, as told by his friend, fellow student and biographer, E. W. L. Davies, is well known after countless repetitions. Nevertheless it is an important part of our story and must again be told in Davies' own words.

At the end of May, when strolling round Magdalen meadow with Horace in hand, but Beckford in his head, he emerged from the classic shade of Addison's Walk, crossed the Cherwell in a punt, and passed over in the direction of Marston, hoping to devote an hour or two to study in the quiet meads of that hamlet, near the charming slopes of Elsfield, or in the deeper and more secluded haunts of Shotover Wood. Before he had reached Marston, a milkman met him with a terrier – such an animal as Russell had yet only seen in his dreams; he halted, as Actaeon might have done when he caught sight of Diana desporting in her bath; but, unlike that ill-fated hunter, he never budged from the spot till he had won the prize and secured it for his own. She was called Trump, and became the progenitress of that famous race of terriers which, from that day to the present, have been associated with Russell's name at home and abroad.

John Russell was certainly impetuous and, throughout his life, was to get into many scrapes as a result. It is entirely possible that the

Trump was the Parson's first terrier, bought in 1819 while he was still a student. This painting, by Mary Palmer, was completed in 1823 and may well have been done from life; certainly, the Parson regarded it as a good likeness.

Ruth Wilford's home-bred Hannah of Clystlands took part in a working terrier show at Marston (where Jack Russell bought Trump), held in 1983 to commemorate the centenary of the Parson's death. She was adjudged the terrier most like Trump.

meeting took place just as the Rev. E. W. L. Davies described. Indeed, Russell read the manuscript of the biography and verified its accuracy. He was a man of the cloth and not inclined to telling untruths but he was also a fox-hunter and fox-hunters are almost as bad as fishermen for stretching and colouring the truth in their pursuit of a good story. It seems to us that, while the story may be truthful, it may not tell the whole truth. Might not Russell have walked towards Marston, which now straddles the A40 to the north-east of Oxford, in the hope of seeing the milkman who, from previous encounters in the hunting field, he knew to own a good terrier? Might it not have been in Russell's mind, alongside Beckford, that he would try to buy that terrier? Moreover, does not Davies' choice of phrase 'a milkman met him with a terrier' suggest that the meeting was not an accidental one but may even have been pre-arranged? It doesn't much matter either way and undoubtedly a chance encounter, guided by the hand of fate, makes a better story than would a more calculated effort to acquire a good terrier which he had already admired. The important thing is that in May 1819 Jack Russell became the owner of a terrier, Trump, who was first to found a dynasty and then a breed.

Russell went on to gain his Bachelor's degree, subsequently his Master's degree and was then ordained. His career in the church did not produce preferment but this does not mean that he was other than a caring and conscientious parish priest. Nor can it be taken as an indication that he was unfitted to a higher office. Whenever he visited Sandringham he was expected to put a sermon in his pocket. He must have been regarded as suitable company and his sermons as suitable spiritual fare for the aristocratic company who gathered there. His career in the church coincided with that of Bishop Henry Philpotts, who was a blatant practitioner of nepotism and was inclined to take leave of the county whenever trouble threatened. He seems to have shared Charles Vancouver's attitude towards hunt-ing. The Bishop made various attempts, few of which were any more successful than they were with the Parson, to prevent his clergy from hunting.

After his ordination the Parson went as curate to South Molton and George Nympton, about ten miles east of Barnstaple on what is now the A361. At that time the two adjoining parishes had over three thousand inhabitants and were together the largest parish over which the Parson would hold sway. His stipend at George Nympton of £60 a year was insufficient to relieve the 'tightness of the chest'

*It is frequently suggested that the Parson did not keep records and,
as a consequence, little can be known about his terriers or their
breeding. In fact, he was an avid letter writer and certainly kept a
diary, which here records his wedding day.*

which he would later use as an excuse for avoiding activities which
he could not afford, and was not nearly enough to enable him to
support a pack of hounds comfortably. This did nothing to deter him
from making the attempt. His second scratch pack consisted of five
or six couple hounds; once more he was able to enjoy following his
own hounds, now supplemented by his own terriers. In 1826 he
married Miss Penelope Bury, daughter of Admiral and Mrs Bury, a
young lady with means sufficient to ensure that, even on the modest
stipend of a rural cleric who made no effort to impress his Bishop
with his ability to fill a more lucrative living, he could continue to
keep hounds and breed terriers. The two were well matched. Penelope was as keen a hunter as was John and, though her name does
not appear among those which populate the history of terriers, must

46

deserve some degree of credit for the Parson's achievements. After his marriage the Rev. John Russell became curate to his father at Iddesleigh. Iddesleigh had less than five hundred inhabitants and is about two miles north of Okehampton and within easy reach of Dartmoor itself. He stayed at Iddesleigh for six years before moving to his own parishes at Swymbridge and Landkey where he was to remain for the next forty-five years, only leaving with extreme reluctance and sadness, after the death of his wife in 1875. Swymbridge, with fewer than two thousand inhabitants, is between South Molton and Barnstaple. Finally came the move to Black Torrington, provided by his old hunting friend and fellow terrier enthusiast Lord Portimore, Master of the Tiverton. From 1879 to his death on 28 April 1883 the Rev Jack Russell was rector at Black Torrington, then with about 700 parishioners, between Hatherleigh and Holsworthy on what is now the A3072.

The bare bones of Jack Russell's career in the church do not even hint at the enthusiasm with which he pursued his interest in foxhunting, indeed in all forms of hunting, and in terriers. Until the very end of his life Jack Russell was a man with an abundance of energy and stamina which enabled him to hunt frequently without in any way neglecting his duties as a parish priest. If his superiors in the church sometimes failed to understand his love of hunting his parishioners were in no doubt as to his qualities as their pastoral leader. At his death over one thousand people followed his coffin to the grave. Parson Jack Russell was as content with his parishioners as he was easy with the nobility. He was a welcome visitor to Sandringham and a special favourite of the Prince and Princess of Wales. He was welcome at Badminton and at many other well known country houses. At once a confirmed rebel but still a staunch supporter of the establishment, he remains a puzzle for those who try to define his character for their own purposes.

Parson Jack Russell, it is often claimed, was opposed to dog shows and at odds with what he saw dog shows doing to Fox Terriers. In fact, although dog shows only became national events when he was a very old man, he was a regular judge not just of terriers but also of hounds. He was happy to accept invitations to judge at West Country shows and was a regular and keen exhibitor. In 1862 he showed at the Bath and West, held in Exeter, and managed to split the Hon. Mark Rolle's terriers by taking a second to their first and third. The Hon. Mark Rolle hunted a pack over what is now the Eggesford country which includes some of the roughest and wildest

*The Parson's sporting life was a very varied one which ranged from
a day out with his own hounds and among his own parishioners to
– as here – informal shooting parties at Sandringham in the
company of the Prince of Wales.*

hill country in Devon. In the following year the Parson was to be
found judging at Bideford and at several other shows where his
opinion about hounds and terriers was respected. All this took place
long before the Kennel Club was founded in 1873 and he was, in that
year, happy to become a member of the new club. There can be no
reason to suppose that he did not fully and enthusiastically support
its purpose and aims. Whatever else he may have been, Jack Russell
was certainly not a hypocrite. He would never have been a member
of an organisation whose aims he did not support.

The May 1883 issue of *The Kennel Gazette* contained an affectionate
obituary to the old man. Almost certainly it was written by the
Parson's old friend, Murchison, a fellow Fox Terrier breeder who, in
this same issue, registered a puppy in the name of Jack Russell, a
touching tribute to his old friend, even though the terrier itself was
not of the old-fashioned type to which the Parson remained faithful.

IN MEMORIAM – THE REV. JOHN RUSSELL

Though fiction in a past generation gave us a Parson Adams, there is no likelihood of a nearer prototype of that worthy than the kind old clergyman who passed quietly away just ten days ago. The resemblance between the country parson of the novelist and the Rev. John Russell ends, however, at the point where both are seen to exercise an influence upon all those with whom they came into contact, and an honesty of purpose to be constantly helping others out of scrapes and troubles. This was the character of John Russell, but he was a greater gentleman than Parson Adams, and his journey through life may be looked upon as an odd mixture between the old fashioned parson, the country gentleman, and the courtier. In his parish he was the adviser and friend of his flock, at cover side or at the agricultural meeting he was hearty and well met with every one, and in the hall or the palace he was polished and affable to a degree. It is no wonder, therefore, that he was a universal favourite, from the prince to the peasant, and it is possible that no one has ever surpassed him as an arbitrator and peace maker in every sort of circle. He would travel third-class from Devonshire to Yorkshire for no other purpose, and whether bringing together broken ties, or preaching a charity sermon, he had a way of his own of reaching the heart that few could equal and no one could surpass. Born a sportsman, he never thought it incompatible with duty to join in every sort of legitimate sport and pastime; and besides being the most genuine foxhunter in the country, it was by no means unusual to see his well-known figure at Ascot or Stockbridge, or on the box of a friend's drag in the coaching season. There was no cant or humbug about John Russell; he performed the duties of his religious profession better than the majority of clergymen, and he was ever ready to join in any thing to promote sport or fellowship amongst sportsmen. The writer of these lines asked him, when the Kennel Club was established, to join as a member, and he was quite delighted with the idea, and has been a member ever since. It will be remembered that Mr Russell judged the Fox Terriers at the Crystal Palace for the club in 1875, and although the old gentleman was not altogether at home with all the requirements of the modern fox terrier, he was greatly pleased with all he saw at the show, and expressed to us the very strong admiration he had for Rattler. Mr Russell's own breed of fox terriers were wire-haired, and his greatest aversion were those that had in them any signs of a bull cross. A real fox terrier, he would say, is not meant to murder, and his intelligence should always keep him from such a crime. Thus, he boasted that the best he ever had never tasted blood to his knowledge, but that they could not lose their way, and that their eye to country and memory was so great that, as soon as

49

hounds were out of cover, some of his terriers had gone ten miles, and reached well-known earths in time to stop a fox from entering a destination that he had been making for. This Mr Russell thought was the highest character that could be found in a terrier, and he would have none that hesitated to go to ground, but he liked them to teaze or worry a fox rather than to kill him or fight him. He said his terriers worked for the pack, and knew as well as he did what they were wanted for. The Jack Russell Terrier was hardly as big as the modern show terrier; in working condition the dogs would not be more than 15lb, and many of them barely that, and five-and-twenty years ago they formed a very distinct type. Since that time they have been crossed on to other strains, and their uniformity has been probably lost, though they live in all descendants of Foiler. Mr Russell started his breed at Oxford when he was eighteen, so something like seventy years ago, and he had his pedigrees that he could trace to from the time he started them. As the oldest fox terrier breeder in England Mr Russell's connection with the Kennel Club was an honour to that body, and we personally regret the loss of a very old friend in the fine old English gentleman who has been recently gathered to his fathers, and that a thousand followed him to his grave that were nearly all of them sportsmen shows that our slight contribution, as well as many others written by staunch friends and admirers, is largely shared by sentiment to the memory of the Rev. John Russell.

It would, perhaps, be wrong to read too much significance into the fact that though Parson Jack Russell was an early and loyal member of the Kennel Club, he appears not to have found the same enthusiasm when the Fox Terrier Club was founded just three years later and in spite of the fact that some of his old friends were among its founder members. Perhaps he found himself out of sympathy with the way in which he saw the breed developing, but a more likely reason for his lack of support was his age and the fact that his preference was for Wire Fox Terriers while in the show ring it was the smooth variety which was attracting all the attention.

Edward Jaquet records that:

Mr Russell joined the Club in 1873, and remained a member until his decease in 1883. At the time of his death he was considered the oldest Fox Terrier breeder in England. He started his strain (the 'Jack Russell Terrier') at Oxford, when he was eighteen and more than fifty years afterwards had pedigrees that he could trace from the time he began to breed them. Mr Russell's terriers in working condition did not scale more than 15lb, some less, and between forty and fifty years ago they formed a very distinct type. He judged Fox Terriers at the Kennel Club Show at the Crystal Palace in June, 1874.

This is not a record of a man at odds with the Kennel Club but of a loyal member who some twenty years after his death still retained the respect and admiration of his fellow members.

4

The Genuine Article

Since well before the Parson's death Fox Terriers have been travelling along at least three divergent lines of development. Many breeds have developed different types for work, show or companionship and in many the original type has totally disappeared. It is not part of either our purpose or intention to attempt to pass judgement. Indeed, it would be very difficult to do so because the criteria on which judgement must be based are confused and contradictory. If some breeders choose to follow a path which takes their dogs away from the origins but makes them better suited for a new career, in the show ring, as companions or in a different activity than that for which the breed was originally developed, there can be no reasonable basis for reproach providing that change is not achieved at the expense of the welfare of the dogs themselves. On the other hand, if others choose to preserve the form of the dogs, and sometimes to do so even though the purpose for which they were originally developed has itself disappeared, there is still no basis for reproach.

The issue is confused in Fox Terriers by the existence of at least three different types. These result from changes made in response to changing tastes, to satisfy changing functional demands and they represent an attempt to preserve what existed in the past. Even the very use of the name Fox Terrier exposes us to the risk of creating confusion. Smooth Fox Terriers and Wire Fox Terriers are two separate, but closely related, breeds derived from the terriers which were used with fox as their quarry. They are not the only breeds which are worked to fox and so cannot be regarded as the only Fox Terriers. Fox Terriers came into existence in response to changing tastes and, during the last 100 years, have themselves been changed in response to continuing changes in tastes. The Parson Jack Russell Terrier represents the old Fox Terrier stock from which the modern Fox Terrier breeds derived and which has been preserved in an unchanged state. It has also produced a variety of terriers, commonly and variously referred to as Jack Russells, which were intended for different purposes than those for which the Parson bred his terriers and which, as a result, are very different from all the terriers which were in existence at the end of the last century.

The situation is still further complicated by use of the term Jack Russell Terrier, by unscrupulous breeders and dealers, to enhance the sale value of any small dog, often of doubtful parentage, and no matter what its make and shape may be. While we were writing this we came across a small advertisement in a local newspaper which offered for sale a litter of 'long coated, black, Jack Russell Terriers puppies, £50 each' which, without use of the Parson's name, would have had to be disposed of, for little or nothing, as the mongrels they undoubtedly were. We also know of instances of allegedly carefully bred Jack Russells being exported, at high prices, whose pedigrees were subsequently shown to be works of fiction. Recently, the growth of interest in longer-legged terriers has induced some breeders to make use of Lakeland Terriers, especially the white ones which appear from time to time, in order to achieve an appearance which is again in fashion. In spite of their parentage, these terriers are still called and still compete at hunt terrier shows as Jack Russells. Indeed, one of the most successful 'Jack Russells' as we write this is the white product of two normally coloured Lakeland Terriers. Recognition will not prevent such practices but it will offer a means by which their effect can be avoided.

The Parson lived through a period during which change was taking place at a speed which had never before been experienced. When he was born railways did not exist but later reached to within forty miles of his home and enabled him to travel the country to hunt, visit his friends and judge at dog shows. On the seas, sail first gave way to paddle-steamers and they, in their turn, gave way to screw-propelled vessels. Gundogs travelled by rail to distant moors and returned at the end of the season to take their place at dog shows. Even in the heavily traditional world of hunting, changes were taking place. Hounds were being bred for speed and dash rather than for dogged perseverance. Hunters, too, were valued for speed, agility and appearance rather than for stamina, even though it was necessary then to have three or even four mounts in order to stay with hounds until nightfall. It was possible to breakfast and dine in London and spend the intervening time hunting in the newly fashionable Shires. Terriers could not be expected to be immune to change. Indeed, they had already changed. When the young Jack

Russell bought Trump he invested in one of the fashionable, pre-dominantly white terriers, which had fairly recently replaced the older coloured terriers in the more fashionable hunting countries. During the Parson's own lifetime this terrier too would come to be regarded as old fashioned.

Charles Darwin showed that isolated populations tend to become differentiated from the populations from which they first sprang. They develop their own characteristics and, as time passes, slowly develop into a separate breed. The opposite influence is to be seen in the way in which improved ease of international communication has tended to erode the use of local accents and customs. In much the same way, the white terriers, developed in response to fashion, were taken up as popular show dogs and refined in a way which radically changed their appearance. The advent of railways also enabled dog shows to attract entries from all over the country rather than just from the immediate locality, and as a result a number of the localised breeds which existed in isolated pockets up and down the country became absorbed into a larger and more standardised population. Breeders and exhibitors no longer just had the example of the best local dogs before them but could see, admire and make use of the best dogs from all over the country. Only in isolated parts of the country or in the hands of breeders who refused to follow the current fashion did local breeds survive.

By the end of the nineteenth century the elegant and refined Smooth and Wire Fox Terriers had become the most popular breed of pedigree dog in the country. The type to which the Parson remained faithful for over sixty years was rather left behind by the changes which had taken place to Fox Terriers. Even so, the two types were not yet so far distant from one another that the Parson's stock was not of value as breeding stock for those who were breeding for the show ring and who retained some interest in working dogs, while the Parson himself, and like-minded breeders, for a long time re-mained prepared to make wise use of the best of the show dogs on their working bitches.

The old-fashioned type was put under still more threat as the use to which it was put changed. Badger digging, then often regarded as an occupation which kept the men folk harmlessly occupied while the ladies enjoyed a pleasant rural picnic nearby, required terriers which were heavier and stronger than those required for work to fox. Weight, size and tenacity were sometimes achieved by means of crosses with Bull Terriers, a cross which the Parson abominated.

Eventually, this pastime produced the Sealyham Terrier, which has itself now undergone a metamorphosis, and a variety of terrier often referred to as a Jack Russell Terrier for which Heinemann and Annie Harris were largely responsible, but which was very different from those bred by the Parson. Fox-hunting had undergone further change and it was no longer deemed necessary, in some countries, for terriers to run with hounds. They could be carried in a bag over the huntsman's shoulder or even chauffeured to within a few yards of the earth. Neither the terriers used for badger digging nor those intended for use with the new method of hunting were required to follow a horse across country. As a consequence, short-legged terriers began to find favour. The best of these were and are bred with care and carry out their tasks in a way which calls for admiration. They are, in every respect, quite excellent working terriers and though they are not the type which the Parson bred or would have found a place for in his kennel, they do not disgrace his name, though their entitlement to its use may be questionable.

The type of terrier bred by the Parson was to be found only in a few old-fashioned kennels in isolated hunting countries, while the elegance of Fox Terriers was widely admired and the courage, perky appearance and jaunty manner of the short-legged, little terriers led to a rapid increase in their popularity. Their popularity resulted in the breed which the Parson had been credited with saving from extinction being once more faced with extinction. What then are the characteristics of the true Parson Jack Russell Terrier? Unfortunately we have few drawings or photographs of the Parson's terriers which would guide us as to their appearance. We do, however, have a picture of his very first terrier.

The picture of Trump (*see* page 44) is dated 18 January 1823 and is signed by Mary Palmer. It was, therefore, produced a mere eight months after Jack Russell had bought Trump and so it is very likely that it was done from life. In addition, we have Davies' description of Trump which again has a ring of a description from life or at the very least one produced with the aid of someone who had seen Trump, and we must remember that the Parson saw and approved Davies' manuscript. The Parson had a prodigious memory: he could memorise the names of an entire pack after a single view in their kennel and would then surprise those whose familiarity was of longer standing by identifying each hound in the field. He may well have added details to Davies' manuscript. Certainly some details could not have been deduced from the picture without the sort of

Exactly the wrong sort, achondoplastic and overmarked.

additional information which only someone who knew the terrier could provide.

Furthermore, we not only have pictures and descriptions of some of the dogs he used on his bitches but, again through Davies, we have the Parson's own assessment of some of these terriers. We have pictures and descriptions of dogs he was known to admire. We have pictures of dogs produced by bitches bred by the Parson himself and by people who might be supposed to respect the Parson's ideal. We also have numerous pictures of Wire Fox Terriers of the period which help to add yet more detail to the picture, the body of evidence, direct as well as circumstantial, is considerable. The accumulation of evidence is sufficient for us to know, with some degree of confidence, precisely what the Parson's terriers looked like. The modern Parson Jack Russell Terrier is neither more nor less than the product of efforts to keep in being the sort of terrier bred by Parson Jack Russell.

Davies said of Trump:

> In the first place, the colour is white with just a patch of dark tan over each eye and ear, while a similar dot, not larger than a penny piece, marks the root of the tail. The coat, which is thick, close, and a trifle wiry, is well calculated to protect the body from wet and cold, but has no affinity with the long, rough jacket of a Scotch Terrier. The legs are straight as arrows, the feet perfect; the loins and conformation of the whole frame indicative of hardihood and endurance; while the size and height of the animal may be compared to that of a full-grown vixen fox.

The painting itself depicts a useful sort of terrier, though perhaps not one out of the very top drawer. The markings are exactly as Davies describes but, though her coat is obviously not a smooth one, only Russell himself, or someone who had seen her, could really say what its texture and density were like. The legs and feet look good, though perhaps the hocks are a little higher than is strictly desirable in a terrier intended to follow hounds, while the feet have more affinity with those of a hound than those of a cat. The loins certainly look strong and long enough to impart the sort of flexibility a terrier needs underground. The ribs are carried well back and are not so deep as to impede the terrier in restricted places. The skull appears to have good width, and the muzzle short and powerful. The neck might be inclined to stuffiness and be shorter than is ideal, but there is no suggestion that the fault lies in the shoulders which appear to have good length and angulation both in upper arm and shoulder. Maybe the topline would not satisfy a purist but the slight suggestion of an arch over the loin is indicative of an ability to gallop with hounds. The ears appear to have been cropped, an operation to which the Parson was vehemently opposed and to which his terriers were never subjected. The tail is docked and carried gaily, perhaps rather too gaily. Trump's imperfections may have dimmed over the years in the Parson's fond memory but there is no doubt but that the painting depicts a very serviceable terrier who could hold her own in the field or in the show ring alongside the Parson Jack Russells of today.

Davies is also a reliable source of other clues to the appearance of the Parson's terriers and to the way they were worked.

> Russell's country is technically known as a hollow one; that is, a country in which rocky fastnesses and earths, excavated by badgers, abound in every direction. Consequently, on every hunting day a terrier or two invariably accompanied him to the field; and certainly no general ever depended with more trust on the services of an aide-de-camp than on those of his terriers. If in chase they could not always live with the pack, still they stuck to the line, and were sure to be there or thereabouts when they were wanted. . . . Entered early, and only at fox, Russell's terriers were as steady from riot as the staunchest of his hounds; so that, running together with them, and never passing over an earth without drawing it, they gave a fox, whether above ground or below it, but a poor chance of not being found, either by one or the other. A squeak from a terrier was a sure sign of a find, and there was not a hound in the pack that would not fly to it, as eagerly as to Russell's horn, or his own wild marvellous scream. . . . This steadi-

ness from riot was, of course, the result of early education on one object – the fox; nor did Russell consider it needful to train his terriers by progressive steps, according to the plan adopted by Dandie Dinmont.

This evocative passage tells us that the Parson's terriers were expected to run with hounds, as was the custom in those days. There was no time for a terrier which needed to be carried on the huntsman's back and no opportunity for it to be chauffered to the earth as is often the case today. Russell's terriers needed the speed, endurance, agility and intelligence to stay in contact with hounds over a demanding country.

They were also expected to be 'steady from riot', as must any dogs be which are expected to make their own way across country. The so-called 'terrier spirit' which is nowadays too often seen and is sometimes actively encouraged in the show ring, would make them useless for any sort of work. In the Parson's day, a useless terrier or a useless hound would be hanged; nowadays they may receive a kinder fate but not one which is any less final. Russell would not tolerate any hound or terrier in his kennel which was at all riotous or quarrelsome. Once more, Davies' reliable testimony is available. He said that:

> In any pack of Russell's, hunted by him during the last fifty years, the fate of a hound touching on such riot would have been quickly sealed; on returning to his kennel I can almost hear him say to old Will Rawle, his faithful and devoted henchman for forty years, 'Will, that hound eats no more of my meal, mind that'; and the culprit would henceforth disappear from the scene.

A riotous terrier would have been equally unwelcome among the Parson's hounds.

In terriers, as with people, unprovoked and indiscriminate aggression is, unless a symptom of mental sickness, a sign of cowardice and stupidity. The Parson's terriers were neither cowards nor stupid. From 'a hundred anecdotes [which] might be related of the wondrous sagacity displayed in the chase by Russell's terriers', Davies selects just a few. One concerns the way in which Tip, one of the Parson's favourites, was able to employ knowledge of the locality to anticipate the route likely to be taken by a hunted fox and to be at the mouth of the earth in which he had intended to take refuge even before the fox arrived. We have seen terriers do precisely the same thing, though how they are able to know the likely route of a fox which might leave a covert on a strong run away from the earth is a mystery. J. Fairfax Blakeborough, in an article on 'Terriers and Terriermen' which appeared in the January 1912 issue of *The Foxhound*, describes the importance of terrier men who have a similar ability.

> It is the mission of the runner, by hook or by crook, by short cut and knowledge of the run of foxes, to be 'there or thereabouts' with the pack, so that if their quarry seeks refuge in an unstopped sanctuary he may have his leader-straying charges handy to expel him.

Jack Russell's terriers were, however, not intended to murder their fox. He is said to have taken pride in the fact that some of his best terriers never tasted blood but achieved their eviction by harassing and chivvying their fox. It was partly for this reason, as well as his abhorrence of riotous behaviour in his kennel, that he was so vehement against the introduction of Bulldog or Bull Terrier blood. It is likely that Heinemann's own inclination to introduce Bull crosses was the result of a preference for a harder terrier. Davies said:

> The bulldog blood thus infused, imparts courage, it is true, to the so-called terrier; he is matchless at killing any number of rats in a given time; will fight any dog of his weight in a Westminster pit; draw a badger heavier than himself out of his long box; and turn up a tom-cat possessed of even many lives, before poor pussy can utter a wail. But ferocity of that blood is in reality ill suited – nay, is fatal – to fox-hunting purposes; for a terrier that goes to ground and fastens on his fox, as one so bred will do, is far more likely to spoil sport than promote it; he goes in to kill, not to bolt, the objects of his attack.
>
> Besides, such animals, if more than one slip into a fox-earth, are apt to forget the game, and fight each other, the death of one being occasionally the result of such encounters. Hence Russell may well have been proud of the pure pedigree he had so long possessed and so carefully watched over. Tartars they were, and ever have been, beyond all doubt; going up to their fox in any earth, facing him alternately with hard words and harder nips, until at length he is forced to quit his stronghold and trust to the open for better security.

What Davies describes is a terrier which is courageous but not quarrelsome. Unfortunately, nowadays a quarrelsome nature is too often confused with a courageous one. Badly scarred terriers are paraded as though the inability to work, if that is how their scars are received, without receiving severe punishment was somehow commendable. In the ring, terriers are goaded to display aggression in order to show their so-called 'terrier spirit' which would condemn them for any sort of serious work. So-called terrier spirit is often no more than a display of hysterical, almost pathological, behaviour which should be as heavily penalised in the show ring as it would be in the field.

'Entered early, and only at fox . . . early education on one object – the fox.' Precosity is still a characteristic of the Parson Jack Russell Terrier. When other breeds are still very dubious about anything approaching serious work or even of entering an untenanted earth a young Parson Jack Russell Terrier may be keen to the point of fool hardiness. In thoughtless or callous hands this youthful enthusiasm sometimes results in a youngster receiving dreadful and needless punishment from an older and wiser fox and how the chest of a boastful terrier swells when he exhibits the results of his own ignorance and callousness. It is interesting though that this precosity has survived intact for well over a century.

Davies here stressed that the Parson's terriers were entered only to fox, though it has to be said that in his early life he had a reputation for hunting anything that moved. Wisdom and discrimination, however, eventually overcame his wild enthusiasm. The Parson's terriers might have been allowed to run off surplus energy in pursuit of a rabbit, though hunting rabbits can lead to indiscretions which can be of severe embarrassment in the field. There is no evidence that the Parson was at all interested in working badger. His terriers did not have the sort of strength, build or aggression which is necessary for badger. They were intended to work fox and only fox and it is significant that Trump should be said to be the size of a full-grown vixen.

Elsewhere, Davies suggests that the Parson followed the fictional Dandie Dinmont's method of introducing terriers to work: 'I had them, a' regularly entered, first wi' rottens, then wi' stots and weasels, and then wi' tods and brocks; and now they fear nothing that ever cam' wi' a hairy skin on't.' The curriculum is one which is, broadly, followed by many a terrier intended for general work, but it must be borne in mind that its author, Sir Walter Scott, knew little about hunting and was, in any case, describing a terrier which was not intended for work with hounds. What Scott, through Dandie

60

Dinmont, refers to as 'entered' is not what Davies and the Parson would regard as fairly entered, but it might well have been a preliminary stage in a terrier's education.

Davies' descriptions tell us a great deal about the character and temperament of the Parson's terriers but, Trump apart, tell us little about their appearance. Nor does the illustration which appears as the frontispiece to Davies' biography of the Parson add reliable information. The drawing of the Parson was taken from a photograph and the terriers were added according to what Baird thought appropriate. In fact, they appear to have been modelled on show Smooth Fox Terriers of the time.

Fortunately, other evidence is available. We have already mentioned Jock as the winner of the Birmingham Show in 1864, and we know quite a lot about this famous old Fox Terrier. One of his many owners was Thomas Wootton, who said that 'so good did my old friend, the Rev. John Russell, of Devonshire fame, think of him, he had the dog over twice to serve his wire-haired bitches'. These visits must have taken place between 1860 – when Jock was about twelve months old and able to mate bitches – and 1871, when he died. We know that on one occasion he mated two of the Parson's bitches. Obviously the Parson had a very high regard for Jock and for his progeny.

Details of one visit are contained in a letter which the Parson wrote to Wootton.

> I have put one bitch to Jock and shall put another – although she is only nine months old – a rather precocious young [lady] you will say – tomorrow or next day; and Lord Portsmouth's huntsman will send him on Saturday. I have never seen this bitch – she is seven years old and of my purest blood, and I hope she may not miss. I never saw a sweeter animal than Jock, so perfect in shape, so much quality. He is as near perfection as we poor mortals are ever allowed to feast our eyes on. His temper is so beautiful and his pluck undeniable, for I had to choke him off a fox.

Then follows a description of an incident to which we will return when we have examined Jock in greater detail. It is difficult to imagine a less equivocal statement of what the Parson regarded as his ideal than is contained in his letter.

Rawdon Lee provides us with a very full description of Jock who, he says, was:

bred by Jack Morgan, who, when the dog was pupped some time during 1859, was huntsman with the grove. The Kennel Club Stud Book gives the breeder as either Captain Percy Williams, who was then master of the grove, or Jack Morgan; but the uncertainty of the month in which the terrier was born, and the little thought given to terrier pedigrees at that time, make me extremely sceptical as to Jock's pedigree, as I am of most of the early stock terriers. Anyhow, Jock has left his mark behind him, and also been the means of handing down to posterity the names of his sire and dam, the former being another Jock (also Captain William's), and the latter, Grove Pepper, huntsman's terriers both of them we may be sure. In show form Old Jock was just about 18lb. weight, standing a little high on his legs, which gave him an appearance of freedom in galloping. His colour was white, with a dun of mixed tan mark on one ear, and a black patch on the stern and at its root. He was not what one would at the present time [in 1893] call a 'varminty-looking' dog, i.e. one with an unusual appearance of go and fire and gameness in him – he was a little deficient in terrier character. His ribs were well sprung, and his shoulders and neck nicely placed. When in this condition he had the appearance of a rib short; but his hind quarters and loin were strong and in union with the other parts of his formation. To some modern tastes he would appear a little loaded at the shoulders; his forelegs, feet and stoutness of bone were good, and his stifles strong and well turned. His ears well placed, neither too large nor too small and he had a nice, strong jaw. With increasing years he grew a little full in the cheeks. All round Jock was a symmetrical terrier, and no specimen of late years has reminded me so much of him as the dog Rattler, who did so much winning. Jock, who is said to have run seasons with the Grove Hounds, had his tail cut, but the portion left on was longer than one usually sees at the present day.

So Jock, bred in hunt kennels from working stock, was more strongly built, wider in the chest, stronger headed and less 'varminty' than was regarded as ideal only twenty-four years after he was whelped. Elsewhere Lee also faulted Jock for not having 'a black and tan head to recommend him'. Already fashion had changed, though not so much as to prevent dogs which resembled Jock from doing their share of winning. It is interesting that Rattler, who reminded Lee of Jock, was the Parson's winner when in 1874 he judged the Kennel Club's Crystal Palace Show. Perhaps he also reminded the Parson of his old favourite. In any case, in making Rattler his winner the Parson was doing no more than agreeing with the opinion of other judges (what price his alleged discord with what was happening in

Old Jock was a terrier for which the Parson had the highest regard and on at least two occasions had in his kennels to mate his bitches.

the ring?). Rattler was whelped in 1871 and at five weeks of age was sold for five shillings and a canary. At a year old he became the property of Mr Fletcher for £17. From 1873 until 1879 he was virtually unbeatable in the ring, in spite of being well up to size, and became known as 'The Dreaded Rattler'. At stud he was regarded as disappointing largely because his progeny were of the working type from which he was bred and so did not conform to the refined standards which were then emerging. Perhaps one of the reason's why the Parson liked him so much was that he carried a lot of the Parson's own blood lines and perhaps this was also the reason for the prepotency which made him such an unfashionable sire.

Lee's doubts about Jock's breeding cannot now be resolved with total certainty but there seems to have been no dispute but that his dam was Grove Pepper. Lee's suggestion that Captain William's Jock was his sire is disputed in the first volume of the Fox Terrier Stud Book, published in 1889, which quotes Luke Turner as saying that 'in my mind there is none or little doubt, about Twister being Old Jock's sire'.

The same letter also shows that the Parson's kennel contained yet another Fox Terrier which had made an appreciable impact in the show ring. This terrier was Tartar. The letter continues with an explanation of how the Parson came to know of Old Jock's pluck.

Since they came here I have kept both Tartar and Jock chained up in two separate loose boxes, because they are warmer than kennels. Yesterday morning I gave Jock a run before I went to meet hounds and after my return from hunting I did the same for Tartar. He went with me very kindly, as he had frequently done before; indeed, they both recognised my voice and were mad to come to me whenever they heard it; when suddenly without the least provocation, he started back and ran full tilt back to the stable, the door of which was open, and in one moment fastened upon Jock, I caught hold of him immediately, put his foot in my mouth, and bit it with all my force, choking him with my left hand at the same time; and no harm – or very little – would have happened had not Jock resented the insult and had him across the nose. This enabled Tartar, when I freed him from Jock's foreleg, to seize his hindleg. But I soon released him and took Jock in my arms. The whole thing annoyed me dreadfully, and I am sure you will believe jealousy is the cause of the mischief.

The Parson was probably being far kinder on Tartar than he deserved. Tartar had enjoyed a misspent youth which made him prone to fighting, and to kill anything which moved. Tartar took his gameness to extremes: not only did he have a fight with Jock while the Parson was in charge of the pair of them but he was also an inveterate cat killer and not unfamiliar with either the rat or badger pit. He was not the sort of terrier which would have enjoyed a permanent home in the Parson's kennel or which could have been allowed to run with hounds, but his indiscretions were tolerated in the knowledge that they were unlikely to be passed on to his offspring and that he would have no opportunity to play havoc among hounds.

Once more, we have Rawdon Lee's detailed description of the dog. He was:

full of go and fire, a hardy-looking, strongly built terrier. . . . Tartar, 17lb in weight, was a pure white dog, excepting for a light patch of pale tan over one eye, unusually compact in build – a pocket Hercules in fact, with a back as muscular and strong as is the neck of a mighty Cumberland and Westmoreland wrestler. A little wide in front was the old dog, but straighter perhaps on the forelegs than Jock, and with better feet. The latter, far the longer and more terrier-like in head, was beaten in size of ears, mode of carriage, and in neatness of hind quarters. Tartar was a peculiarly elegantly moulded dog behind, notwithstanding the amount of muscle he showed, and he stood neither too high on his legs nor the contrary. . . . Both Tartar and Jock

These three famous old Fox Terriers – Old Jock, Grove Nettle and Tartar – all have close connections with the Parson. Jock and Tartar both mated the Parson's bitches and Nettle is the product of his breeding.

had fair coats, that of the former, the harder and smoother, and no doubt he was much the gamer of the two.

We will select just one more piece of evidence to demonstrate just what sort of terrier the Parson admired and spent sixty-five years trying to breed. Not only did he make use of the best of the old-fashioned Fox Terriers when mating his bitches, but his breeding stock was also in demand by some of the top kennels of Smooth Fox Terriers, including Thomas Wootton's and Henry Fitzwilliam's. When, towards the end of his life, the show ring began to extend its interest beyond the smooth variety to the rough coated terriers which he bred, it was to Jack Russell that the top kennels turned for breeding stock. One of these belonged to yet another hunting crony, Master of the Carlisle Otterhounds, William Carrick. Carrick's Carlisle kennel of Wire Haired Fox Terriers began with a dog called Venture, a dog which almost certainly carried blood from the Parson's kennel, and from which judges at Curzon Hall in 1872, more accustomed to the elegance of the refined smooth variety, had withheld a prize 'for want of merit'. Indeed the Wires were, for some time, so unfashionable that, in order to compete at shows they sometimes had to show in the non-sporting classes, a fact which could not have been calculated to impress their very sporting owners.

Venture was soon joined in the Carlisle kennel by the bitch Lill Foiler, bred by Thomas Wootton, by Troilus – a dog who went back both to Juddy, a bitch bred by the Parson and to Jock – out of Wasp, another bitch bred by the Parson whose pedigree contains little that was not bred by the Parson. Lill Foiler can reasonably be said to be a product of the Parson's many years of skilful breeding.

It is a fascinating exercise to trace Lill Foiler's pedigree back through the Parson's terriers. She was born in 1883 and bred by Thomas Wootton to whom the old man had given her dam, Wasp, who was out of almost pure Parson Jack Russell breeding. (At the same time, Wootton also received Pussy as a gift but she was later sold for £40 to Mr S. E. Shirley, founder of the Kennel Club. It is salutary to remember that the founder of the Kennel Club owned a genuine Parson Jack Russell Terrier!) Wasp was by Tip II, by Tip I out of Fuss, which takes us as far back as we can go on the sire's side. On the Wasp's distaff side was Moss II, by the Rev. Gibson's Bitters out of Moss I, which the Parson bred in 1869. Moss I was by Old Hornet, by Earl Fitzwilliam's Trap out of Grove Nettle, and out of Juddy, bred by the Parson in 1868. Juddy was by Grove Willie, by Grove Tartar out of Grove Nettle, and out of Vic, bred by the Parson in 1860, by Grove Tartar out of Old Nettle.

Mated, in 1884, to Trick, a dog of mixed and doubtful breeding, Lill Foiler produced Carlisle Tack who, mated to Vice, produced Carlisle Tyro. Tack carried a great deal of the Parson's oldest blood lines as did Tyro, if in a slightly diluted form. Both were said, by Rawdon Lee

Carlisle Tack, out of a bitch which carried several lines to the Parson's own breeding and described by contemporaries as very like the Parson's own terriers, was both a successful show dog, at a time when rough coated terriers were not in fashion, and a good worker.

Carlisle Tyro was Tack's son and is very much of the same type. He achieved notoriety as a result of having his ears virtually surgically altered and it is interesting that the ears of the Parson's terriers seem to have offended the show-ring purists.

and others, to resemble closely the Parson's own terriers and they are, perhaps to a greater extent than any others, the models on which the modern Parson Jack Russell Terrier is built. A lot is known about the appearance of both these dogs for not only are descriptions and drawings available but we also have photographs which are somewhat more informative than those now available of Jock. Rawdon Lee wrote:

Skipper, bred by Mr and Mrs W. Sayner and owned by Mr J. Waters, is a replica of Carlisle Tack and shows how well the type has been preserved for more than a hundred years.

Mr and Mrs P. Lloyd Edge are the owner–breeders of Ryemill Fudge who is a female counterpart of Carlisle Tack and Tyro.

Here is Mr W. Carrick's prize dog, Carlisle Tack; look at him, and does there appear to be any reason to doubt his gameness? A terrier every inch, built on racing lines almost, without any lumber about him, and with powerful jaws; the artist having flattered him in the latter respect as he has done in coat. His weight was 17lb, he was all white in colour. . . . His chief defect lay in his scantiness of coat on his sides and ribs, and down his legs, but what there was was of good, hard quality.

Of Tack's son, Tyro, Rawdon Lee said that:

This was a white puppy called Carlisle Tyro, just about the right size for his age, 17lb in weight, and allowed to be the best of his kind seen. . . . Tyro took after his sire in beauty and keenness of expression, but was a little stronger in jaw, possessed smaller ears, and excelled him in quantity of coat. . . . Tyro's shoulders and loins, too, were powerful; his stern was neatly set on, his stifles were well turned, and his forelegs and feet were very good, though he at times stood not quite straight on them, which fault, if it were one, prevented him having that wooden and stiff appearance nearly all the absolutely straight-legged terriers possess. I should have liked Tyro a little better had he had more hair down his legs.

Sadly, William Carrick's star did not remain in the ascendancy for long. It was alleged that Tyro's ears, or possibly just one ear, had been surgically tampered with and, though it was not proved whether the scar on which the accusation rested was the result of surgery or of an accident and even though it was widely accepted that if the ear had been deliberately tampered with, the operation was not carried out under William Carrick's instructions or even in his knowledge, the result was that the Kennel Club disqualified Tyro from all his wins. For his part, Carrick resigned his Kennel Club membership and took no further part in show-ring activities. Would the evolution of the Wire Fox Terrier have taken a different route had he and his terriers remained in the ring?

When the Parson died he was generally and rightly recognised as the oldest and one of the foremost breeders of Wire Fox Terriers in the country. From 1819, when he acquired Trump, to his death in 1884, he had devoted himself to breeding outstanding Wire Fox Terriers. So successful was he and so rapid were the changes taking place around him that his strain had reached the stage at which it could be regarded a a distinct breed. Indeed, even during his life his terriers were referred to not as Wire Fox Terriers but as Jack Russell Terriers. A period of sixty-five years is a very long time for any breeder to be active. For such a talented breeder it provided more than ample time to establish and fix a distinctive strain, and his fellow breeders were happy to recognise the Parson's singular contribution. What is not mentioned, either in his obituary or in

Dick, who was bred in the Pytchley Kennels in 1921 and owned by Nancy Turrall who remembered him as a great character and very game. Dick, apart from being more heavily marked than is desirable, is exactly of the type which was favoured by the Parson.

*There is an appreciable difference between the size and shape of a
modern Wire Fox Terrier and the Parson Jack Russell Terrier.*

recent histories of the breed, is that it was the Parson who was
credited with having saved the breed from extinction during the days
when all eyes were on the smooth variety. Thomas Pearce, in 1872,
recorded that 'the breed would have died out I am persuaded, but for
Rev. John Russell, of Dennington, near Barnstaple, North Devon,
who has always declared them to be the best of good terriers, and his
opinion carries great weight.'

It is entirely fitting that this fine old breed should be preserved in
its original form as one of the very best working terriers, as a natural
show dog of extraordinary quality and as an ideal rural companion.
It is also entirely appropriate that the Parson's name should be com-
memorated in the name of the terrier which he developed.

5

Campaign for Recognition

Parson Jack Russell bred Fox Terriers. He made use of the best of the show winning Fox Terriers in his breeding programme and was, for a few years at the end of his life an enthusiastic judge, who travelled great distances to deliver his opinion at shows run under Kennel Club rules. He became a member of the Kennel Club in the year of its foundation and numbered among his closest friends many who also supported the Club's aims. Three things prevented him from playing an even fuller part in the new organisation's activities. When it was formed, in 1873, he was already an old man, albeit a remarkably vigorous one, and it can hardly be expected of any 78 year old that he throw himself whole-heartedly into any new venture no matter how worthy. The Parson, though saved from the penury which resulted from using his very small stipend to assist his son over the consequences of an ill-judged business venture by Lord Poltimore's generosity, still suffered from the 'tightness of the chest' which he had, throughout his life, excused himself from participation in ventures which he believed to be beyond his means. The third, and possibly the most important drawback, was that though the hunting and sporting fraternity were showing their terriers with enthusiasm, it was the smooth variety which had found greatest favour in the ring. Jack Russell's terriers were rough coated and it was hardly likely that he would divert the aims of a sixty-year-long breeding programme in order to accommodate the new fashion. However, rough coated Fox Terriers did, slowly, find favour and at the end of his life the offspring of his terriers were not only forming the foundations on which some of the most successful kennels were built but were also producing terriers which were making their mark in the show ring.

Already the Smooth Fox Terriers had evolved along lines which were different from those to which the Parson adhered but, although on one occasion he gave vent to a wildly improbable series of accusations about how they were bred, he remained prepared to offer his

This study, entitled 'Man's Best Friends', of three Fox Terrier heads was made by John Arnold Wheeler some time during the 1860s. Already, the Smooth Fox Terrier in the centre shows signs of the refinements which were to turn it into a very different animal but the rough coated terriers which flank it are very much of the old type which the Parson bred.

This companion study of three Foxhound heads shows that even without the allegedly pernicious influence of the show ring, the demands of fashion can appreciably change.

opinion as a judge and there were undoubtedly a number of the top winning dogs which earned his admiration as well as some which, in spite of the changes which were taking place in the breed, were very like his own terriers. Obviously he preferred rough coated to smooth Fox Terriers, though he mated his bitches to smooth coated dogs, and he may have been fearful that the rough variety would follow the fashionable road travelled by the smooths. In fact, Wire Fox Terriers did, though more slowly, follow a similar path and by the time the Kennel Club was a hundred years old the two breeds had, in common with many others, undergone a transformation.

In fact, this change had begun to take place before the end of the nineteenth century. Even when the Parson died, in 1883, his strain was regarded as being sufficiently different from others in the breed almost to justify being regarded as a separate breed. In the next few years, during which time Fox Terriers became the most popular show dogs, the differences became even more acute and by 1909 were sufficient to warrant Cruft's Show putting on classes specifically for working terriers. The existence of the classes does suggest a degree of acceptance and possibly concern at the way in which Fox Terriers were already developing. This concern was further emphasised by various attempts to start clubs which would encourage interest in working terriers and would support classes at shows which catered for genuine working terriers. Concern about the way in which Fox Terriers were splitting into different types suitable for work or show is not new. It has existed since before the beginning of this century.

The changes which are wrought in many breeds are often condemned by those who give the matter little thought. Change, without a conscious and determined effort to prevent change, is inevitable. It might take a course which some regard as undesirable but to condemn change *per se* is both unreasonable and unrealistic. If we examine all the breeds which are recognised by the Kennel Club we will find that some – Deerhounds, Irish Water Spaniels and Mastiffs are good examples – have remained unchanged because that is what their breeders want. Others have evolved in ways which have changed their appearance. The Bulldog is often cited as an example of the destructive influence of the show ring but in fact the Bulldog had developed what many now regard as its present exaggerations long before it was much, if at all, involved in shows, and certainly long before any national shows or the Kennel Club came into existence. Change was, in this case, the result of being

73

It is tempting to assume that the friendship between the Parson and the Prince of Wales and their mutual regard for terriers would have led to the Prince owning one of the Parson's terriers. In fact, as King Edward VII, his most famous terrier, Caesar, which followed his coffin to the grave, was bred by the Duchess of Newcastle. It does, however, serve to demonstrate that, even by 1910, the Wire Fox Terrier required even more skilful grooming than was available in the Royal household if a pristine appearance was to be maintained.

deprived of contact with the activity for which Bulldogs were originally bred, coupled, perhaps, with a very Victorian regard for exaggeration and useless ornament which improved veterinary skills, for the first time, made possible. There are other examples of breeds which have changed, or which appear to have changed, but more often than not the changes are more apparent than real and result from nothing more than different methods of grooming. The Poodle is a good example of this group.

Breeders face a series of choices. They can, as Dalmatian and Staffordshire Bull Terrier breeders have done, preserve their breed for an activity which no longer exists or, they can, like Sealyham and Scottish Terrier breeders, direct the breed's evolution along a very different route which may take the breed a long way from the purpose for which it was originally developed or, as in the case of Poodles, change appearances by means of changed styles of hairdressing but without radically changing the dog itself. All three courses have their supporters and their critics but all must be allowed their own validity. All, in any case, are the product not of some

Kennel Club dictum, but of what breeders themselves choose to do. During the last hundred years Fox Terriers have changed in basic shape and have adopted different styles of hairdressing. They are now very different from the sort of terrier which the Parson bred.

After the Parson's death some of the terriers which bore his name also underwent a considerable change. Within a few years they were being bred with short, often crooked legs, and with large heads, and their colouring was being changed to allow more black and tan than the Parson regarded as desirable. They were being bred, not to run with hounds or even for fox-hunting, but for badger digging, an activity in which the Parson had no interest. The changes were every bit as dramatic as any to be found in any officially recognised breed and, as so often seems to be the case, it was the new type which appealed to the public and which, as time passed, came to be regarded as the true representatives of the breed. These sprightly little terriers became enormously popular as Jack Russell Terriers. They were regarded as the genuine article and terriers of the type bred by the Parson were forced to take a back seat.

However, these little terriers and the popularity they had attained carried the seeds of their own fall from grace. Many were bred to satisfy the demand for pets and they were bred without thought or care. What was happening to them is precisely what has happened to so many breeds which have caught the public imagination. A particular type of breeder is attracted by the profit to be made by the ready sale of large numbers of puppies; there is little or no thought for quality, only for quantity, and, as a result, the standard begins to fall. Problems are ignored and hereditary disease gains the foothold it needs to spread. Eventually what was, rightly, regarded as a fine breed gathers a very different and unenviable reputation. Popularity falls and a few faithful, responsible breeders are left to do what they can to pick up the pieces.

It must be accepted that, in the past, Kennel Club recognition has offered only a flimsy defence against the worst effects of popularity and exploitation but some defence, even if it is able only to keep a nucleus of breeding stock free from contamination, is far better than none at all. There are also indications that the Kennel Club, making good use of computer technology, is determined that it will, in future, provide a far more effective defence against the undesirable effects of commercialism and popularity. Criticism which may have been deserved in the past has now lost much of its validity.

The pros and cons of Kennel Club recognition were fully discussed in the late Betty Smith's book, *The Jack Russell Terrier*, published in 1970, and possibly the first book to be devoted exclusively to this very popular breed. The author recognised the dangers of un-controlled popularity, of indiscriminate breeding and of a loss of contact with the work for which the breed was originally bred but, on balance, suggested that the breed would benefit from Kennel Club recognition. This may well have been the first tentative move towards recognition but it was doomed to progress no further. At that time, many breeders were implacably opposed to recognition and not always without good reason. The breed itself was far too divergent in type to satisfy the Kennel Club that it was a true breed. Furthermore, as the book itself demonstrates, what was then regarded as a typical Jack Russell Terrier was very far removed from the type produced by Parson Jack Russell himself. It is doubtful, though, if this would have carried much weight with the Kennel Club providing that other conditions could be met.

It is perfectly understandable that breeders should be reluctant to forego the freedom they then enjoyed in order to accept the restrictions and additional expense which would be consequent on official recognition. It is understandable, too, that they would look askance at what had happened to a number of recognised breeds. For their part, the Kennel Club was right to be very cautious about recognising a breed which contained such a wide divergence of type, in which at that time, there had been little or no attempt to record and verify pedigrees and which seemed determined to ignore the existence of a growing catalogue of hereditary diseases.

During the next decade, however, a change took place which could not have been anticipated in 1970. The dwarf, often deformed, terriers which had been popular for so long began to lose favour and the type bred by Parson Jack Russell began to reassert itself. There were problems in accommodating the two types, and for some time Breed Standards tended to err on the side of laxity rather than defining, as is their intended purpose, precisely what characteristics were to be regarded as desirable. Standards tried to find ways of accepting both the traditional fourteen-inch terrier and the nine-inch dwarf. Working terrier shows began to separate the two into their own classes but judges were given no guidance, other than their own taste, as to which should be regarded as correct. A number of breeds contain both standard and miniature versions, a few even manage to produce three different sizes. None, however, produces two totally different types of dog and yet remain determined to present themselves as a single breed. Such divergence of type made eventual recognition seem increasingly unlikely and the views of opposing camps tended to polarise. Arguments, for and against, became submerged in special pleading and determination not to lose face, position or influence.

In July 1973 a report appeared in *Shooting Times* which illuminates what was then taking place.

> I think I am right in suggesting that at long last the mini-terrier boom is over and though stunted oddities are still seen as 'popular pets', serious hunting folk are at last doing their best to revert to a terrier higher in the shoulder, narrower in the chest and more like the original Russell standard.

A report in Shooting Times *in 1973 described Mick Clarke's terrier, which had just won the overall championship at the Bisley and Sandhurst Terrier Show, as 'as close to the Russell standard as one is likely to see'. It was terriers such as this and the judges who were able to recognise their quality which helped to revive interest in the old type.*

As an example of my contention, at the recent Bisley and Sandhurst Hunt Terrier Show there was not a single short-legged terrier to be seen in the eleven classes; indeed, the judges remarked to me that the standard was exceptionally high and that they had little hesitation in selecting as overall champion Mick Clarke's splendid terrier – as close to the Russell standard as one is likely to see. Let's hope that the trend has now been reversed, but let us pray that this type of terrier is confined to hunting circles and does not achieve fame or fortune with the general public.

The trend which had kept the short-legged, often deformed terriers in favour had certainly been reversed, except in the minds of the general public and some who might have been expected to know better. Though the 'stunted oddities' virtually disappeared from the scene, it was their image which the public retained as that of the true Jack Russell Terrier. The image was a remarkably resilient one and was still to be found among members of the Kennel Club's General Committee when, fifteen years later, they were asked to consider the question of official recognition for the Parson Jack Russell Terrier.

During the 1970s, a number of approaches were made to the Kennel Club by some of the clubs which were, by now, catering for the breed's interests, but none were deemed worthy of more than the briefest consideration. In 1983 the South East Jack Russell Terrier Club itself made an application for recognition of its own short-legged, rather heavily boned and heavily marked variant of the breed. The application was rejected but the South East Club had made the issue of recognition a real one. Their efforts inspired the formation of the Parson Jack Russell Terrier Club, dedicated to achieving recognition for the type of terrier bred by the Parson himself. By 1986 the Club felt that the time had come to test the water and so made its own application for recognition of the classic fourteen-inch, fourteen-pound working terrier. The application was given very serious consideration and, though it was eventually rejected, the terms of the Kennel Club's rejection gave reason for hope.

The Kennel Club decided that 'the time was not right for recognition'. It seemed that the application had foundered for a number of reasons. In an effort to listen to all sides of the case, it called a meeting at which those who opposed recognition, for a wide variety of good and bad reasons, were far more strongly represented than were those who had made and supported the application. The tenor of their objections, perhaps not unwittingly, gave the impression that there was little agreement as to the type of terrier which had most right to be regarded as a typical representative of the breed. Some of the types harboured unenviable catalogues of hereditary disease and these the Kennel Club had no wish to encourage. There was still too little reliable evidence of the existence of well-documented pedigrees, of a well-supported club registration system or even of a Standard which closely defined a single desirable type. Furthermore, the negative arguments, both from within the breed and its variants and from Fox Terrier breeders, which opposed recognition, were perhaps given more weight than they deserved. All felt themselves under threat by the prospect of recognition.

Fox Terrier exhibitors and the exhibitors of other recognised terrier breeds, particularly those which were not numerically strong, did not relish competition in the show ring from a terrier which would eventually probably command the sort of numbers which Fox Terriers themselves used to enjoy. Neither were the supporters of the recognised terriers, which had drifted a long way from the type which could be used for work, happy at the idea that another genuine working terrier would join the Border Terrier in the group and would inevitably invite comparisons and provoke questions which would be difficult to answer effectively.

The Jack Russell breeders who opposed recognition did so for a number of reasons. Some feared that recognition would inevitably lead to the breed's ruin as a working terrier. They were accustomed to small, informal events and to commensurate standards and had no desire to face tougher competition. Nor were they keen to enter a larger pool in which their own positions of influence might be under threat. Some also groundlessly feared that recognition would bring them under Kennel Club authority whether they liked it or not. Their opposition was perfectly understandable but the point was entirely missed that recognition would not change anything for them unless they chose to become involved in Kennel Club licensed events and registration. The system of working terrier shows would continue unchanged and their participation at these would not be threatened. Those who sought recognition were disappointed that the dice had been so heavily loaded against them and that the Kennel Club had not only failed to understand the situation fully but had, apparently, made little attempt to gather, at hunt, working terrier and breed club shows, the first-hand knowledge which would enable the application to be given balanced consideration. Only the terms of the rejection offered some slight hope for the future.

By rejecting the application, the Kennel Club denied access to a reliable registration system as a means of validating pedigrees, to methods for assessing and controlling the incidence of hereditary disease and for publishing the results, to a set of rules supported by effective disciplinary procedures which would enable some control over malpractice at shows to be exerted and to means by which the international development of the breed could be influenced by British breeders. It had ignored growing fears that increased opposition to fox-hunting would, if successful, result in the total loss of the purpose for which the breed was developed and of most of the shows on which the breed traditionally relied. It might well have been argued that by denying recognition the Kennel Club was itself acting against the spirit and intention of its own objectives which begin with the statement that 'the objects of the Club are to promote in every way the general improvement of dogs'. Certainly, it would be very difficult for the Kennel Club to argue that a refusal of recognition promoted the improvement of the Parson Jack Russell Terrier, though others would undoubtedly do so.

There was one further matter which refusal did not address. What were described as Jack Russell Terriers were sold in large numbers not just in Britain but throughout the world. Almost any small mongrel, preferably, though not necessarily, predominantly white could have its market value enhanced if it was described as a Jack Russell Terrier. There were even cases of overseas breeders paying high prices for allegedly pure-bred Jack Russell Terriers which subsequently gave birth to puppies which betrayed their parents polyglot origins. There were others which were reputed to be the offspring of well-known dogs which their owners denied had ever been used by the breeders of the exported puppies. Official recognition would have helped to put an end to this sort of dishonesty and by its refusal the Kennel Club left the public exposed to those who were exploiting the Parson's name and reputation.

The rejection, though not unexpected, provoked a heated discussion in which Ruth Hussey-Wilford, Secretary of The Parson Jack Russell Terrier Club, took a prominent part. In an article published in *Our Dogs* she wrote:

> The Kennel Club recently issued a Press Release, from which I quote: 'Non-recognition of the Jack Russell Terrier – the General Committee decided it was not appropriate to recognise the breed at the present time.

The Parson Jack Russell Terrier Club had not applied for recognition of the Jack Russell Terrier, a name often given to any Hunt type terrier which is predominantly white. The Club applied for recognition of the original type of working Fox Terrier. . . . Surely Kennel Club members, with all their knowledge of the world of dogs, must know the difference between a 'Jack Russell' and a Parson Jack Russell Terrier. Did they completely misunderstand the application or did they have pressure put on them by people from similar breeds who did not want our terrier to be recognised?

Mrs Hussey-Wilford's questions remained unanswered but they did provoke a considerable discussion. By November *Our Dogs* was able to report progress overseas and that in the Australian National Kennel Council's *Gazette* one of their most influential members, Mr J. Crowley, who had represented Australian canine interests at the World Conference, wrote what has come to be regarded as an invitation to Australian Jack Russell breeders to apply for recognition. He pointed out that the lack of recognition in Britain, the breed's country of origin, need be no impediment to Australian recognition. The Border Collie, another British breed, had been recognised in Australia thirty years before it was achieved in Britain, and there was, in Mr Cowley's opinion, no reason why the Jack Russell should not, if necessary, follow the same course.

A number of meetings between the Jack Russell Terrier Club of Australia and the Australian National Kennel Council followed and the terms on which recognition was likely to be granted were thoroughly explored. In America, a slightly more circumspect course was being pursued with the Jack Russell Terrier Breeders Association of America taking steps to ensure that all its procedures were in accord with what the American Kennel Club require after recognition but, in effect, being content, for a while at least, to await developments in Britain.

During the next couple of years the resurgence of the old Parson Jack Russell Terrier continued, both among those who sought Kennel Club recognition and those who opposed it. The problems associated with the previously popular dwarf terriers were brought into sharper focus and they fell further out of favour. Most significantly, in terms of Kennel Club interest, moves by overseas kennel clubs, notably in Australia, America, Holland and India, towards recognition also began to gather pace. It was beginning to seem very likely that the Parson Jack Russell Terrier would be offi-

81

cially recognised overseas before it received recognition in its homeland. Such a situation would not only have embarrassed the Kennel Club but would have resulted in problems with the export of unregistered terriers and the import of registered terriers which the Kennel Club might then have to allow at its shows. Continued refusal of recognition could have created its own very difficult problems. At the same time opposing arguments were effectively answered in a way which satisfied the Kennel Club's doubts, while the Kennel Club itself became more aware of the situation and the breed's needs.

The situation faced by the Parson Jack Russell Terrier and the Fox Terrier in the 1980s was precisely the same as that faced by the King Charles Spaniel and the Cavalier King Charles Spaniel in the years prior to the war. It was realised that the King Charles Spaniel had, over the years, evolved into a very different dog than that found at the court of King Charles. An American exhibitor, Roswell Eldridge, offered a £25 prize for dogs shown at Cruft's from 1926 to 1930, to the exhibit which most resembled the old breed. The same dog, Mostyn Walker's Ann's Son, won the prize for the first three years but by then a number of enthusiasts, led by Amice Pitt, had set to work to reproduce the old type. So successful were their efforts that a club was formed in 1928, the breed was given official recognition in 1944 and gained championship status in 1946. In 1987 the 'modern' King Charles Spaniel produced 248 registrations while the restored 'old-fashioned' Cavalier King Charles Spaniel produced 9,110 registrations. In the face of these figures it is perfectly understandable that the owners of modern Fox Terriers, now very far from the popularity they enjoyed during the early years of the century, should have been concerned about recognition of the old type.

It could be argued that overseas developments, during the mid-1980s, were also partially instrumental in getting the Parson Jack Russell Terrier recognised. Both the Kennel Club of India and the Raad van Beheer op Kynologisch Gedied in Holland simply went ahead and accepted registrations of Parson Jack Russell Terriers. Both were members of the Federation Cynologique Internationale whose influence extends over many countries and which had already shown a readiness to recognise breeds in the countries within its jurisdiction. Even the Kennel Club in Britain had found that it could not refuse to accept the breed on its obedience register, though it did insist on calling them cross breeds, much to the justified annoyance of their owners.

Disappointing though the outcome of the 1986 application may have been to some, it did pave the way for smoother progress in the future. Continuing discussion about the subject appeared in Sheila Atter's weekly breed notes in *Our Dogs*, and this influential paper pursued a consistent editorial policy which argued the case for recognition. As a result, problems, real as well as imaginary, were faced and overcome and the opposition to recognition was seen in its true, reactionary light. By the end of 1988 it began to be apparent that the Kennel Club and Parson Jack Russell Terrier owners might soon find themselves in a very invidious position if recognition was not granted before too long. The Parson Jack Russell Terrier Club, following informal sounding which indicated the likelihood of a favourable outcome, therefore, made a further application for recognition towards the end of 1988. The application went through the usual careful and lengthy process of consideration and the meeting between the Kennel Club's General Committee and representatives of the Parson Jack Russell Terrier Club was a very different occasion than the previous meeting had been.

Once more the arguments were rehearsed. Here was a terrier which had been bred with care for many years, which formed a distinct type and which reproduced that type. The Club's registration system was able to authenticate pedigrees and had already produced a method by which preferred breeding stock could be recorded differently from stock which might be less suitable for breeding. The Breed Standard though based on that produced by Heinemann in 1904, had been set out in the form which the Kennel Club had adopted in 1986. Its phraseology had been deliberately tailored, even to the extent of adopting suitable and relevant phrases from the Standards of other working terrier breeds, to produce a result which the Kennel Club would find acceptable but without, in any way at all, sacrificing what was of importance to the breed. One of the stumbling blocks to earlier applications had been the existence of a Standard which not only failed to define a desirable type but seemed at pains to encompass almost any terrier whose owner might wish to regard it as a Jack Russell. The far tighter Standard was a necessity if type was to be preserved and was something which would be welcomed by the Kennel Club.

At its meeting on 11 April 1989, the Kennel Club's General Committee formally considered the application and decided that, subject to the Parson Jack Russell Terrier Club's acceptance of certain conditions, the application should progress further. These conditions involved a thorough examination by the Kennel Club of the breed club's registration system, an insistence that the Standard must be amended to make it clear that it did not embrace terriers under twelve inches and the acceptance of a series of conditions, more stringent than had previously been applied to newly recognised breeds.

The announcement that the Kennel Club was making progress towards recognition of the Parson Jack Russell Terrier did not pass unnoticed by the general press. *The Times* was soon thundering about an alleged rumpus. Its report quoted Major General Martin Sinnatt, Secretary of the Kennel Club, whose words were chosen for their accuracy rather than their diplomacy:

> These people in the Parson Jack Russell Club have the successor of the real 14-inch terrier that Jack Russell bred. . . . They are not the short-legged little sawn-off things which rush around horse show car parks and bark at you and steal chicken legs from your sandwiches.

Mrs June Laker, Secretary of the South East Jack Russell Club – the Club which had made the 1983 application – expressed a view which demonstrated how little the process or its implications was understood:

> We do not wish to be dictated to by the Kennel Club. We want to run our own breed in our own way. They say their dogs are the dog the Parson bred but the Parson bought his first terrier from a milkman in Oxford market. No one knows what he really got up to because his records disappeared.

The unfounded fear that the Kennel Club, using some undisclosed power, would be able to dictate to those who have no wish to avail themselves of the opportunities which recognition would offer, was one shared with many others and was, perhaps, one of the reasons why opposition to recognition remained so implacable. It was used in a letter circulated to club members in an attempt to dissuade them from supporting recognition and was even used to persuade Jack Russell Terrier owners in America to oppose a process which could not possibly have had any effect on the activities and values they regarded as important. The Kennel Club neither would nor could force anyone to do anything. Recognition would extend the opportunities available to Parson Jack Russell Terrier owners if they chose to avail themselves of these new opportunities but it would not at all affect the opportunities which have been available in the past, though it would provide a valuable insurance against the future. Unreasonable fears of the unknown; a reluctance to face the challenges and accept the opportunities which recognition would offer; a fear that recognition would lead to a loss of markets for terriers of mediocre quality and dubious breeding sold at high prices by dealers; and a well-justified recognition that many of the less creditable practices by which some dealers, breeders, judges and exhibitors maintained their positions would be curtailed by Kennel Club authority were perhaps the main reasons for continued opposition to recognition.

At the same time, many people who had previously kept their attitude towards recognition carefully hidden showed themselves to be strongly in favour of it. At a time when its officers needed to devote all their attention to satisfying the Kennel Club's questions, the Parson Jack Russell Terrier Club found itself inundated with expressions of interest in recognition, applications for membership and for registration from terrier owners all over the world. Throughout May and June of 1989 an exchange of correspondence between the Kennel Club and the Parson Jack Russell Terrier Club made steady progress towards recognition. The Club's records were minutely examined, suggestions for slight changes to the Standard were made and various other points were ironed out so that at its meeting in autumn 1989 the Kennel Club finally gave official recognition to the breed which its old member had originated over one hundred years previously.

6

Breed Standards, British and American

The Breed Standard of any breed represents an attempt to describe the characteristics, both physical and temperamental, which together produce the ideal dog of that breed. Some Breed Standards, particularly those favoured by the Federation Cynologique Internationale, are extremely verbose without producing a clearer picture of the ideal than do some more concise Standards. In Britain, the Standards of all recognised breeds were revised by the Kennel Club in 1986. The aim was to arrange each in the same format to facilitate ease of reference and to remove any descriptions which, by calling for exaggerated or extreme characteristics, might encourage the production of unhealthy animals. At the same time, the opportunity was taken to reduce the length of all the Standards by eliminating what, in the Kennel Club's opinion, were unnecessary words and to do so even to the point of misuse of the English language. Having completed this exercise, the Kennel Club then laid claim to the copyright of all the Breed Standards and is now in a position to exercise complete control over both their content and use, not just in this country but in all countries where British copyright is respected. Consequently, the Standard which is eventually accepted by the Kennel Club will be the product of negotiations between the Kennel Club and the Parson Jack Russell Terrier Club in which the Kennel Club will have the right of veto sparingly, carefully and responsibly exercised.

In America, the situation is slightly but significantly different in that copyright for the Breed Standards is vested not with the American Kennel Club but with individual breed clubs. It is they who control the content of the Standard and the way in which it can be used. In America, if recognition results in a perceived need for a changed Standard, all the changes will be made by the breed club. Other countries, particularly those which owe allegiance to the FCI, tend to make use of the Standard which is used in the breed's country of origin, which means that it is the British Standard which will be most widely used throughout the world, thus enabling British breeders, through the Kennel Club, to exert influence and control over the international development of the Parson Jack Russell Terrier.

The Kennel Club has not yet undertaken what little editing might be deemed necessary to tailor the Standard produced by the Parson Jack Russell Terrier Club to suit their particular tastes and needs. In fact, very little editing should be necessary because the Standard was produced in accordance with the Kennel Club's own format, avoids any suggestion of encouraging exaggerated characteristics and is already concise. However, the present Standard is only the most recent to evolve from a process which was begun by the Parson himself. What must be regarded as the first Standard for the breed was produced by the Parson in 1871.

Parson Jack Russell's 1871 Standard

A small energetic terrier of from 14/16lb in weight, standing about 14 inches at the withers, legs straight as arrows; a thick skin, a good rough weather-resisting coat, thick, close; and a trifle wiry, well calculated to protect the body from cold and wet, but with no affinity to the wiry jacket of a Scotch Terrier. It is certain that a good horse or dog cannot be a bad colour, but I prefer a white dog. The bitch 'TRUMP' was white with just a patch of dark over each eye and ear, with a similar dot not larger than a penny-piece at the root of the tail. Feet should be perfect, the loins and conformation of the whole frame indicative of hardihood and endurance. The size and height of the animal may be compared to a fully grown vixen. Every inch a sportsman, the dog must not be quarrelsome. As regards height, some people prefer them to be rather more on the leg if they are to run with the hounds all day.

What the Parson left out of the Standard is almost as interesting as what he put in. There is no mention of anything, other than colour, which could be regarded as of no more than cosmetic importance; every single requirement has functional importance. There is no mention of ears. The ears of the Parson's terriers were said to have been inclined to fly, a defect which landed William Carrick in trouble. There is even no mention of the shape of the head and none of the tail, either its length or carriage. Some people have suggested that the Parson was as opposed to docking as he was to cropping. Even so, as a first attempt at a Standard the document is admirable and valuable. It contains much which should, somehow, be incorporated into any new Standard. Especially the requirements of thick skin, rough, white, weather-resistant coat, hardihood and endurance, weight and size and amiable disposition which now differentiate the Parson Jack Russell Terrier from other fox terriers.

Then, in 1904, Arthur Heinemann produced another Standard for the breed. It was far fuller than that of the Parson's, as was perhaps to be expected from a practising journalist. It also describes a terrier which is somewhat different from Heinemann's own. He appears to have been able to expound the verity of one particular type while producing a quite different type himself; perhaps that too was a product of his career in journalism.

Heinemann's 1904 Standard

Head

The skull should be flat, moderately broad, gradually decreasing to the eyes. Little stop should be apparent. The cheeks must not be full. Ears V-shaped and small, of moderate thickness and dropping forward close to the cheek, not by the side. Upper and lower jaws strong and muscular and of fair punishing strength. Not much falling away below the eyes. The nose should be black. The eyes dark, small, and deep set, full of fire, life and intelligence, and circular in shape. Teeth level, i.e. upper on the outside of the lower.

Neck

Clean and muscular of fair length gradually widening to shoulders.

Shoulders

Long and sloping well laid back, at points, clearly cut at the withers.

Chest

Deep but not broad.

Back

Straight and strong with no appearance of slackness.

Loins

Powerful, very slightly arched, fore ribs moderately arched, back ribs deep. The terrier should be well ribbed up.

Hindquarters

Strong and muscular, full from droop, thighs long and powerful, hocks near the ground, dog standing well up on them. Not straight in the stifle.

Stern

Set on high, carried gaily but never over back or curled. Of good strength and length. A 'pipe cleaning' tail or too short is most objectionable.

Legs

Perfectly straight showing no ankle in front. Strong in bone throughout, short and straight to the pastern. Fore and back legs carried straight forward when travelling, stifles not turned outward. Elbows should hang perpendicular to the body, working free to the side.

Feet

Round, compact, not large, soles hard and tough, toes moderately arched, turned neither in nor out.

Coat

Dense, a trifle wiry, abundant. Belly and undersides not bare.

Colour

White, with acceptable tan, grey or black at head and foot of tail. Red brindle or liver marks are objectionable.

Symmetry, Size and Character

Terrier must present a gay, lively and active appearance. Bone and strength in a small compass are essentials, but not cloggy or coarse. Speed and endurance must be apparent. Not too short or too long in leg. Fourteen inches to withers for the ideal dog, thirteen for a bitch. Weight when in working condition about fourteen pounds, but a pound more or less entirely acceptable. Conformation that of an adult vixen.

Disqualifying Points

Too short, too leggy, legs not straight, nose white, cherry, or spotted considerably with these colours. Ears prick or rose. Mouth under or over shot. Excessively nervous or savage.

Using this Standard as their starting point, the Committee of the Parson Jack Russell Terrier Club produced its own Standard in 1984. During the next five years this Standard went through a period of evolution; passages which were imprecise were tightened up to respond to the breed's particular needs. The final amendments made by the Parson Jack Russell Terrier Club in May 1989 were intended to bring the Standard into line with those of other recognised breeds and were principally concerned with format, the removal of ambiguities, reinforcement of important points and fleshing out of those which were perhaps too terse. Nothing which would affect the breed's appearance or working ability was changed; indeed, such changes as were made were all intended to prevent change.

British Breed Standard

Characteristics

A workmanlike, active and agile terrier, built for speed and endurance. Well balanced, with a length of back from withers to root of tail to be much the same as from withers to the ground. Strong head, bright, keen expression. Scars and injuries resulting from work or accident are acceptable unless movement is impaired.

The opening words of the old Standard drew attention to the importance of type by emphasising that this is the Standard of the Parson Jack Russell Terrier and not of any other working terrier, no matter how good it might be. These introductory words are now omitted as they are from all Kennel Club Standards. This we regard as a pity because they helped to emphasise the importance of type, and, unless type is maintained, any breed can, almost imperceptibly and unknowingly, be changed into a very different animal than that which the Standard attempts to define. The Parson Jack Russell Terrier represents an attempt to perpetuate the type of terrier which the Parson bred, of which he was so rightly proud and for which he was, equally rightly, renowned. It follows, therefore, that protection of the type bred by the Parson is of the utmost importance. There must be absolutely no question that, subsequent to recognition, these aims will be in any way changed either by the pressure of changed fashion, the desire for show ring success or in the name of so-called improvement.

The final sentence represents the breed club's attempt to guard against any tendency by judges who have no experience of work to regard legitimate scars as a disfigurement which should be penalised. However, it should also be said that scars of unknown origin should not be regarded, as is sometimes the case, as badges of courage. Too often, heavy scarring indicates a terrier which is foolhardy or an owner who is callous of its well-being. Judges should neither penalise an acceptable level of scarring nor regard it as a proof of a terrier's working qualities.

Characteristics

Essentially a terrier with the ability and conformation to work underground and to follow a horse.

The Standard does not say that those qualities required of a working terrier bred to run with hounds are desirable or to be encouraged. It says that they are essential; without them the terrier would be useless. Unfortunately, but understandably, it must assume that its readers have some knowledge of what those qualities are.

91

A terrier well built for work but insufficiently racy to run with hounds.

Temperament

Bold and friendly at all times.

The previous version of the Standard laid emphasis on boldness and confidence, qualities which the breed, even at a very early age, takes to the point of foolhardiness and even arrogance. Nervousness is to be discouraged, as is cowardice, a quality which can only truly be assessed at work, though a clever judge may infer cowardice from a terrier's behaviour in other situations. A reference to 'over-aggression' has sensibly been deleted and replaced by a call for a friendly disposition. Aggression in a working terrier, particularly one bred to run with hounds, should be directed only towards its legitimate quarry. Any display of aggression towards anything other than its legitimate quarry must be regarded as a quality which would detract from its value as a working terrier.

A very typical head – strong, broad, with a powerful muzzle and an intense expression.

Head and Skull

Should be flat, moderately broad, gradually narrowing to the eyes. Little stop should be apparent. The length from stop to nose should be slightly shorter than that from stop to occiput. Nose black.

What is here described is a head very different from that of the modern Fox Terrier. A head which might be summarised as 'workmanlike', though use of that word should not imply a lack of quality or the presence of any coarseness. The flat, moderately broad skull provides adequate room for brains as well as good anchorage for the muscles which drive a rather short, strong muzzle.

In a white terrier with no more than a small amount of light tan markings there may be a tendency towards a liver- or flesh-coloured nose. Both the eye clause and that which describes the nose guard against any loss or dilution of pigmentation.

Eyes

Deep-set, dark with keen expression.

The eyes of any terrier tell a lot about its character. In a Parson Jack Russell Terrier they flash with mischief and impart a slightly quizzical expression which may at times be fiery, but should never be hard. Previous Standards have variously described the eye, or rather the aperture formed by the eyelids, as round and almond shaped. The present Standard avoids the trap of describing a shape which might give rise to an abnormality. A round or protuberant eye would be susceptible to damage, an almond-shaped aperture could easily give rise to entropion; both are, therefore, discouraged.

Ears

Small, V-shaped, dropping forward and carried close to the head.

Ears are set on the side rather than the top of the head and should have no suggestion of being pricked. They drop forward close to the cheeks in order to protect the inner ear from incursions of debris when the terrier is below ground. What remains unsaid is that the ears should not rise above the level of the skull as do those of the modern Fox Terrier. Nor is there any mention of thickness, which should be moderate. A thin ear is easily damaged and a thick leather, if damaged, takes longer to heal.

Mouth

Jaws strong and muscular. Teeth – scissor bite, i.e. strong even teeth with upper teeth closely overlapping the lower teeth.

The clause which describes the head and skull defines the length of the muzzle. Here the description is amplified by emphasis on the need for strength. No guidance is given as to shape but a narrow or pointed muzzle would be unlikely to have the necessary strength. The need, in a working terrier, for big, evenly spaced teeth is obvious. It is likely that the description of a scissor bite will be amended by the Kennel Club by the insertion of their standard, if incomprehensible, clause which is intended to describe a scissor bite. The clause defines a scissor bite as one with the 'upper teeth closely

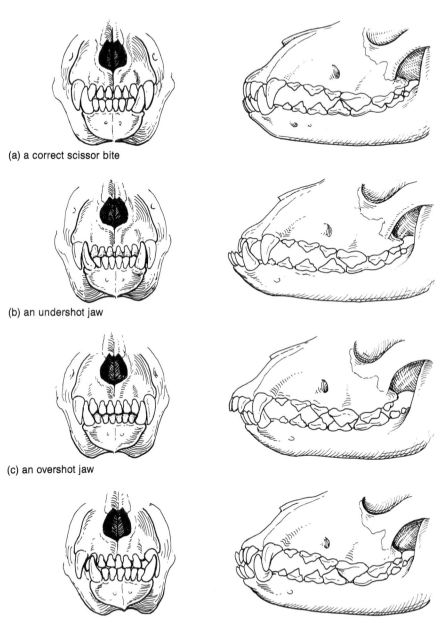

(a) a correct scissor bite

(b) an undershot jaw

(c) an overshot jaw

(d) a wry mouth – perhaps the worst fault of all

A correct jaw, an undershot jaw, an overshot jaw and a wry mouth – perhaps the worst fault of all. A scissor bite best withstands the wear and tear of work.

95

overlapping lower teeth and set square to the jaw'. It should be noted that the Standard contains no suggestion of any tolerance for under or overshot jaws or even of unevenly placed teeth.

Neck

Clean and muscular, of good length, gradually widening to the shoulders. (The terrier, when working underground, should be able to extend its neck to enable its mouth to reach beyond its paws.)

The length of the neck is often indicative of shoulder construction. A short, stuffy neck is the product of upright shoulders which would restrict a dog's movement both above and below ground. The requirement that the mouth should be capable of being extended beyond the front paws is a necessity to all working terriers if their feet are not to be exposed to undefendable attacks by foxes when the terrier is below ground. A good length of neck allied to well-laid shoulders provides for this in the best manner. Other unacceptable ways of achieving the same effect would be to have an exceptionally long neck or exceptionally short legs.

Forequarters

Shoulders long and sloping, well-laid back and clearly cut at the withers. Legs strong and straight with joints in correct alignment. Elbows hanging perpendicular to the body, working free of the sides.

The shoulders of any breed which are expected to run with hounds across a difficult country and then to work below ground in restricted spaces are very important. An upright construction or lack of adequate length in either the lower or upper arm would not only restrict movement above ground but would also reduce necessary flexibility below ground. A shoulder which produced a stilted or hackney action rather than the ideal, flowing 'grass cutting' movement could not be regarded as correct.

The clause encapsulates in a few words all that is necessary to say about the forequarters. Reference to straightness and to the need for joints to be correctly aligned might be seen as a reaction against the bow-fronted, heavy-jointed terriers which some people might, wrongly, still regard as typical of the breed.

Body

Chest of moderate depth, capable of being spanned by average size hands, behind the shoulders. The length in comparison to the height of the terrier to give a balanced image. The loin slightly arched.

A terrier's ability to manoeuvre in restricted places is not to any significant degree affected by its length of leg. If short legs were necessary in order to manoeuvre below ground then foxes would either not venture below ground or would have short legs. It is the chest which tends to limit the sort of places which can be regarded as accessible. In any breed intended to gallop across country, a depth of chest, to give good heart and lung room, is an advantage. However, too much depth must be regarded as an encumbrance to a working terrier, as must any degree of spring of rib which inclines the terrier towards being barrel chested. The traditional way of measuring a working terrier's ribs is to span it behind the shoulders. Of course,

This terrier has a very short coupling which would reduce its ability to manoeuvre underground.

hands vary in size; here the reference to average hands must be regarded as a reference to average-sized masculine hands.

The reference to a slightly arched loin, in order to provide additional strength, does not mention the need for a strong loin of fair length in order to provide the flexibility which a terrier needs underground. Short-coupled terriers are at a disadvantage in tight places because of their inability to manoeuvre.

We are not entirely happy that 'balanced image' gives sufficient guidance as to length in relation to height. Dachshund breeders regard their breed as presenting a balanced image; so do those who breed the ultra-short-backed modern Fox Terriers. Balance, like beauty, seems to lie in the eye of the beholder. A Parson Jack Russell Terrier has neither a short back nor a long one. In outline he is slightly longer, from withers to root of tail, than he is high, from ground to withers. Why the Standard does not say so we cannot imagine.

Hindquarters

Strong and muscular with good angulation and bend of stifle. Hocks near the ground giving plenty of drive. Looking from behind their hocks must be straight.

Once more, reference to the need for straightness might be regarded as a reaction to deformities erroneously regarded by some as breed characteristics. A well-muscled Parson Jack Russell Terrier is a little power-house of energy, and moves with considerable drive, imparted by strong quarters and hind legs which should neither be straight nor over-angulated. Low hocks tend not to produce excessive angulation and are a desirable part of the construction of any dog intended to cover great distances over rough ground.

Feet

Compact with hard pads, turning neither in or out.

The earlier version of the Standard referred to cat-like feet, but of course no dog can possibly have cat-like feet. The need for tightly and thickly padded feet which will enable a terrier to work over rough terrain is obvious – thin and open feet are easily injured. There is a saying 'no foot, no hound' which stresses the need for good feet on a hound; the same is true of a working terrier.

Tail

Strong, straight and set on high. Customarily docked with length complimenting the body while providing a good handhold.

Parson Jack Russell Terriers are customarily docked and there is, as illustrations in this book demonstrate, a current fashion to dock tails shorter than will leave enough for a 'good handhold', sometimes a useful means of assisting or persuading a terrier to leave an earth. Tails are straight, not curved and certainly not kinked, and carried, when the terrier is on the alert, with that jaunty pride which is associated with the breed. Though they are set high they should not be carried squirrel fashion over the back.

The phrase 'customarily docked' responds to the growing antagonism, with the European Community, welfare organisations and the veterinary profession, to what is increasingly regarded as an unnecessary mutilation. In two Scandinavian countries docking is already prohibited and it is no more than prudent to anticipate that

A low-set tail alters the entire topline.

it may eventually be prohibited in Britain. If that does happen, there will be a need to decide what the correct natural tail for a Parson Jack Russell Terrier should be and perhaps to place greater emphasis on efforts to breed the naturally short tails which are to be found in some strains of the breed.

Gait/Movement

To be free, lively and well co-ordinated with straight action in front and behind.

Any terrier which is expected to run with hounds must be capable of speedy, efficient movement. Any exaggeration such as a hackney action in front or poor drive behind would reduce both speed and efficiency. The movement of a Parson Jack Russell Terrier is like that of a well-trained athlete – bouncy on his toes, deceptively easy and very economical.

Coat

Rough, a trifle wiry or smooth. Dense with belly and undersides not bare. Skin must be thick.

The Parson bred terriers with wiry jackets. He made use of terriers which were regarded as having smooth coats but these smooth coats

Pauline Hancock's owner-bred Ragford Rascal shows some degree of the coloured flecking which is associated with the traditional Welsh Foxhound.

Ridley Redstart, bred and owned by Sheila Atter, is a smooth coated bitch, but still with the hard, close, short jacket which affords protection in the field.

were not soft or silky; they were hard, close and weather resistant. The same qualities should be present in a rough coated terrier – coats should be hard and dense. A thin jacket offers poor protection against wear and weather. Parson Jack Russell Terrier exhibitors denigrate what they regard as the excessive hairdressing practised on some breeds and discourage it in their own. A terrier, nevertheless, must be clean and well groomed whether it is to attend a show or join hounds at a meet. A dirty, ungroomed coat does not improve a terrier's ability to work and is suggestive of nothing other than a careless owner. It is, perhaps, reprehensible that we cannot resist the temptation to point out that neither the hardness not cleanliness of a coat requires the use of chalk or of any other foreign substance.

In addition to a dense, thick jacket a working terrier needs a thick skin, as protection against injury and cold. An underlay of fat should not be confused with a thick skin.

Colour

Predominantly white with black and/or tan markings.

This clause is, in our opinion, the least satisfactory in the Breed Standard in terms of the qualities which Parson Jack Russell regarded as important. From the rather heavily marked Trump he developed a strain of dogs which were either totally white or which had tan marking confined to the head and the root of the tail. In other terrier breeds in which the Standard calls for a predominance of white, there is a tendency to accept very heavy coloured markings. If this were to happen to the Parson Jack Russell Terrier one of the qualities which he valued would be lost. Perhaps, at this stage in the breed's development some tolerance of heavily marked terriers might be reasonable, providing that temporary tolerance does not lead to permanent acceptance.

Though the Standard does not say so, brindle is unacceptable, being strongly indicative of the recent introduction of foreign blood, most probably from a Staffordshire or Bull Terrier.

Size

Height ideally 35–36cm (14in) at withers for dogs and 32.5–33.5cm (13in) for bitches but none should be more than 2.5cm (1in) under these heights.

The classic ideal for a working terrier is fourteen pounds and fourteen inches, a convenient and easily remembered formula which metrication effectively destroys – 6.3504 kilograms and 35.56 centimetres does not have quite the same ring to it. The height measurement is, of course, taken from the ground to the point of the withers when the terrier is standing upright. The weight, to which the Standard surprisingly makes no reference, is for a terrier in hard working condition. Reference to weight along with the minimum allowable height would reinforce the difference between the Parson Jack Russell Terrier and the dwarf terriers which have made use of the Parson's name, and would leave these terriers free to pursue their own development without fear of confusion with the recognised breed.

Faults

Any departure from the foregoing points should be considered a fault and the seriousness with which the fault should be regarded should be in exact proportion to its degree.

This clause, included in all Kennel Club Standards, is intended to quantify faults according to their degree. It does not, however, give any guidance as to the relative importance of different faults. In a working terrier any fault which would prevent it from doing the job for which the breed was intended must be regarded as far more serious than one which has no such effect.

Note

Male animals to have two apparently normal testicles fully descended into the scrotum.

This final clause in the Standard is another which is contained in every Kennel Club Breed Standard. It represents an attempt to discourage a hereditary condition which not only reduces a dog's fertility and so places the breed's future at some risk but which also predisposes a dog to the growth of tumours.

The American Standard is understandably more verbose than the British version. America has no tradition of using terriers in the way which the Parson used them. Matters which might need no more than an inference in the British Standard are rightly spelled out in some detail in the American Standard. It contains some, relatively minor, differences from the British Standard but these are grammatical rather than indications of any broad disagreement on fundamental principles. What is important is the general agreement which exists between the two Standards. Here, surely, is evidence of a firm international intention to maintain a single type of terrier. It is not necessary to make any attempt to interpret the American Standard; what has been said already should suffice. It is included because of the way it extends appreciation of the breed.

Ridley Reckless was bred by Sheila Atter in Lincolnshire, Beau Jeste Golly by Melissa Wineholt and Terrie Hartleib in Pennsylvania. Both were whelped in May 1988 and show that their type is not just to be found on one side of the Atlantic. Apart from having a common grandfather, the two puppies are unrelated.

American Breed Standard

General Appearance

An alert, active, predominantly white terrier confident in attitude but never shy or vicious. Balanced in height and length, of medium size and bone suggesting strength, agility and endurance. The dog is a working terrier and must possess sufficient length of leg to follow a fox hunt on foot and a chest small enough to go to ground to fox, their natural quarry.

Size, Proportion and Substance

The height that gives overall balance is usually between twelve and fourteen inches at the withers. (The ideal height of a mature dog is fourteen inches at the withers and bitches thirteen inches at the withers.) Terriers with heights either larger or smaller than the ideal are not to be penalised provided other points of their conformation, especially balance and chest span, are consistent with the Breed Standard. Balance is the keystone of the terrier's anatomy. The chief points for consideration are the relative proportions of skull and foreface, head and back, height at withers and length of body. The terrier should be of medium bone, not so heavy as to appear coarse or so light as to appear racy. The conformation of the whole frame should indicate substance and endurance; the size and height may be compared to an adult vixen European Red Fox.

Head and Skull

Should be well balanced and in proportion to the body. The skull should be of moderate width at the ears, narrowing to the eyes. There should be a defined stop but not over-pronounced. The length of the muzzle, from the nose to the stop, should be slightly shorter than the distance from the stop to the occiput. The jaws upper and lower should be well boned and muscular, of fair punishing strength, excessive muscular development so as to appear 'cheeky' is objectionable.

Nose

Must be black and fully pigmented.

Eyes

Almond shaped, small, not protruding, dark in colour, full of life and intelligence, showing an intense expression. Dark rims desirable. Anything approaching light or yellow eye is objectionable.

Ears

Small, 'V'-shaped drop ears of moderate thickness, carried forward close to the head with the tip so as to cover the orifice and pointing towards the eyes. Button ear.

Teeth

Comparatively large teeth with a scissor bite.

Neck

Clean and muscular of sufficient length to provide balance to the dog, gradually widening to blend well into the shoulders. The dog when working underground should be able to extend its neck to enable its mouth to reach beyond its paws.

Shoulders

Long and sloping, well laid back and clearly cut at the withers.

Body

In overall length to height proportions, the dog appears approximately square and balanced.

Chest

Narrow and of moderate depth, the front legs set not too widely apart, giving an athletic, rather heavily chested appearance. The maximum size is a hand span of approximately 14in behind the point of the elbow. (When measured with a tape at this point, the measurement will be larger.) Chest should be flexible.

Ribs

Fairly well sprung, oval rather than round, not extending past the level of the elbow.

Back

Strong and straight, laterally supple, the loin slightly arched.

Tail

Set high, strong, carried gaily, but not over the back or curled. Docked so the tip is approximately level to the skull, providing a good handhold.

Forelegs

Strong, straight with good bone and joints in correct alignment. Elbows hanging perpendicular to the body and working free of the sides. Pasterns firm and nearly straight.

Hindquarters

Strong and muscular, smoothly moulded with good angulation and bend of stifle. Hocks near the ground giving plenty of drive. When viewed from behind the hocks must be straight.

Feet

Round, cat like, very compact, the pads thick and tough, the toes moderately arched pointing forward, turned neither in nor out.

Coat

Smooth: Flat but hard, dense and abundant, belly and undersides of the thighs should not be bare. Rough: Double-coated, short, dense undercoat covered with a dense wire-like top coat, belly and underside of the thighs should not be bare.

Colour

White should predominate with black or tan markings or a combination of these, tri-colour. Heavy body markings are not desirable.

Disqualifications

Vicious behaviour. Mouth over or undershot. Brindle markings, prick ears, brown or white or liver nose, cryptorchid.

Faults

Excessively nervous or aggressive. Mouth under or overshot. Weak jaws. Down at the shoulder. Barrel ribs, out at the elbow, narrow hips. Legs not straight. Cow-hocked, straight stifles. Unsound movement, dishing plaiting, toeing. Price, tulip, propeller or rose ears. Brown, white or liver nose. Silky or woolly coats. Brindle or liver markings. Overly short, curly or squirrel tails. Weak voice. Lack of muscle or skin tone. Evidence of foreign blood. Yellow or light eyes. Facial wrinkles. Heavy body markings.

Note

Scars and injuries resulting from work should not prejudice a terrier's performance in the show ring unless they interfere with its movement or ability to work. Shyness should not be confused with submissiveness. Submissiveness is not a fault. No single point of the Standard should be over-emphasized.

107

Measuring a Terrier's Chest by Spanning

Carefully measure one's hand span, thumb to thumb, forefinger to forefinger. Find out where, on one's span, 14in is measured. Span the terrier's chest from behind, raising only the front feet from the ground, and compress gently. Now span behind the terrier's elbows and around the smaller rigid part of the chest. The central part of the chest will usually be larger, but this part is more flexible and compressible.

Comparisons between Standards

Comparisons are said to be odious but one of the comparisons which is inevitable is between the old Fox Terrier Standard and the Standard now intended to describe the old-fashioned Fox Terrier which is the Parson Jack Russell Terrier. Perhaps the most significant is that, though protesting the need for a terrier to 'gallop and stay, and follow his fox', the original Fox Terrier Standard allowed for terriers up to 20 pounds (9kg) in weight. The Parson's terriers seldom scaled more than 15 pounds (6.8kg), and the touchstone for most working terrier men is 14 pounds (6.4kg). Even this very first Standard allowed a weight which was 25 per cent greater than that which is generally regarded as ideal by working terrier men.

Since, as we have suggested, the true Parson Jack Russell Terrier is an old-fashioned Fox Terrier preserved in the form perfected by the Parson and his hunting cronies well over a hundred years ago, it is surely valid to ask in what way it differs from the modern Smooth and Wire Fox Terriers. Differences there certainly are, but these differences are not the result of accidental or unintentional development. They stem, in the main, from the way in which, during the latter part of the nineteenth century, the Smooth Fox Terrier was refined in order to satisfy those who had turned it into the most popular show dog. For the Wire Fox Terrier the same process came somewhat later, during the 1920s, and now appears to have gone far further because of the way in which the breed is trimmed for the show ring. Appearances, however, can be deceptive and there is, in fact, little structural difference between the modern Smooth and Wire Fox Terriers. Nor should there be, because prior to 1986, the two Breed Standards were identical, except in reference to the coat. Now they describe the same animal, using slightly different words.

108

Comparison between the three standards will help to identify the differences.

The clause which describes the breeds' characteristics stresses that the Fox Terrier must be alert, quick of movement and on tiptoe of expectation of the slightest provocation. These are the qualities necessary to achieve success in the show ring but are not necessarily desirable in a working terrier. The Parson Jack Russell Standard stresses the importance of working characteristics and looks for boldness and confidence, while discouraging unprovoked and indiscriminate aggression. Parson Jack Russell Terriers should be capable of amicable relationship with other dogs whether in the field or the show ring.

The significant difference between the heads is that the Parson Jack Russell's is required to be 'moderately broad' whereas in both the Smooth and the Wire Fox Terriers the phrase used is 'moderately narrow'. In the Parson Jack Russell 'the length from stop to nose should be slightly shorter than that from stop to occiput' whereas in the Wire there is 'little difference in length between skull and foreface'. In the Wire, excessive 'muscular development of jaws' is regarded as undesirable and unsightly. A strong jaw is necessary to a working terrier.

The eyes of a Parson Jack Russell Terrier were described as 'almond shaped'. Those of both the Smooth and the Wire Fox Terrier should be 'as near circular in shape as possible'.

In the Smooth, the chest is required to be deep, in the Wire the brisket is described as deep. The Parson terrier should have a chest 'of moderate depth, capable of being spanned'. Excessive depth would restrict a terrier's ability to work underground.

Both the Smooth and the Wire are required to have short backs, with the Wire also being 'very short coupled'. Shortness is also stressed in comparison with 'a short backed hunter'. Excessive shortness in back and particularly in coupling reduces the 'flexibility a terrier will need when it is working in restricted spaces underground as well as the freedom of movement, stamina and agility necessary to run with hounds.

The description of movement in both the Smooth and Wire Standards appears to suggest precision rather than freedom and economy. The stress in the Parson Standard is on freedom, economy and co-ordination.

In all three, the words used to describe the coat stress density, though the Wire Standard also suggests that about one and a half inches of coat is required on the withers. Density rather than profusion of coat is more important to a dog intended to work in winter weather. Grooming a Parson Jack Russell Terrier does not require the skill which is lavished on Wire Fox Terriers and does not result in terriers which look very different when they appear in the ring than when they are at work or live as companions. The coat of the smooth coated Parson Jack Russell is appreciably harder than is acceptable for the Smooth Fox Terrier and the skin should be appreciably thicker.

The descriptions of what are regarded as desirable colours are very similar in all three breeds, though it will be found that in the Parson Jack Russell Terrier heavy, coloured markings are in practice less readily accepted than they are in Fox Terriers.

The classic formula for a good working terrier of any breed is fourteen inches (36cm) at the shoulder and fourteen pounds (6.4kg) in weight. This requirement is based on an empirical assessment of what is required in the hunting field. The Parson Jack Russell Standard suggests that bitches might be an inch shorter and, presumably, a pound lighter. The Wire Fox Terrier Standard suggests an ideal of fifteen and a half inches (39cm) and eighteen pounds (8.2kg) for dogs and slightly less for bitches. Smooth Fox Terriers range between fifteen and seventeen pounds (6.8–7.7kg) for bitches and sixteen and eighteen pounds (7.3–8.2kg) for dogs. The modern Fox Terrier is appeciably bigger than the Parson Jack Russell Terrier. The original Standard for Fox Terriers set a maximum weight of twenty pounds (9kg), over 30 per cent heavier than the Parson's terriers, and it may well be that present differences are, in this respect, less marked than was once the case.

The sum of all the differences, some minor, others of greater importance, especially when set alongside the work which a terrier is intended to carry out, result in the overall appearance of each of the three fox terrier breeds being very different. The difference need not and should not invite odious comparisons. Fox Terriers have chosen a particular path, the Parson Jack Russell Terrier has chosen a different path. Neither has a monopoly of right or wrong.

7

Caveat Emptor

Before you buy a Parson Jack Russell Terrier or, indeed, any animal you must decide whether you are a fit owner. Can you give one the attention, the living conditions, the food and the exercise it will need and deserve? Are you prepared to face the cost of its upkeep, which over the years will add up to many times the original purchase price? Are you prepared to face all the attendant costs such as fencing, housing, insurance and veterinary treatment? Are you prepared to accept the restrictions and responsibilities which ownership of any animal involves? Are you willing and capable of training it and subsequently keeping it under proper control so that it is neither a nuisance nor a danger to others? If the answer to any one of these questions is not an unqualified, convinced and honest affirmative then you need read no further. You should abandon the idea of becoming the owner of any animal and should certainly not contemplate buying a Parson Jack Russell Terrier. If, as we hope will be the case, you are quite sure that you will be able to discharge all the responsibilities and expenses of a caring dog owner, you could make no better decision than to buy a Parson Jack Russell Terrier.

Buying a Puppy

First of all you need to identify your own needs. What sort of ambitions do you harbour? Is it your intention to breed, to show or to work your dog? Perhaps you intend to try all three or maybe you are simply looking for a lively and healthy companion. The choice is yours but a word of warning about that choice. Far too many people decide that they have no ambition to breed or show and accept a second-rate dog simply because it is intended *only* as a pet. They later find that their interest in the breed has developed in such a way that breeding and showing now seem attractive activities. These new ambitions, however, are frustrated by the fact that they have got a

111

terrier which is not good enough for either. Worse still, they may have a dog of which they are very fond but in which, as a result of knowledge acquired since it was bought, they can take little pride. They will have learned enough about the breed to realise that their beloved pet is a thoroughly mediocre specimen and will have to live for several years with the consequences of an unwise decision to accept second best. So, whatever are your present ambitions and whatever you imagine to be your longer term ambitions, you should, at the very outset, ensure that you buy a first-class Parson Jack Russell Terrier.

Do you want a dog or a bitch? Dogs tend to be a little more self-assertive, more boisterous and more demanding than the female of the species, though in such a confident breed as the Parson Jack Russell there is probably not much to choose between dogs and bitches in this respect. Bitches come into season twice a year and need, during these times, to be kept especially secure if they are not to be mated either by a wandering dog or as a result of escaping and going in search of male companionship. Bitches present this problem twice a year but dogs are attracted by a pretty face at any time.

One solution to this problem would be to have the dog or bitch surgically neutered. The veterinary profession and leading welfare organisations devote considerable energy and expense to persuading dog owners to have their pets neutered. The aim is to reduce the population of stray and unwanted dogs. It is, of course, irrefutable that a neutered dog or bitch cannot produce unwanted or any puppies. If they were in the habit of straying for sexual reasons, neutering may reduce their wanderlust, though it will not have any effect if they wander in search of sport or food or simply to relieve the tedium or to satisfy curiosity. There are times when neutering is necessary to relieve some health or psychological problem, but it is, in our opinion, never justified to submit a well-cared-for and responsibly owned dog to the trauma and the risks, both immediate and long term, no matter how small they may be, which are an inevitable concomitant of any surgery unless there is a very good reason for so doing. To recommend that dogs should be neutered simply so that they can be allowed to wander the streets without inconveniencing their owners with unwanted puppies is, in our opinion, professionally unethical for vets, uncaring for welfare organisations and irresponsible and callous for dog owners.

Furthermore, if you do decide to have your dog or bitch neutered you must expect some change in its character and even in its appearance. It will be more placid and less assertive and as a result will tend to become more corpulent unless you are mindful of its diet. Vets deny this, but the fact remains that neutered dogs are more likely to become obese than are entire ones. The coat may become woolly rather than harsh which will reduce your chances of success in the show ring, and, of course, any ambitions to breed must be forgotten. Even ambitions to show must accept the fact that the Kennel Club (though not working or hunt terrier shows), does not usually allow neutered animals to be shown. If it is necessary, desirable or convenient to postpone a bitch's season or even to prevent seasons altogether, there are perfectly harmless products which will do so without the need to resort to surgery. If, by some mischance, a bitch is accidentally mated, an injection carried out soon after the misalliance will prevent her from having puppies. Neutering is an irreversible step, and no matter what persuasion you face from whatever source, should never be undertaken lightly.

Having weighed the choice between dog and bitch according to your own preferences, you next need to examine your reasons for buying a Parson Jack Russell Terrier. If it is your intention to breed you will, of course, need a bitch. She should be well bred, from a family which has produced good stock over a number of generations and be free from hereditary defects, with parents which enjoy a similar freedom and which are sound and typical representatives of the breed. You should be satisfied with nothing less.

If your intention is to involve yourself in the show world, you might decide on either a dog or a bitch. Dogs are, perhaps, easier to show in that their career is not interrupted by bi-annual seasons or by pregnancies, false or real. A dog's self-assertiveness may catch the judge's eye more often than do the less obvious qualities of a good bitch. Dog classes at shows are often smaller than those for bitches, though the quality may be higher. You are most likely to get a dog which will achieve success in the ring from someone who has previously produced successful dogs. You will want the very best representative of the breed you can find; only the best should be regarded as good enough. There is no point in embarking on a show career if you have encumbered yourself with a third-rate dog and, if you choose to do so, you should not blame your lack of success on incompetent or dishonest judges but on your own lack of discernment.

If it is your ambition to become involved in work, the choice between a dog and a bitch is less relevant. A small bitch can reach

113

places which would be beyond the range of a larger dog, while a dog might be of more use in a big, deep earth. Once more, you will want a sound, healthy and typical representative of the breed and, while you might prefer to buy one bred from parents of proven working ability, there has seldom been a real Parson Jack Russell Terrier bred which, given the opportunity, would not work.

Let us, for the moment at least, assume that, whatever your ambitions are, you have decided to buy a puppy. From this flow three matters in which there is no room for compromise. You must never buy a puppy which is less than eight weeks old; you must never buy one from anyone but its breeder; and you must never allow your heart to have more influence than does your head when making the purchase. Puppies, even of a hardy breed like the Parson Jack Russell Terrier, need time in which to achieve full independence from the care which their dam provides. To deprive a puppy prematurely of this care will result in a maladjusted and poorly reared puppy. Puppies are also vulnerable to infection and especially so to infections which are different from those they may have faced in their own home. Changing home, especially for the first time in their lives and at a very young age, involves stress, and stress reduces resistance to infection. A puppy which is younger than eight weeks may not be sufficiently robust to combat any such problems. You might also wonder whether a breeder who is willing to expose puppies to such unnecessary risk may not also have given them indifferent attention during the first few weeks of their lives. You might be well advised to look elsewhere.

A puppy which has already changed home once, or for all you may know twice or more, and which has been carried round the country, exposed to cold, hunger and infection, is more than likely to be incubating infections which, along with their attendant heartache and expense, you would wish to avoid. Such puppies may turn into very expensive purchases before they are restored to health and might be heart-breaking if residual damage remains after the disease has been treated. A soft heart which overrules a wiser head and leads you to purchase a young puppy from a dealer could result in disappointment especially if you intend to breed or show your dog. Does the dealer really know that the pedigree he hands to you is the one appropriate to your purchase and not to one of the perhaps dozens of other puppies which pass through his hands? Are you quite satisfied that both the puppy's parents were Parson Jack Russell Terriers? Never buy a puppy from a dealer.

Buying an Older Dog

Perhaps you don't want a puppy at all but would prefer an older dog. Buying an older dog means that you will avoid the uncertainty of trying to predict how a puppy might develop. You will not have to face the problems of rearing a growing and demanding youngster. You will avoid the period when the risk of juvenile disease is at its greatest. You may be buying a dog which is already well trained, though you must also consider the possibility that you may be buying one which its owner has decided is untrainable. Ask yourself why a young adult should be for sale. There are several possible genuine reasons but a great many more which should give rise to caution. Breeders will often keep the most promising puppies in a litter until they are sure which is the best and which they will want to keep for their own purposes. At this stage the others may be available for sale. They may be very good indeed and entirely suitable for your purposes especially since the unpredictability of puppyhood will have passed. On the other hand, the faults which make them less good than the best may also make them unsuitable for you. *Caveat emptor*, let the buyer beware.

Sometimes a dog or bitch which is no longer required as a show dog or for breeding will become available. These often make excellent companions and seem to appreciate the individual attention they receive in their new homes but, of course, their breeding and show careers and working lives are behind them and they must be regarded as potential companions only. Older dogs also sometimes become available as a result of some mischance in their lives. Their previous owners may have died or for other good reasons may no longer be able to keep them. The poor dog may simply have fallen on hard times through no fault of its own, though it is prudent to consider the possibility that it may be available because it is, in some way which is not immediately apparent, an incorrigible rogue. Once more decisions are best made by the head and not the heart.

Sadly, not every breeder is a paragon of care and responsibility but, at least, if you buy from a breeder any complaint you may have can be targeted with accuracy and is far more likely to receive sympathetic treatment. This is especially so if the breeder is one who registers puppies with the Kennel Club, which has the power to discipline those whose standards fall below an acceptable level. The courts too offer protection against dishonesty and are taking a far keener interest in the sale of dogs. Buying with care should avoid any need to make use of the courts, but both buyers and vendors should be aware of the sort of protection which the courts offer. You are also less likely to encounter problems and will have a source of reliable and concerned advice if you buy from a good, well-established breeder. Find one with a good reputation which they are anxious to maintain. Most breeders will not lead you astray and will offer an excellent after-sales service which extends well beyond puppyhood.

Finding a Reputable Breeder

The first step could be to contact the Kennel Club or the Breed Club. Either will be able to put you in touch with reliable breeders, perhaps even in your area. If you are intent on breeding or showing, you may already have visited a number of shows and will have begun to draw up a short list of the breeders whose stock especially appeals to you. In this respect, the catalogues produced by Kennel Club licensed events, which provide the registered name, date of birth, name of sire and dam, name of breeder and name and address of the owner of every exhibit at the show, will be of particular value. Hunt terrier shows never produce catalogues and the few working terrier shows which do so offer only meagre and not always reliable information. It is, however, at the terrier shows run by the local hunts that you are most likely to find people actively involved in work and so best able to put you in touch with a breeder who produces good working stock.

Having identified likely breeders, the direction your own ambitions are likely to take will indicate the next step. If you are intending to breed or to become involved in the show scene, you must buy from a breeder whose stock is registered with the Kennel Club. To buy unregistered or unregistrable stock simply means that you can neither become involved in Kennel Club licensed events nor produce stock which can be involved; you will, in effect, have restricted both your range of interest and the market for your puppies. If Kennel Club events do not figure in your ambitions, you might buy from a breeder who produces unregistered stock though you would then forego all the protection which the Kennel Club might provide.

The next step is to make your requirements known to the breeder. There may be puppies available straight away (though the best breeders tend to have a waiting list), and you can make an appointment to go and see them. At this point, you enter territory requiring expertise which you may not have. You have three choices available: you can do your best to acquire some basic expertise (since you are reading this book you are already doing so), you can rely on the breeder to guide you or you can take a reliable expert with you to look at the puppies. If you have chosen your breeder well you will have little need of rapidly acquired expertise and no need of an imported expert.

Make sure you arrive at the appointed time, as all breeders are busy people, especially so when they have young puppies to care for, and they will not appreciate an early arrival or a tardy one. For many breeders selling puppies is the least enjoyable part of breeding. For many, perhaps the best, the primary purpose of breeding is to produce a good puppy for themselves and selling surplus stock is an unwelcome concomitant. The breeder will, from the outset, be deciding whether or not you are a proper person to have one of their precious puppies, while you will be deciding whether or not any of the available puppies are likely to suit your requirements. It's a process of mutual assessment. While staying well within the bounds of common courtesy, see how clean and well maintained the terrier's quarters are; dirty food containers, small, dirty or unlit runs and kennels should all raise your suspicions. How many old dogs, well past the age at which they can make a profitable contribution to the enterprise, are there about the place or is the breeder only interested in profitable dogs? Do all the dogs seem happy, in good condition, clean and well fed? Do they mingle as part of one big, happy family? If not, make your excuses and look elsewhere.

If all seems well, look at the puppies. Is their bed clean? Are they and their dam well cared for and content? Do they bounce up to you with all the confidence of young things accustomed to people and with no reason to fear them? Are their eyes clear and sparkling, their coats glossy and their bodies plump and well filled? If you have any reason for doubt, look elsewhere, and do not allow yourself to be persuaded that though one or two puppies look unwell the one you like seems healthy. In practice, if one puppy in a litter is ill, then if the rest are not already ill the chances are that they soon will be.

If you are thinking of breeding, your first purchase will be intended as the foundation of your kennel. An unwise first purchase will provide a very shaky foundation indeed. You may need to start again or to spend years correcting the faults which were bought with your first purchase. If you are looking for a potential show dog, why begin with one which already has obstacles to overcome? No one has yet bred the perfect dog, though some claim to do so regularly. Do not buy, as a potential show dog, a puppy which already has obvious faults. If you want a worker, isn't it better to start with one whose parents have already proved their worth in the field? If you want a companion wouldn't a confident and healthy companion be better than a shy and unhealthy one?

By the time the puppies are eight weeks old they will have left their dam, but you will want to see her to assure yourself of her good health, her temperament and that she is a sound and typical representative of the breed. However, you should realise that she will not be looking her best at this time and may be suspicious of your interest in her offspring, so may not be as well mannered as she normally is. If you can also see the sire, then so much the better, but it is likely that he will belong to another breeder. In this case, it might be prudent either to see him or in some other way assure yourself of his quality before you look at the puppies.

The breeder will, of course, be a confirmed devotee of the breed; his or her enthusiasm will be apparent but you should beware of any exaggerated claims either for the breed itself, the kennel or for any individual puppy. Parson Jack Russell Terriers have their limitations as well as their virtues; neither the breed as a whole nor individuals within the breed are perfect, though some owners may choose to think so. A breeder who, out of sheer enthusiasm or for some more sinister reason, gives you false information is exposing him or herself to subsequent action at law should any of those claims fail to materialise and you would be very prudent to take any exaggerated claims with a large pinch of salt. We have known breeders who had never owned, let alone bred a champion, confidently guarantee that their puppies would become champions. Others, who neither show nor work their terriers, will happily advertise them as 'show and working stock' and there is a tendency among others to use meaningless but impressive descriptions such as 'champion stock' or 'champion bred'. Not all these and other phrases are used with the intention to deceive, some are simply the result of misguided enthusiasm or ill-judged emulation of poor examples.

What you should expect from the breeder is an assurance that the puppies are healthy, that they have not been in contact with any infection and that neither of their parents suffer from or have, in the past, transmitted any hereditary disease. The process of registration should already have begun and may even be complete by the time the puppies are eight weeks old. The breeder will be able to provide you with an accurate four-generation pedigree, and some with more enthusiasm or time at their disposal may even provide one with five generations. Indeed, some breeders even undertake the mammoth but enjoyable, interesting and informative task of preparing ten-generation pedigrees for their favourite terriers. A four-generation pedigree contains the names of thirty ancestors, five generations increase the number to sixty-two and ten generations contain 2,046 names. It takes a lot of enthusiasm, a lot of time and a lot of information to complete a ten-generation pedigree.

Pedigrees can be confusing documents which convey little to the new dog owner. They are, of course, simply records of the dog's ancestry through the last few generations but they are indispensable to any breeder and of great interest to every dog owner. At first they may be simply no more than a list of names, but as your knowledge of the breed increases so you will come to be able to put faces to some of these names, to follow their progress in the ring, and to see what sort of success your puppy's relations have achieved. When you come to breed you will find that pedigrees become documents to be studied with care, weighed and assessed. They are one of the tools which enable breeders to plan future generations.

In addition to a pedigree and registration documents you should expect to receive written evidence of the worming regime, of any vaccinations which have been undertaken and instructions which will help you to care for the puppy during your first days and weeks of ownership. If all the assurances and paperwork seem in order, if you are satisfied that all is well and if one of the puppies appeals to you, your search for a Parson Jack Russell Terrier may be at an end. All that remains now is to purchase the puppy.

Good puppies are not cheap but in the long term they are very much cheaper than bad ones. You should be very wary of any pro-posed arrangements which offer a reduced initial price in exchange for some degree of control being retained by the breeder. Such arrangements often take the form of what are known as *breeding terms*, by which you undertake to mate the bitch, often to a dog of the breeder's choice, rear the subsequent litter and then give one or more, usually the best, to the breeder. In extreme cases such arrange-ments even extend to subsequent litters. It requires only a moment's thought to realise just how expensive a bitch will be if you are expected to pay even a reduced purchase price, eventually to pay a stud fee to have her mated, go to the considerable expense and effort of rearing the puppies and then part with one or more without any return. You would be very wise to avoid buying a puppy on breeding terms but, if you decide to do so, you must ensure that the contractual agreement between you and the breeder is unambiguous and legally binding on you both. All breeding-term arrangements are, to some extent, unsatisfactory but those which are based on vague and unenforceable agreements can too easily end in troublesome disputes or even expensive court battles.

If you are buying an older dog you should expect this to be reflected in the price. An adult youngster of established quality and ready to begin a career in the ring or the nursery is likely to be very much more expensive than a puppy. An older dog or one which has fallen on hard times might well be much cheaper, the prime consideration being an understanding and permanent home. Problems are very seldom encountered as a result of Parson Jack Russell Terriers being unable to adjust to a new home but such problems as may arise are most likely to be encountered with older dogs. You should expect, therefore, that an older dog will be offered on a short trial, to be returned and the purchase price fully refunded, though not your attendant expenses, should you have genuine reason for complaint.

If you are wise you will pay for the puppy outright and unconditionally, collect all the relevant documents and say your farewells. You will have become the owner of a Parson Jack Russell Terrier puppy, and will have taken the first step towards realising your ambitions.

8

Care and Maintenance

During the fifteen thousand or so years in which dogs have been sharing man's home they have adapted to our needs and wishes in all sorts of remarkable but not always obvious ways which we are far too inclined to take for granted. There is, nowhere on earth, any other species which has adapted so well to life with man. Not even, it sometimes seems, man himself. No other species is used for such a wide variety of purposes nor shows all the variation of size and shape to be found among domestic dogs. Dogs, which are a social carnivorous animal, have adapted to what is, in terms of their own species, often a solitary existence, to a diet which is seldom that of a carnivore and may sometimes, and unsuitably, be entirely vegetable. They accept a lifestyle which is very different from that to which they were originally accustomed and for which, it might be said, they were intended. Until very recently man has, with all his customary arrogance, tended to expect dogs to conform entirely to his lordly wishes. He has had little interest in the needs of dogs except in so far as satisfying these needs improved their utility. Certainly, he had little or no interest in dogs as companions and little or no concern for their well-being. His religious and political mentors had taught him that since dogs had no souls their suffering in the name of sport or at work was of no consequence and had even argued, when this philosophy was eventually called into question, that contemplation of their suffering could increase man's own ability to withstand suffering with dignity and courage. If dogs had any status it was as servants or slaves. There is now a growing but belated readiness to accept that by recognising and respecting what dogs need we will derive far more benefit from their companionship.

Only with the work of Konrad Lorenz and Niko Tinbergen was a real start made on the study of animal behaviour and an attempt made to understand what it had to tell us about animals of all sorts. In a very few years the work of animal, and especially of canine, behaviourists has made great advances. Veterinary surgeons now

121

make use of these specialists, which the popular press delight in regarding as canine psychologists, when faced with patients with behavioural problems, and the work of authors like Michael Fox, Desmond Morris and James Serpell has brought much of this fascinating new study within the reach of ordinary dog owners. It is not within the scope of this book even to attempt to précis this huge and fascinating topic. It is sufficient, perhaps, just to stress that a Parson Jack Russell Terrier is a dog and not a small and oddly shaped human being. He is also a dog which has, because of the job for which he was originally bred and for which he may still be used, retained a certain intelligence and independence of spirit which some other breeds may have lost. It would be a nonsense to try to turn a Parson Jack Russell Terrier into a servile and fawning lapdog, to expect instant and unthinking obedience or to demand that its sporting instincts should be entirely suppressed. There are well over four hundred breeds of dog in the world, so there must be at least one to suit the needs of every dog owner. Those who own a Parson Jack Russell Terrier should respect its particular character and not try to change it into something else. Indeed, the very existence of the breed is a result of over a hundred years of determined effort not to allow the sort of terrier which the Parson bred to be changed in any way.

Kennel – Indoors or Outdoors?

Let us assume that you have arrived home with a healthy, bouncy Parson Jack Russell puppy of about eight weeks of age. You will, of course, have bought it from a responsible and caring breeder who will be happy to provide a good after-care service which will ease your introduction to dog ownership. You will already have prepared a place where the puppy can sleep and enjoy some privacy away from the demands of other young members of the family and you will ensure that this need for privacy is respected. You will have stocked up with some suitable food. Obviously, the first decision to be made after you have decided to acquire a puppy is whether it will live in the house or in an outdoor kennel. The companionship and interest which a dog living in the house both gives and receives are valuable, but there may also be times when it is better for both the dog and its owner that it should be in comfortable and secure accommodation out of doors. Perhaps, like the Parson himself, you

A traditional kennel makes a very unsuitable home for a terrier. The doorway is too large to protect the interior against bad weather and too small to make cleaning easy. The floor is close to the ground and would be cold and damp. The absence of a secure run or door would mean that the occupant would have to be chained if it is to be prevented from wandering.

will find that the best solution is to provide accommodation which will enable the dog to be indoors sometimes and out of doors at other times.

An outdoor kennel, with a floor area of about three feet (1m) by four and a half feet (1½m), will accommodate one or two terriers. It must be dry, secure, light and warm, and sited so that it is not exposed to the full force of the wind or to the full heat of the sun. It should not be placed where other buildings or trees will make it damp. If the dog is to spend any appreciable amount of time in it, it must also have access to a secure run, at least twice as big as the kennel, covered or not. Such kennels are not cheap, but it is a false economy to pick the cheapest which is likely to be made of feather-edged boarding or even thin plywood. Better to spend a little more and get a kennel which is not only lined but can be made even more comfortable by the addition of further insulation between the two skins. Look for a kennel which offers no sharp internal angles to injure, invite chewing and is difficult to clean. If you can also find a make which provides a variety of arrangements, can easily be extended and which also offers replacement parts, then so much the better. You will also quickly learn to appreciate a door big enough and tall enough to facilitate easy access for cleaning. A kennel which can be easily dismantled for thorough disinfection or for moving to another place also offers advantages which less adaptable structures do not possess.

Within the kennel a raised bed, well filled with some dry and clean bedding, will add to the comfort of the occupants, and for young puppies, in cold weather, some form of heat is also necessary. An infra-red heater is probably the safest as well as the easiest to control but, of course, this relies on the availability of electricity. This will also provide a source of light which will be appreciated on dark winter mornings and evenings. For the run itself, remember that it must confine a very active terrier. A six-foot (2m) fence should be enough providing that the terrier cannot dig under it. A base of concrete or paving slabs will avoid this possibility as well as making cleaning easier if adequate drainage has been provided. A covered run is a boon in winter and in wet weather but most Parson Jack Russell Terriers have enough sense to keep themselves warm and dry by retreating into their kennel through a convenient 'pop-hole' if they have the opportunity to do so.

Indoors, the criteria are precisely those which should be applied to an outdoor kennel. Warmth, freedom from damp, privacy, easy cleaning, and security, most of which characteristics are usually already provided for the comfort of the house's non-canine occupants. It is only fair, particularly in houses which contain young children, to provide the dog with a place it can regard as its own, to which it can retire for rest and privacy and which is respected as a haven by all the house's other occupants. Dog beds come in all shapes and sizes. What you will need, especially for a young puppy, is one which can be easily cleaned, which is not easily damaged or, if damaged can be repaired or replaced, and which will not be a source of possible injury to its occupant. Equipment firms have yet to produce anything which makes quite such a good bed for a young puppy as does a strong, clean cardboard box, preferably one which has not contained soap powders, detergents or other products which might irritate. Cardboard boxes are cheap to acquire and easy to replace when soiled or damaged. Time enough for something more elegant when the puppy has learned clean habits and has ceased to be destructive. For an older dog timber is warm, easily repaired and easily cleaned. The same cannot be said of either wicker or plastic, and plastic has the additional disadvantage that, if chewed and swallowed, sharp indigestible pieces can have tragic consequences.

There are several choices available when it comes to selecting bedding. Outdoors, wood shavings, preferably from white wood unless you want your white terrier to be stained an unusual colour, are excellent. Hay or straw are less good because they might harbour parasites and disease and will also, when damp, stain a white coat. Some straws, particularly barley, also contain very sharp seeds which can be a source of problems. Newspapers also suffer from the fact that newsprint leaves a white dog looking very grey. Towels, blankets, particularly those which are especially manufactured, under various trade names, for dogs, are all excellent both indoors or out. They offer no problems of disposal and are easily kept clean.

Nutrition

Before you arrive home with your new puppy you will also have taken the precaution not only of finding out about its diet but of ensuring that the larder is well stocked. Most breeders ease the transfer to a new home by supplying enough of the food to which their puppies are accustomed to last for a couple of days and if, at least for a few days, you do not impose, on top of the need to adapt to a new home, the need to adapt to a new diet your puppy will be the better for it. Indeed, throughout a dog's life dietary change is often at the root of upset and illness. We, too often, tend to impose our tastes and need for variety on what we assume a dog will like, and even some dog food firms, who should and do know better, may seek to increase their sales by offering an unnecessary degree of variety of tastes and recipes. Once you have found a diet which your dog enjoys and on which it thrives you should never change without very good reason. You should not, however, ignore indications that change may be necessary.

Most good pet-food firms offer foods which have been carefully formulated to be especially suitable for puppies or for old dogs, for dogs which are working or under stress or which are obese. There are diets which take account of particular infirmities or which are especially suitable during convalescence. All these conditions may indicate a need for change but otherwise constancy to one well-chosen, carefully balanced food is by far the best policy. Feeding dogs was, in the Parson's day, largely an art depending on skilful mixes of the various foods which were available. Little was known about a dog's actual nutritional needs but a skilled feeder, using experience and some mysterious sixth sense, somehow managed to provide his charges with a diet which kept them fit and healthy. Nowadays, feeding is no longer an art but an exact science. A dog's nutritional needs at all stages of its life are precisely known and precisely satisfied by the best of the foods which are on the market. Providing that a dog is being fed one of these diets in the right quantities, the most likely source of problems is not to be found in inadequacies but in surfeit. Research has, rightly, tended to concentrate on the dangers of diets inadequate in essential vitamins, minerals and trace elements. More recently the dangers of excess have begun to be investigated and publicised.

Every high street now contains at least one shop which offers us nostrums for which almost miraculous qualities are claimed. Similar concoctions are available for dogs and cleverly worded adverts seek to persuade us that without these supplements our dogs will not be properly cared for. In our desire to do our very best by them we may give so many supplements as to actually endanger their health. Thus cod-liver oil, which is a source of vitamins A, D, and E, and seaweed tablets, which are a source of iodine, are both toxic, if given to excess. Vegetable oils, rich in essential fatty acids, are capable of destroying vitamin E, and even bone meal, a source of calcium phosphorus, may be toxic and can, if given to excess, lead to malformed bones.

An excess of calcium can lead to skeletal abnormalities, joint problems and lameness, especially in growing puppies. It can result in zinc, magnesium and phosphorus deficiences and can lead to lactational tetany in pregnant bitches. Too much phosphorus can produce calcium deficiencies; iron in excess results in poor appetite, weight loss and damage to the digestive tract. Too much vitamin A also reduces appetite and leads to weight loss, pain, damage and distortion of long bones and joints. Too much vitamin D produces bloody diarrhoea, vomiting, lassitude and rapid respiration, calcification of soft tissues and deformed jaws and teeth.

The list is not exhaustive but serves to illustrate the dangers that a well-meaning owner can expose a dog to by giving mineral and vitamin supplements to excess, and, even if these stages are not reached, the cost of feeding is considerably increased to no good effect. Dr Ian Burrows, a well-known canine nutritionist, has said that:

> Supplementing an already balanced diet can at the very least take an unnecessary toll on the owner's purse, with excess nutrients being excreted. At this level no real harm is done and no doubt the owner's need to provide extra care is satisfied. . . . However, a balanced diet cannot, by definition be bettered nutritionally. Owners should, therefore, be made aware that their long-term kindnesses or pursuit of some wonder treatment may not merely be wasteful but could actually cause harm. Supplements are an unnecessary addition to prepared pet foods.

The cost of feeding a dog is often exaggerated as a deterrent to impulsive buyers but, the cost need not be exorbitant especially for a relatively small breed such as a Parson Jack Russell Terrier. It can be appreciably reduced by buying in bulk. The difference in unit cost between even just one tray of tins and a few tins bought at a supermarket, or a 22-kilo bag of dry food bought from an authorised distributor and a pound or two bought at the local pet shop represents a worthwhile saving as well as an added convenience whether you have one dog or several.

There is a danger that new owners of a puppy may underestimate its nutritional needs or that, when the puppy is mature, its puppy needs will give a false indication of its adult needs. Puppies grow at a prodigious rate. Even a Parson Jack Russell Terrier puppy will, day by day, increase its weight more quickly than does a human baby and will reach its adult weight in a matter of months. Such a rapid development not only needs good food but it needs a relatively large amount of food. An eight-week-old puppy may need about two or even three times as much food as an adult. This should be given in several small feeds rather than one large one. This gargantuan appetite may remain when the puppy is adult, but the need for this amount of food will no longer exist and if food intake is not regulated the result will be an obese and unhealthy terrier. Obesity may well be one of the major sources of non-infectious illness in dogs and is arguably also the source of a great deal of unintentional cruelty. An over-fed Parson Jack Russell Terrier is a pathetic creature, a misery to itself and the target of pity of all those who appreciate the breed's qualities. The owners of obese dogs cannot realise the degree of cruelty they are inflicting, nor can they realise what lies behind the glances they attract as they slowly parade their unhappy animal down the street.

We are all, to some extent, weight conscious these days. Some go in for counting calories which, for dogs, is a very simple method of keeping them in good condition, since we can do the counting while they have to endure the results. The ease is increased because most proprietary diets, certainly all the best, publish the calorific value of their products. It thus becomes a simple matter to devise a diet suitable for a fourteen-pound (6.4kg) terrier. However, we must remember that the dog needs variety throughout the various stages of its life. From weaning to being about half grown (about four or five months old) it will need about 1100kcal, in late pregnancy about 750kcal is needed and in peak lactation about 1800kcal. For normal adult maintenance about 550kcal is sufficient, increased for a dog which is working hard for a living or getting more than average exercise.

Health Care

It will depend largely on the puppy's age as to whether it has received all the necessary protective vaccinations before it joins your household. If it has been vaccinated make sure you know precisely what it is protected against, what vaccine has been used and that you get, from the breeder, a form signed by the vet who carried out the vaccinations. Some breeders carry out their own vaccinations, getting the vaccines cheaply from some compliant source. Doubtless they ensure, as do vets, that the vaccines are stored and used in ways which protect their efficiency, but if anything goes wrong – and things occasionally do – you will have little hope of redress if the vaccines were not administered by a vet.

Vaccination works by imposing what the immune system interprets as a threat of disease and produces antibodies in order to repel the threat. Puppies, if they suck early and well from their mother, receive immunity from her, but during the ensuing weeks this maternal immunity slowly subsides so that by the time a puppy leaves the nest at eight weeks of age it may be virtually unprotected. It is vital, therefore, that such a puppy is not put at risk by being

Only when a puppy is fully vaccinated should it be allowed to mix with other dogs or play where other dogs have been.

taken anywhere where other dogs, whether healthy or not, have recently been and that it receives its protective injections at the earliest possible moment. We cannot stress too strongly that if your puppy is not already fully protected you should contact your vet and ensure that it receives protection as quickly as possible.

Your puppy should also have been well wormed before you bring it to your home but you will need to ensure that it remains free of parasites both internal and external. In fact, it is a simple matter to ensure that a puppy is and remains totally free of any parasites which might pose a threat to its owners or, for that matter, to anyone else. Only ill-cared-for dogs habitually harbour parasites.

Nowadays, many breeders take steps to ensure that their breeding bitches are free from parasites before they whelp. This means that puppies are not born with parasites and enables them to thrive better. Those that do not do so will begin worming the puppies when they are about a fortnight old and will continue to worm them at regular intervals until the puppies go to their new homes. By this time they should harbour no parasites but, since reinfestation is always possible, a regular routine of worming should continue throughout their lives. There is a wide variety of preparations available over the vet's counter. Some are specific to one parasite, others control a wide range; they come in the form of tablets, powders and liquids to be given with, after or before food. The

129

particular regime will depend on what your vet supplies and should be scrupulously followed if it is to have optimum effect.

We might next turn our attention to the equally unpleasant subject of ectoparasites, all those tiny, and not so tiny, creatures which creep and crawl through the coat and over the skin to torment dogs and revolt their owners. Fortunately, vets are very well equipped to deal with these problems. They can supply sprays, lotions, baths, tablets and even injections which will kill and deter all the parasites your dog is likely to encounter. Regular use of these will ensure that your dog is not host to unwelcome visitors.

Most parasites which live on their host's skin are, because they are so obvious, especially on a white Parson Jack Russell, much more easily controlled and less of a threat to health than are those which live within their host. Vigilance, attention to hygiene and regular treatment will get rid of and deter the reintroduction of most of these unwelcome visitors – fleas, lice, ticks and mites – in all their repulsive variety. In addition, we must consider mange mites, which live not on the skin but in it and so offer a more serious challenge to eradication.

Fleas

Fleas are not only the intermediate host of one species of tapeworm but also live by sucking the blood of their hosts, thus causing irritation, skin problems produced by the dog's attempts to relieve irritation by scratching, and possibly allergic dermatitis. Fleas are picked up from other infested hosts or, since eggs and even adults can live for long periods away from their host, from places in which infested animals have been, no matter how briefly. Signs of infestation include scratching, the brown spots of flea excreta in the coat and the rapidly moving fleas themselves. Control by means of regular grooming and the use of sprays and washes is simple and effective, providing that reinfestation is prevented by attention to hygiene in the kennel and home.

Lice

Lice, or nits, also feed on the blood of their hosts. They are slow moving and unable to survive long away from their hosts. Infestation is therefore directly from an infested animal. Control is precisely as that for fleas.

Ticks

Ticks can be picked up by dogs which are exercised on land which has contained sheep, foxes, badgers or hedgehogs. They are small brown insects which attach themselves to the dog, usually on its head. They rapidly become suffused with the blood on which they feed and can then grow to about the size of a finger nail. Ticks cause no apparent irritation or harm but are, obviously, offensive. If ticks are simply pulled off the dog the mouth parts may be left behind and may subsequently become infected. Swabbing with surgical spirit, alcohol, ether or a similar substance like nail polish remover is said to be very effective, and will often loosen their grip to facilitate easy removal. If dogs are in regular contact with sheep, dipping them when sheep are dipped is an excellent method of tick control and is one reason why some terriers which appear at summer hunt terrier shows may have a yellow cast to their coats. Sheep dip, though an effective means of control against a number of parasites, is not designed to enhance a dog's appearance.

Mites

Mites come in various types, all very small. Harvest mites *(Trombicula autumnalis)* are red; rabbit fur mites *(Cheyletiella)* are grey and look like slow-moving cigarette ash. Both cause irritation and are controlled by application of the appropriate spray or wash.

Canker

Otodectes cynotis is the mite often responsible for the condition in dogs which is often referred to as canker, in which the inner ear is intensely irritated, producing frantic scratching which itself may produce lacerations and subsequent infection. Treatment by the introduction of the appropriate preparation is easy and usually effective. Subsequent reinfestation is prevented by keeping ears clean and regularly dosed. However care should be exercised to make sure that the problem is not the product of ear mites, as there are other causes of canker which are less easily treated. Some dogs with restricted or deeply folded inner ears may be especially susceptible to ear infections. In some cases, it is possible for minor surgery to remove the abnormality and so reduce the likelihood of infection.

The armoury against all these pests increases all the time. Some products are not only effective against several species but also leave residues in the coat which deter subsequent reinfestation. Even so, regular grooming and clean living conditions remain the first and most effective line of defence.

Grooming

By far the best way of keeping a check on your dog's health and well-being is during what should be a daily grooming session. Of course, a Parson Jack Russell Terrier needs little more than a quick brushing to remove any dead coat or foreign bodies in the coat but regular grooming also enables you to check teeth, eyes, ears, anal glands, feet, the dog's weight and to ensure generally that it is in good health. The early signs of an impending problem are far more easily dealt with than after the problem has been allowed to become intractable.

In order to groom your terrier you will need a fairly stiff brush, a comb, a pair of sharp scissors and nail clippers. Use of the brush and comb surely need no explanation, the scissors will be used for trimming any long or tangled hairs, and the nail clippers will be used as often as is necessary to keep the nails short. Grooming a Parson Jack Russell Terrier requires neither great skill nor takes a long time. The best time to groom a dog is perhaps when it has just returned from exercise. It may then be wet and need drying or have collected a passenger or two, or perhaps some vegetable matter may have become entangled in its coat. All are matters best dealt with promptly before they can cause problems.

Exercise

A Parson Jack Russell Terrier will enjoy all the exercise you can give it – the harder the better. This is not a breed intended for a sedentary life. By far the best form of exercise is provided by running free in play with another dog but, in the absence of a companion, retrieving a ball or stick is almost as good. Long walks where your dog can run free to play and explore are to be preferred to a sedate walk along the street, which, to a Parson Jack Russell Terrier, hardly qualifies as exercise at all.

Free exercise is physically and mentally invigorating in ways which a sedate walk on a lead can never be.

With a comfortable bed, a good diet, regular grooming and adequate exercise you can look forward to a long and mutually happy association with your pal.

Ageing

Dogs, just like the rest of us, if we are fortunate, grow old. Ageing is inevitable and irreversible but at least some of its worst effects can be postponed or palliated by the right treatment. By the time a dog has reached about eight years of age its physical state is about equivalent to that of a fifty-year-old person, at about twelve years old it becomes a pensioner and should be regarded as very aged when it has reached fifteen. In Britain, dogs who have passed their seventh birthday are, for show purposes, regarded as veterans. By that age, a healthy Parson Jack Russell Terrier should not have begun to show any of the attributes usually associated with advancing age. In Scandinavia a more realistic attitude has introduced classes for dogs over ten years old by which time they might be expected to have begun to show signs of advancing decrepitude. Given reasonable good fortune and good care, Parson Jack Russell Terriers are a relatively long-lived breed. Fifteen is not uncommon and even eighteen is not unknown.

However, advancing age does call for some modification of care. Older dogs have greater need of a warm, dry bed. They require less strenuous exercise, though not to the extent that deterioration of muscle tone which age produces is accelerated by too little exercise. Hearing may become less acute, though it is surprising how many dogs which are apparently deaf to instructions can hear even the slightest rattle of a food dish. Keeping ears clean and free from infection will tend to delay deterioration. Eyes too may become less efficient and the development of nuclear sclerosis, seen as a bluish haze across the eye, is to be seen in many elderly dogs. It is untreatable and irreversible and should not be confused with cataract which occurs less frequently in dogs than in man, except as a result of hereditary factors in some breeds. Cataracts are treatable. Dogs with failing vision – even totally blind ones – adjust well and, by making use of their other acute senses, are able to get around without too much difficulty. An understanding attitude on the part of their owner, familiar surroundings free from hazards and they seem perfectly content.

Less content, perhaps, are dogs with tooth or gum disease. Dogs which began life with large, evenly spaced, correctly aligned teeth are less prone to oral problems. Those which have been worked may have suffered tooth or jaw damage, as might those which have been allowed or encouraged to chew hard objects. Equally, dogs which, for whatever reason, have been fed a diet deficient in roughage or with insufficient calcium may be expected to show early signs of tooth deterioration. Keep a watch on teeth – a dog cannot tell you when its teeth are aching – and watch for signs of pain or discomfort especially when the dog is eating. Dental care can avoid many of the problems which decaying teeth can produce.

Older dogs may be subject to kidney deterioration, leading to a need to drink more water and to incontinence, which is distressing for a properly house-trained dog as it is for owners. Special diets may retard further deterioration. The digestive system too will be less robust than it once was and the diet should be adjusted accordingly. Respiration and cardiac problems are best kept at bay by controlling weight and providing adequate exercise. Perhaps, for an ageing dog, the biggest threat to health comes from stress, physical or emotional.

The loss of companions, periods away from home, changes in diet or routine – all impose stress, which is best avoided if possible.

Eventually, the time will come when an owner must consider whether the dog's quality of life has deteriorated to below acceptable limits. At this stage, the owner has the duty to relieve the dog of further suffering by having it humanely killed. It can never be easy for a caring owner to part with an old friend but to prolong a life which is never free from pain and from which all pleasure has departed simply in order to postpone an unpleasant and painful task cannot be regarded as a kindness. Dogs have no foreknowledge of death and so avoid the fears to which man is often subjected. An intravenous injection, given by a vet, induces sleep and peaceful cardiac arrest. Your old friend's suffering is at an end and you can console yourself by the knowledge that you have done your dog a final kindness.

9

Breeding

The breeders of Parson Jack Russell Terriers should regard themselves as heirs to a proud tradition. It is they who accept the
responsibility not only of trying to match the high standard set by the
Parson but of undoing all the harm which has been done by those
who, for so many years, have exploited his name. Breeding Jack
Russell Terriers not only offers the same challenges which must be
faced by anyone who seeks to breed quality livestock, but might, in
addition, be regarded as something of a crusade. Parson Jack Russell
Terrier breeders, especially at this important time in the breed's
history when the eyes of all the breed's countless thousands of
admirers all over the world are on them, must set an example which
will silence those who regard the terrier as nothing more than a
small, predominantly white mongrel. At the same time they can
silence, once and for all, those who argue that Kennel Club recognition is the first step towards perdition, or worse, and that as a
consequence of recognition the breed will rapidly become unsound,
effete and useless for working.

If your purpose in breeding Parson Jack Russell Terriers is to make
money, you should realise that there are a number of other breeds
which offer a far better chance of making a profit. If you are
determined to breed dogs for profit, then for the sake of the Parson
Jack Russell Terrier as well as for the sake of your own purse, choose
another breed or, better still, find another way to become rich. If you
are determined to breed Parson Jack Russell Terriers for profit, consider first the cost of buying a bitch and of keeping her until she is
mature, and consider the cost of mating her and of rearing her
puppies. Even if she has a large litter and they are reared without
problems and sold without difficulty you will not show a profit on
your first litter. You might then decide to set aside any thought for
the bitch's welfare and breed another litter at her next season and
perhaps even carry on with this callous regime. Here you will encounter a difficulty because if you wish to sell Kennel Club

Registered Parson Jack Russell Terrier puppies details of your breeding performance will be published in Kennel Club publications. You cannot hope to conceal your activities from those whose attitude to the breed is more caring than your own or from officials who may have an interest in your undeclared income. You must be prepared to accept the consequences of your activities.

When the young Jack Russell strolled towards Marston on that May day 170 or so years ago we do not entirely believe, as he and Davies would have us believe, that he was wandering aimlessly. It seems far more likely that he knew that in Morton lived a man who bred good terriers, whose reputation was well established locally, and who might just be persuaded to sell one. Perhaps Jack Russell already had his eye on a particular bitch and had decided that, though his undergraduate means were far from extensive, he would

Mr E. Rich's home-bred Somervale Danny is descended through John Hodder's breeding from Heinemann's own terriers and then from Snow's and the Parson's. The type has not changed in over a century.

make the milkman an offer he could not refuse. Whatever the truth of the matter, at the end of that day Jack Russell possessed a bitch which delighted his eye and which would be very likely to breed him some good puppies.

Prospective breeders of today are no more likely to come across the terrier of their dreams during an aimless stroll than was Jack Russell, but they do have the advantage of being able to travel the length and breadth of the country to shows and to visit established breeders in order to find the sort of bitch which should provide a good foundation for their kennel. No prospective breeder should be satisfied with anything less than was Jack Russell. To start a kennel on the basis of a mediocre animal is to encumber the enterprise at the outset with a load which only time, expense and considerable talent, allied to more good fortune than breeders can usually rely on, are likely to remove. Better by far to start without such a load, there will be problems enough without taking one on before breeding has even begun.

Those with a long purse might prefer to begin their kennel by buying an adult bitch, perhaps one which has already produced some good puppies. But beware, such bitches seldom change hands and may do so for reasons which the previous owner may choose to conceal. A bitch whose previous breeding performance has been less than satisfactory is more likely to come on the market than is one which has produced and reared, without undue difficulties, litters of healthy puppies. We have even heard the tale of a spayed bitch being sold on breeding terms to an unsuspecting prospective breeder.

So it seems that the safest course might be to start with a promising bitch puppy – safest perhaps but by no means infallible. You might well go (as you should) to immense trouble to locate and buy a well-bred, well-reared and promising bitch puppy out of a line you know to have produced good stock in the past, which has no history of untoward hereditary, fertility or whelping problems only to encounter some problem or other which has not previously been encountered in that family. One of the very few certainties about breeding any animal is that you will slowly work your way through every problem in the book and will, sooner or later, encounter problems which are raising their heads for the first time. Breeders have to overcome such problems and take whatever steps are necessary to avoid them in the future. If you are going to be a successful breeder you will need an ability to preserve your optimism and enthusiasm in the face of all sorts of unexpected problems. It is easier to overcome them after some success rather than at the outset but it

The characteristically heavy down face and bulky muscles of the bull breeds tend to persist in terriers which carry bull blood.

is not in the nature of problems to wait until you are properly equipped to deal with them before they make their unwelcome appearance.

It has been said that the Parson selected his breeding stock by testing a terrier against some particularly demanding quarry and then, because the test would have made that terrier unsuitable for breeding, breeding from its sibling. Such a course of action would have been very foolish and the Parson was not a fool. In any case, he did not want his terriers to punish their quarry, or themselves to receive unnecessary punishment; a terrier which was too hard would probably have been discarded and its sibling come under suspicion as future breeding stock. Furthermore, the Parson had every opportunity to see his terriers working in real situations and would have no need to set up artificial tests in order to arrive at an opinion of their mettle. It is more likely that the Parson used the same methods as breeders of Foxhounds used and still do use and which have, over the years, produced a breed which is uniform in appearance, with variations between rather than within packs, which is as physically and temperamentally sound as any animal can be, superbly adapted to its purpose and able to reproduce its like without great difficulty.

This enviable state of affairs has been achieved by rigorous selection practised over the last two hundred or more years. There is a story of a visitor to Hampton Court who was admiring the magnificent lawns. He enquired of a gardener how such perfection was achieved and was told that the process was simple. It was necessary to prepare the ground with care, use the finest seed available and then to feed, weed and mow the grass regularly for about four hundred years. Breeding dogs tends to be a little like that. Success is usually only achieved after careful preparation and selection and several years of effort. There is another analogy which comes from more recent times. In the computer world there is a phenomenon known as 'gigo' which refers to the fact that inaccurate information will produce inaccurate results. The acronym comes from the phrase Garbage In, Garbage Out', and it is a phrase totally applicable to dog breeding.

Breeders of Foxhounds are able to select breeding stock after watching an animal's performance in the field just as the Parson himself would have done. If a terrier has run with hounds for a season or two its soundness cannot be in doubt; if it has worked amicably among hounds, other terriers and farmstock its temperament can be relied upon. If it has been able to carry out the tasks for which it was intended its suitability for those tasks can be accepted and if it is then mated to another terrier with similar credentials the chances are that the offspring will be equally good. Selection against function allows for no clouded judgements interfering with the process, and even if the breeder, as the breeders of Foxhounds and certainly the Parson himself are wont to do, also choose animals which please their eye, no harm is done. Indeed, beauty is often allied to functional efficiency. An efficient racing car has a particular sort of beauty which is absent from the fashionably styled cars made to appeal to a transitory popular taste but lacking efficiency. When ideas of what constitutes beauty become divorced from function they have a tendency to produce grotesque caricatures of the real thing. Sadly, some breeds, including terrier breeds, have already followed this path but it is a path no Parson Jack Russell Terrier breeder would ever want to follow.

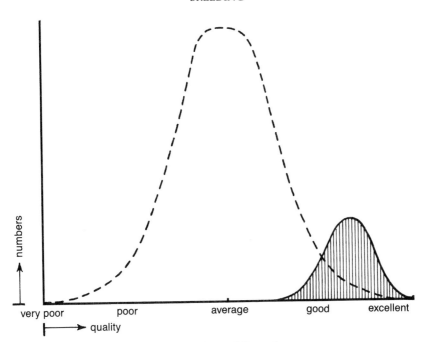

The distribution of quality in any strain always follows the same curve. Good breeders seek to shift the curve towards greater quality so that even with reduced numbers more good and excellent dogs are produced.

Most modern Parson Jack Russell Terrier breeders do not enjoy the advantages which selecting breeding stock against function confer. They must rely entirely on their own judgement and our judgement is, like the accuracy of our watches, not invariably reliable. Good judgement is more likely to be achieved against a background of knowledge, indeed judgement cannot be exercised without knowledge, but knowledge does not always improve judgement. There will always be very knowledgeable breeders whose judgement is subverted by a tendency to minimise the importance of faults found in their stock or even to deny that they exist. All they will ever achieve is the perpetuation and probably the increase of these faults.

Hereditary Disease

Fortunately, modern breeders do have some advantages which were not available to the Parson. They can make use of a series of schemes run by kennel clubs in association with veterinary practitioners which are intended to reveal the existence of hereditary disease and so enable breeders to reduce the incidence of these diseases by breeding only from unaffected stock. Hereditary disease is an emotive subject which tends to produce reactions which are based on neither thought nor fact. About two hundred defects which may be inherited have been identified in dogs. About three thousand have been identified in people. No species on earth is, or can be, free of hereditary problems. The good breeder faces this fact and ensures that the incidence of hereditary disease is minimised in the stock he produces. Hereditary disease is not a problem among well-bred Parson Jack Russell Terriers. Most of the hereditary problems which have been found in what were described as Jack Russell Terriers were not found in the type bred by the Parson; there is every chance that these problems were confined to the dwarf terriers which masquerade as Jack Russells. Nevertheless, every responsible breeder will want to do everything possible to avoid hereditary disease and many submit their breeding stock for tests as a matter of course.

A number of problems which are or may be inherited have been identified in what were described as Jack Russell Terriers. In the absence of a comprehensive and reliable registration system, which only the Kennel Club can provide, there is no way of knowing whether all or even any of these problems occurred in pedigree Parson Jack Russell Terriers or how extensive the problems may be. Nor is it possible to control and reduce their incidence. Until it becomes possible to assess the true incidence of these diseases in stock of known pedigree it is probably sufficient for breeders to be aware of their existence and be vigilant for their unlikely appearance. The problems which have been diagnosed in what were described as Jack Russell Terriers include: cardiac defects, cerebellar ataxia, cryptorchidism, deafness, epilepsy, glaucoma, invertebral disc protusion, lens luxation, microphthalmia, oesophagal dilation, patella luxation, skin disease, swimmers and undershot jaws.

Those which certainly occur, though very infrequently, in Parson Jack Russell Terriers include:

Cryptorchidism

This is a condition in which one or both testicles is not fully descended into the scrotum. Retained testicles tend to develop tumours, and a dog with both testicles retained is infertile. The mode of inheritance is complex and not fully understood. Cryptorchids should not be used at stud and their parents and siblings of both sexes should be regarded with suspicion.

Deafness

Deafness is often associated with all white dogs, though it can occur in dogs of any colour. Once more, the mode of inheritance is not fully understood. Deaf dogs should not be bred from.

Lens Luxation

Lens luxation may be caused either by trauma or be the result of an inherited condition. People who indulge in violent sports such as boxing may suffer from lens luxation and it is possible that its occurrence in Parson Jack Russell Terriers has a similar cause. Breeders should be aware of the problem and treat any dog which has lens luxation with suspicion.

Patella Luxation

Patella luxation or, crudely, slipping kneecaps, is usually associated with toy breeds and is seen infrequently in short-limbed Jack Russells but is not entirely absent from the Parson Jack Russell type. Its presence becomes apparent because of the peculiar hopping action of one or both hind limbs. Once more, the mode of inheritance is complex and not fully understood. Dogs which suffer from patella luxation should not be bred from but here there is a problem because simple surgery can cure and effectively hide the defect, thus allowing infected dogs to be unknowingly used for breeding. The problem occurs with other diseases and in other breeds, and, in an attempt to prevent it, the Kennel Club introduced a Code of Ethics for breeders which authorises veterinary surgeons to report to the Kennel Club any operations which might obsure the existence of a problem which could be transmitted to the next generation. Details will then be recorded on the dog's registration certificate and will be publicly available.

Should tests, scientific or empirical, indicate the existence of a hereditary defect or perhaps even a defect which may have some hereditary disposition, the simple and straightforward course is not to breed from that animal. In some breeds such a course would lead to the rapid extinction of the breed because no dogs are free from hereditary problems but that is not the case with Parson Jack Russell Terriers. Breeders can select stock which is known to be free of problems and by doing so will keep problems at bay. When problems do arise they can best serve the breed not by attempting to sweep them under the carpet, where they will create an obstacle which will trip up other unwary breeders, but by being open and honest about the situation. Breeding only from the very best may be a difficult route to follow but it is the only safe one. About 10 per cent of all the dogs registered by the Kennel Club are used for breeding. Unfortunately, breeders do not always use the best 10 per cent. They tend to breed from what they have available rather than face the unpalatable fact that what they have available may not be good enough to breed from. They are the ones who perpetuate mediocrity. Those who select their bitch and her mate with rigorous care are the ones who will produce the stock which will be admired and who will gain the respect of their fellow breeders.

Genetics

Having introduced the subject of scientific assessment of potential breeding stock and made some mention of genetics we should, perhaps now go on to discuss a branch of knowledge which was unavailable to the Parson. He lived at a time when knowledge of genetics was both rudimentary and often misleading. Indeed, many breeders remain in a similar state. We heard, only recently, of a well-known breeder and judge who made public claim to having begun his own career before the existence of genetics. The Parson may well have been every bit as well equipped as are many modern breeders even though he may have believed, as did many of his contemporaries, that a bitch mated to a dog of a different breed could not henceforth produce pedigree puppies. He may well also have believed that pre-natal influences would affect the nature of unborn puppies just as Joseph believed that planting parti-coloured sticks in a field would induce the birth of parti-coloured calves. He might even have subscribed to the view that phases of the moon, or the course of the stars would have their effect for good or ill and, as a man of religion, would certainly have subscribed to the advice on breeding which is contained in the Old Testament book of Leviticus.

144

Indeed, many of our modern attitudes towards what are regarded as line breeding or in-breeding stem from this particular source. What are largely moral precepts laid down over 1,500 years ago are still sometimes paraded as modern scientific fact.

Thomas Hardy in his 'Moments of Vision' put the matter of inherited characteristics most succinctly:

> I am the family face;
> Flesh perishes, I live on,
> Projecting trait and trace
> Through time to times anon
> And leaping from place to place
> Over oblivion.
> The year-heired feature that can
> In curve and voice and eye
> Despise the human span
> Of Durance – that is I;
> The eternal thing in man
> That heeds no call to die,

It is doubtful if the suspiciously received discoveries made by Gregor Mendel in 1866 and which were to form the basis on which the entire and complex edifice of the science of genetics now stands, had filtered down to Devon before the Parson's death. Even if they had, they could have had little practical influence on methods which had been tested and proven during the previous sixty years. Indeed, though it will, in some quarters, be regarded as heresy to say so, the science of genetics, though explaining many things which were previously a mystery and helping us to predict others which previously came as a surprise, pleasant or otherwise, may seldom have practical bearing on the decisions made by Parson Jack Russell Terrier breeders. Such hereditary problems as do occur have either a very complex mode of inheritance or one which is not fully understood and so are best treated by the avoidance of known or suspect carriers.

The perpetuation of desirable characteristics is best achieved by breeding only from dogs which carry those characteristics, while the elimination of faults may be achieved by carefully seeking out breeding stock which does not carry those faults. Parson Jack Russell Terriers are a natural breed in which virtues are dominant over faults. By breeding to good points, the incidence of bad ones will be reduced, though never eliminated. Simply by avoiding breeding from any animal which shows a recessive problem, the appearance of that problem would be reduced to about one fifth within four generations. By ignoring its existence it would be increased fivefold in the same period. The incidence of carriers (animals which carried and could transmit but did not show the problem) would be reduced by more than half, and, by taking out of the breeding population any animals which threw affected stock, the incidence would continue to decline. This can be achieved without a detailed knowledge of the science of genetics. By selecting the best, breeding only from the best, facing problems as they occur and doing so honestly and openly, the breed can be kept in its present healthy state. This is not to say that a knowledge of the science of genetics is to be despised. No knowledge, no matter how esoteric it may seem, should be despised, but as a practical tool for Parson Jack Russell Terrier breeders, genetics probably has only a limited role to play.

It is certainly useful to know that while dogs with light eyes will never produce dark-eyed puppies, those with dark eyes may produce light-eyed offspring. It is certainly essential to know that rough coats are dominant over smooth coats, which is to say that smooth coated dogs can produce only smooth coated offspring but that rough coated dogs, which carry the hidden characteristic for smooth coats, may produce smooth coated puppies. Breeders who wish to avoid the production of heavily marked puppies will find it useful to know that these are most likely to be produced by heavily marked parents and those who wish to breed terriers of a particular colour, as do Foxhound breeders in some of the most famous packs, will find it useful to know that black-marked parents may produce either black- or tan-marked puppies but that tan-marked parents can only produce tan-marked puppies. It is, perhaps, of less value to know that it is, in genetic terms, quite wrong to refer to either black or tan markings. Technically, black does not exist as a colour in dogs – what seem to be black dogs are in fact very dark brown. All Parson Jack Russell Terriers are some shade of brown, lighter or darker, and, though the colour may predominate, they have white markings, technically known as white spotting. Thus, an all-white dog is probably a dog which is covered by one large white spot!

In-Breeding and Line-Breeding

The moral strictures laid down in Leviticus are largely responsible for having formed our attitudes towards in-breeding and line-breeding, which are simply degrees of incest. Neither are scientific terms with a precise and invariable meaning, and for our purposes we will take in-breeding to mean the mating of close relations and line-breeding to refer to the mating of more distant relations. Both are useful, indeed valuable, tools when used with discretion by careful breeders but both can be dangerous when they are used unwisely. Every puppy inherits half of its characteristics from each parent. Some of these may not be apparent because a dominant characteristic inherited from one parent may hide a recessive characteristic inherited from the other. For example, a smooth coated bitch mated to a rough coated dog will produce only rough coated puppies but they will all carry the hidden genes for smooth coats. If two of these puppies are mated together the result would be approximately one quarter of the puppies with smooth coats and three-quarters with rough coats. Of these rough coated puppies, two-thirds would carry the hidden genes for smooth coats. If two of the smooth coated puppies were mated, the result would be nothing but smooth coated puppies. If two of the rough coated puppies which did not carry the smooth gene were mated, the result would be nothing but rough coats. But if two rough coated puppies which carried the smooth gene were mated, once more the result would be one quarter smooth coats, one quarter rough coats and one half rough coats carrying the genes for smooth coats. If, to make matters still more complicated, two rough coated puppies were mated together, only one of which carried the genes for smooth coats, only rough coated puppies would be born but some, about one quarter, would carry the genes for smooth coats. It is this ability for some characteristics, known as recessives, to remain hidden through many generations which results in the surprises, pleasant and unpleasant, which breeders have from time to time.

The effect of in-breeding and, to a lesser extent, of line-breeding is to reveal the existence of recessive characteristics and it is because of this that both are often blamed for causing problems. In fact, they do not create anything, all they do is reveal what may have been hidden for many generations and, by revealing it, provide an opportunity to eliminate it or increase its incidence. If a mating between a related pair of terriers with good mouths results in puppies with undershot jaws, the problem has not been caused by in-breeding but has been revealed by it. One, or more probably both, of the parents must have been carrying the genes which result in undershot jaws. Consequently, all that breeders achieve who ignore the existence of such characteristics is to hide them temporarily in their breeding stock where they will multiply to emerge at some later date to create havoc. Pretending that problems do not exist does not mean that they go away.

The breeder who makes good and careful use of in-breeding can produce related terriers which have a strong family likeness and which have the ability to reproduce that likeness. That is the value of in-breeding. It allows desirable characteristics to be increased and undesirable ones to be eliminated. There is, however, a price to pay. In-breeding has a tendency to reduce fertility and vigour. In-bred strains may produce better pups than others but they may also produce fewer of them. In the course of several generations they may also become slightly smaller and less robust. The wise breeder protects his stock against these tendencies by unremitting vigilance, rigorous control over the degree of in-breeding and careful control over the selection of breeding stock.

At the end of the nineteenth century, the Editor of *The Fox Terrier Chronicle* attempted to discover what were then regarded as the best ten Fox Terriers. The bitch Dorcas headed the list with thirty-seven votes, Foiler and Jock were well down the list while poor old Tartar never got a vote at all. The exercise was a proof of the way in which the experts had changed what they regarded as a good Fox Terrier since the days when they made their début in the show ring.

Those who are aghast at the whole idea of in-breeding might like to give some thought to the pedigree of Old Foiler, a Smooth Fox Terrier born in 1871 (shown opposite). Not only does Foiler's breeding give the lie to the fallacy that in-breeding is a modern phenomenon only indulged in by people who breed for the show ring but it also suggests that the Parson was not entirely circumscribed by Leviticus when it came to the business of breeding good terriers. Foiler was bought after the 1872 Birmingham show by Henry Gibson who, according to Rawdon Lee, 'always believed in the old-time terriers'. He paid £100, a ransom in those days. Ackerman says that Foiler's dam, Juddy, 'came directly from the Jack Russell kennels', which is a circuitous way of saying that she was bred by the Parson. We know that Juddy was bred by the Parson in 1868. We also know that he bred Grip, or Old Grip, and there is a very strong likelihood that he also bred Old Foiler who was sold, or more likely given, to George Whitemore at the Grove from whose terriers the Parson has derived so much benefit.

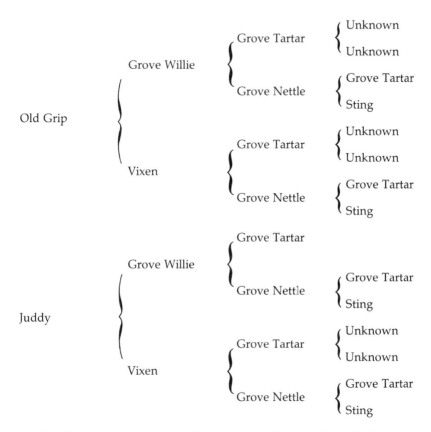

Old Foiler is an interesting dog, out of a bitch which the Parson, in all probability bred. Charles Littleworth of Wembworthy in North Devon, a breeder of the old-style Fox Terriers and huntsman, expressed the view that:

> The fox terrier at the present day [1889] has attained, by 'fine breeding' too great a delicacy and too high an excellency in fineness of coat and bone for really hard work. In many instances the modern standard is only useful for show purposes; perhaps he can kill a rat, and he is elegant as a drawing room companion. . . My belief is that the best strain for work has descended from George Whitemore's (of the Grove) Willie, afterwards called Foiler.

If we assume that by 'fine breeding' Littleworth was referring to what we would nowadays call in-breeding, the comment takes on an interesting aspect because we know of no dog, let alone terrier, before or since, which has been as closely bred as was Old Foiler. Yet Littleworth was the man who is alleged to have bred Foiler. Did he not know Old Grip's and Juddy's pedigrees? Or did he not care? Or is it not more likely that he was just one of those people whose received opinion about in-breeding was not going to be disturbed by the facts but neither was it going to alter the way he chose to breed terriers. It was probably just a case of 'do as I say, not as I do'.

We must not, as is often assumed to be the case, give the impression that in-breeding is practised only by the breeders of domestic animals. In fact, a number of wild animals and insects which breed in herds or colonies are very closely in-bred. A strong male will collect a harem and protect it from all other males. Next year, his harem will include some of his own daughters and this will continue until he is deposed by a younger and stronger male, probably one of his own sons, who will then take over the harem to produce offspring from his mother, aunts and sisters. The ingredient which keeps this closely in-bred stock healthy is rigorous natural selection. Substandard animals do not survive to breed. The breeder must replace natural selection with an artificial selection which is equally effective. This requires an ability to face and accept the existence of problems, to overcome the disappointment which they cause, to deal with them honestly and, if necessary, ruthlessly.

There are probably no more than about a dozen lines of Parson Jack Russell Terriers, each tracing back to a particular dog. Some degree of in-breeding cannot be avoided. It is, therefore, essential to the breed that all breeders exercise the greatest care when selecting their breeding stock.

10

Mating and Pregnancy

Choosing a Mate for your Bitch

To which dog are you going to mate your bitch? A number of courses are available to you. You can seek and slavishly follow advice from those who have persuaded you that they have the necessary expertise. The results may be entirely satisfactory but your own satisfaction will inevitably be reduced by your lack of real involvement in the process of selection. Registration documents will give you credit for being the breeder but in practice the breeder will be the person whose advice you sought and accepted. Alternatively, you might and, we would suggest, should try to acquire the necessary expertise yourself. One of the ways by which breeders tend to keep themselves harmlessly amused is by poring over pedigrees of the dogs which might be chosen as mates for their bitches. The exercise can be an interesting and informative one and especially when it is allied to a detailed knowledge of the dogs in the pedigrees and of their progeny. Working out potential matings on paper and trying to decide what sort of puppies they might produce is one of the breeder's less energetic tasks. A split pedigree book, with its pages divided, top and bottom, to allow the pedigree of likely dogs (at the top) to be aligned with the pedigree of different bitches (at the bottom) are a great help, especially as your information about individual dogs, their ancestors and their offspring begins to increase. Better still is a word processor on which a great many pedigrees can be stored and which offers the facility for information to be exchanged between breeders who are similarly equipped.

On the other hand, you might prefer to choose a mate for your bitch simply on the basis of the dog's appearance. The old truism that 'bad dogs never make good sires' is often shown to contain a great deal of truth but whether you would be better off using a good dog with a poor pedigree or a bad dog with a good pedigree could be endlessly debated if these were the only possibilities available to you. Fortunately, they are not and it is quite possible to find good, well-bred dogs which, given the luck which every breeder needs, should produce good puppies from your bitch providing, that is, that you have chosen your bitch wisely.

Whatever method or combination of methods you adopt, what you will certainly need is information about the available dogs, about their ancestors and about their existing progeny. Going to shows is one way, perhaps the best and certainly the most convenient way, to gather this information. You might choose to store this information in your memory and might be able to do so for a few years and a few dogs but cannot hope to do so over several years and for all the dogs, their ancestors and progeny which, as a good breeder, you will want to consider. It is surprising how often some dog can be forgotten or ignored because memory about his progeny is imperfect. Breeders who keep accurate records, whether in a notebook, on a set of filing cards or on a microchip, have no need to trust an imperfect memory.

You might consider adding to the available information by making use of Kennel Club publications and services which list all registered puppies and their parentage, which also list all winning dogs and their pedigrees and which, on payment of a small fee, will provide you with a list of all the puppies sired by your short-listed dogs. This will enable you to extend and verify your research. In addition, the Kennel Club can supply a pedigree of your chosen dog as well as details of any checks that have been made as to its status in relation to hereditary disease. By this means you can gather a great deal of information about potential stud dogs and can compare the number of outstanding puppies they have produced against the total number produced. You may well want to consider whether a dog which has produced ten well-publicised outstanding puppies out of a total of 100 is as good a prospect as one which has quietly produced five out of a couple of dozen puppies. We would suggest that 'strike rate' is an important consideration.

Whether you choose to use a dog which has particularly impressed you, which has produced puppies you have admired or whether your decision is made after spending hours poring over pedigrees, the choice is yours. If you can find a dog which appeals to you, with a pedigree compatible with that of your bitch, and which has already produced good puppies from bitches related to your own, the decision should be easy. It may be made less easy by the fact that, in the usual order of things, such dogs always seem to live at the other end of the country, a problem which is of far less consequence in Britain than it is in America or Australia. Try to remember, then, that the Parson, in an age when there were no motorways, when railways were in their infancy and he lived over forty miles (64km) from the nearest railway station, was prepared to go the length of the country to find what he considered to be the right dog for his bitches. Most of the time he probably relied on local dogs, most likely on dogs he had bred, but there were certainly times when he had to use dogs which lived at a distance from his kennel. He must have gone to some trouble to get Old Jock and Tartar into his kennel but must have thought that the trouble was well worthwhile. Surely you will not accept any lower standard?

Having made the decision, you will need to ask the dog's owner if your chosen dog is available for mating to your bitch. If your bitch is not, in the opinion of the dog's owner, up to the required standard the answer may not please you. There may also be other reasons why the dog is unavailable: he may be getting on in years and have had his stud work restricted or he may not be at public stud. In this case, you must select another dog, perhaps one of his brothers or sons if you want some particular characteristics, or another dog which features on your list for some other reason. Let us suppose that your chosen dog is available. You then need to discover what arrangements and terms the owner requires. Usually these involve taking the bitch to the dog when she is ready to be mated and payment of a stud fee when the mating has been accomplished. The fee itself varies but is normally reckoned to be between half and two-thirds of the average price of a puppy. In reality, though, the fee is set by the owner of the stud dog and reflects nothing more than his or her assessment of the dog's value, what the owners of bitches might be prepared to pay and his or her eagerness for the dog to be used. The stud fee is a payment for the service of the dog, for its owner's time and trouble, and is not dependent on the production of puppies. The owner of the stud dog cannot be expected to accept responsibility for your bitch's fertility or lack of it, for your decision about when she is to be mated, for her behaviour during the mating and for your subsequent care of her. The owner's responsibility is to provide the services of a fertile dog and to take reasonable steps to effect a mating. Even so, some stud dog owners do offer a second service if puppies do not result from the first. They are under no obligation to do so and it is not a condition on which you can insist. If a second service is offered it will be restricted to the same dog and the same bitch unless the stud dog owner is unusually co-operative.

Do not entertain any arrangements which waive payment of a stud fee but which would involve you in giving up a puppy or puppies when the litter is born. Like breeding arrangements, these are too often a source of trouble and, in any case, result in a mating which might cost twice, or even more than twice, the going rate. Even worse, they may result in you having to part with the best puppy in the litter, perhaps even the only good one, in which case the whole exercise will, from your point of view, have been no more than an expensive waste of time and effort. You will have bred a litter and have nothing to show for it except an older bitch and a good puppy in someone else's hands.

The Oestrous Cycle

By the time your bitch has had two or three seasons you should be able roughly to predict when she is likely to come into season. Bitches usually come into season at six-monthly intervals but some may have a slightly shorter or a longer interval between seasons. The interval can also be changed by having produced a litter at the previous season, by the use of hormones which suppress seasons, by the weather or by the oestrous cycle of other bitches with which she is in contact. You might be able to indicate to the owner of the stud dog that your bitch is due in season in a certain month, you might even indicate what part of the month, but greater accuracy is neither possible nor necessary. Even so, the information will provide the stud dog owner with an indication as to when to expect your bitch, and you with a rough guide to the time when puppies may be born. It is surprising how many first-time breeders will blithely arrange a mating and only subsequently realise that the pups are due to be born when they intend to be away on holiday or have some other prior commitment.

Having made the decision that you are going to breed from your bitch, you should ensure that she is, as well as being a good and healthy specimen of the breed, in good condition. Obese bitches are not only less likely to conceive but are also far more likely to experience whelping problems than are those in good condition. Equally, a thin bitch may not have the necessary reserves to enable her to rear a litter without undue difficulty. It pays to go to some trouble to ensure that your bitch is in tip-top physical condition, is free from parasites and that all protective vaccines are up to date.

Then comes what always seems to be the long wait until your bitch shows signs of coming in season. Wild canine bitches come into season once a year, as do some primitive domestic dogs. Some breeds may come into season at four-monthly intervals but six months is regarded as more usual in most breeds, though the interval can be varied by a number of factors both within your control and outside it. A mild winter and warm spring may bring bitches in season early, while cold weather may delay them. The presence of other bitches in season may provoke what some breeders refer to as the 'me too syndrome', whereby the seasons of bitches in one kennel tend to coincide. Your bitch's season may also be delayed if she has been or is in ill health or if you have made use of any of the hormonal injections to delay or suppress seasons. These are sometimes used so that a winning bitch can continue to be shown through the time when she would normally be in season or, perhaps, to postpone a season which otherwise occurs at an inconvenient time. The manufacturers and some vets do not recommend the use of hormonal injections on breeding bitches but, in practice, apart from making the timing of the next season unpredictable, their use appears to have no untoward effects.

Your bitch will have had at least one season and probably two before you mate her and so you will have had an opportunity to observe the signs which indicate an imminent season. Since, for the owner of any bitch, and especially for any breeder or potential breeder, the oestrous cycle is of the utmost importance, it is necessary to understand something of its nature. The cycle itself, which, as we have said, usually occupies a six-monthly period, consists, as far as the bitch is concerned, of four distinct phases. There is the anoestrous phase in which overt and covert sexual activity are quiescent. This, depending on the length of the cycle, usually lasts for about two months. Towards the end of this period an increase in oestrogen levels begins to prepare the bitch for the next stage and may result in some behavioural changes. The bitch may become quiet or restless, she may take an increased interest in her genital regions, and may, especially when out at exercise, urinate frequently, though usually passing no more than a drop or two of urine. It may well be that this is a means by which she advertises her approaching condition to likely suitors and so is something which the vigilant owner should respond to with increased security.

Some owners may attempt to disguise their bitch's approaching condition from wandering attendants or at shows by the use of chlorophyll tablets or scented sprays. To do so underestimates both the sensitivity of a dog's nose and the ability of a wise stud dog to recognise such diversionary tactics. We have known stud dogs which would respond sexually to the cans of sprays intended to deter them and which seemed totally unaware that in-season bitches had been liberally sprayed in an attempt to hide their condition. When a bitch shows signs of coming into season she should be left securely at home. Certainly, she should not be taken to shows where her condition will make her move and show less well than normal, excite stud dogs, cause curiosity among bitches, acrimony among their owners and do nothing for your own popularity.

Anoestrus is followed by the pro-oestrous stage, lasting about nine days, during which the bitch's reproductive organs are undergoing changes which will enable her to conceive. Some further behavioural changes may be noticed at this time but the most obvious changes are that the vulva will become swollen and will, in normal circumstances, emit a blood-suffused discharge. In some bitches, especially those which do not keep themselves clean, this may be sufficiently copious to stain furniture and it may be convenient, as well as more secure, to consign the bitch to a kennel for the duration. Some bitches, however, perhaps cleaner than the rest or for some physiological reason which has not yet been fully explained, may have what breeders refer to as 'silent seasons' in which the discharge is colourless. It then takes a very observant breeder or a vigilant dog to realise that the bitch is coming into season since the only visible sign may be a very slight swelling of the vulva. During this time, which lasts for about nine days, the bitch will be especially attractive to dogs and to other bitches and may go through the motions of mating with either.

She cannot, however, conceive until pro-oestrus gives way to oestrus, a short period which may last no more than a couple of days, during which the vulva may be greatly enlarged and the discharge pale yellow. About two days after the start of oestrus, in practical terms two days after the discharge has become clear, the bitch should be fertile and ready to be mated. It is possible for pro-oestrus and oestrus to be more precisely defined by taking swabs from the bitch, and these will assist the owners of bitches which have silent seasons, but for most practical purposes observation of outward signs remains sufficient to indicate to the breeder when the bitch is

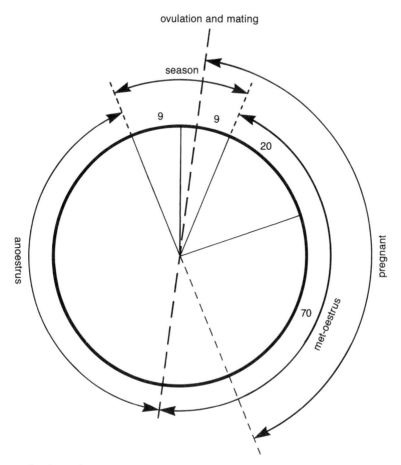

ovulation and mating

season

9 9

20

anoestrus

pregnant

70

met-oestrus

The reproductive cycle.

ready to be mated. Perhaps the most reliable indication, and certainly the most obvious, is when the bitch begins to present herself, perhaps to another bitch, her owner, the household cat or, in a well-controlled situation, to a dog. She will frisk rather skittishly, turning this way and that before arching her back and curling her tail to one side to expose and protrude her vulva. Once this behaviour has been seen, the bitch should be mated within a few hours. Some bitches may 'stand' for the dog for as much as two days; others may be receptive for a couple of hours. It is during this period that she will ovulate and must be mated if she is to conceive. Delaying or anticipating the mating in order to fit it in with a time more convenient for the owner, or the owner of the dog, is to ignore the entire biological process and will reduce the chances of conception taking place. If you simply want your bitch to have the experience of being mated then by all means allow your convenience to dictate matters but if it is your intention to breed some puppies you must be guided by nature and your bitch.

Depending on whether or not the bitch has been mated and has conceived, the next stage of the cycle will be either pregnancy (*see* page 164) or met-oestrus, in which hormonal changes may produce all the signs of pregnancy – the 'phantom pregnancy' which is the bane of the lives of many breeders and exhibitors. If the bitch has not been mated, or rather if she has failed to conceive, met-oestrus will, after about ninety days, give way to pro-oestrus, and the cycle will have come full circle. However, if she has been mated, the cycle will be interrupted by a developing pregnancy.

For bitches which, since puppyhood, have lived without contact with other dogs, mating can be a traumatic experience and any trauma will also reduce the chance of a successful mating. The opportunity to play regularly with other dogs will not only make your bitch happier but is also likely to increase her receptiveness when she comes to be mated. Isolation is not a normal or happy state for any dog or, indeed, any living thing. It will certainly pay dividends to ensure that your bitch is well adjusted towards other dogs. If she lives alone, take her to a few training classes or to a few dog shows.

Mating

When you have decided that your bitch is ready to be mated she should be taken to the dog, his owner having been given good warning of your impending visit. You would not be pleased after a long journey to find that the dog is not available any more than the stud dog owner would be pleased by the arrival of a bitch to be mated at a time for which other plans have been made. It is customary to take the bitch to the dog and only in very rare and privileged cases are the arrangements which the Parson enjoyed with Jock and Tartar available. If distance is a problem you may make arrangements to send the bitch to the dog and for her to enjoy his company for a few days. If no other arrangements are possible, this may be satisfactory but in our experience a bitch taken from her customary home, subjected to a long journey and then kept in unfamiliar surroundings is less likely to conceive than is one for whom arrangements have produced a minimum of upset.

It might well be that you want to use your own dog or will be asked to make him available at stud. You will not want to do so and are unlikely to be asked to do so by serious breeders unless he is good enough. There is no reason ever to use mediocre stud dogs. If you do intend to use your own dog you may be concerned at the effect which this might have on him. It will certainly make him more self-assertive and, perhaps, less likely to tolerate other dogs on his territory. It may, especially, when house bitches are coming into season and after strange bitches have visited the house, make him less clean about the house. He is likely to reinforce ownership of his territory by cocking his leg indiscriminately and so is, perhaps, better confined to a kennel and run. Otherwise, his stud work will make little difference to him. It will, though, make a difference to you. You will be providing a service for which you will charge a not inconsiderable fee. The service will be used by a variety of bitches and a similar variety of owners. A young and virile dog is capable of mating a bitch every week but you will find that, because of the normal oestrous cycle and the preferences of breeders, there will be spring and autumn peaks of stud work. You must regulate matters so that your dog is not used on different bitches on consecutive days and should, if his use is not more than three days apart, inform the owner of the second bitch of the time of his previous use.

Overuse will reduce his fertility, and loss of fertility will make him and you much less popular. It is also in his and your interests to select his bitches with some care. You will find that all the bad puppies he produces are blamed on him while credit for the good ones is claimed by the bitch's owner. Notwithstanding the attraction of several stud fees, a few top-quality puppies will, in the long run, be far better than a large number of mediocrities. In our experience it is the less good bitches which are most difficult to mate. These are the ones that arrive too early or too late in the bitch's season, with owners who are inexperienced and perhaps using the production of puppies as a sex lesson for a large family, all of whom arrive to witness the event. The bitch may not be accustomed to other dogs and you may well find yourself spending more than one evening trying to mate a reluctant bitch. Even a substantial stud fee is poor reward for all your and your stud dog's efforts, especially if the subsequent litter, as is likely, does him little credit.

We have heard stud dog owners justify mating their good dog to substandard bitches on the grounds that if they were to refuse to do so the bitch would go to a substandard dog and the breed would therefore be harmed. The argument is a facile one. You are not responsible for what others may or may not do. Your responsibility is to your own and your stud dog's reputation. These will be enhanced by producing outstandingly good puppies and will be harmed by mediocrity. Do not be tempted by greed or by any other reason to accept mediocre bitches.

The mating itself is not something which can be run to a strict timetable. You should allow ample time for a proper courtship, lengthy consummation and for the exchange of all the necessary documentation afterwards and you should expect the stud dog owner also to have made adequate time available. Stud dogs, and sometimes their owners, may be rather idiosyncratic creatures which perform best only when certain conditions are available. You should be prepared, within reason, to comply with the owner's suggestions. The basic procedure of a mating might be that, having arrived at the appointed time and made your presence known, you would give your bitch an opportunity to relieve herself and become familiar with her surroundings. The stud dog owner will indicate where the mating is to take place and what is expected of you. It is preferable that you are present at the mating or, at the very least, that you have an opportunity to observe it, and your help will usually be welcomed. Indeed, some stud dog owners seem to expect the bitch's owner to do all the work while they make little or no contribution to the exercise.

Let us suppose that the mating is to take place on the lawn, in anticipation of which you will be suitably, by which we mean practically, dressed, though the mating could just as well take place in a dog run, a shed or even, exceptionally, in the comfort of the house. The lawn, weather permitting, is perhaps the best place because this will allow the dog and bitch to become acquainted and to indulge in a brief courtship which will ease the mating considerably. The two will run around together, playing and frisking, the dog sniffing the bitch's vulva and she being very coy. The dog is likely to urinate frequently, reinforcing his boundaries and establishing his proprietorial claim to the bitch. At times he may appear to have no interest in the bitch. Patience may be called for until he decides to approach the bitch and she to accept his advances. You will observe the arched back, curled tail and presented vulva of a bitch ready and willing to be mated and will see the dog stimulating himself by sniffing and licking her rear end prior to mounting her and beginning the thrusting motions which will effect a mating. A great deal of licking and half-hearted thrusts, followed by a rapid dismount and further perambulations round the garden may indicate that the bitch is not ready to be mated, that you have left things too late or that the dog, for some other reason, lacks enthusiasm. More patience will be required.

It is not wise to use a dog at stud before he is fairly mature (at about ten months old), after which he might be rested for a month or so. It is also customary for the owner of a dog being used for the first time not only to provide him with a receptive and experienced bitch but also to waive the stud fee or, at least, to defer payment until the birth of the puppies. If the first mating goes well, it will make a great difference to the way in which the dog subsequently performs and so to his use as a stud dog. A young or otherwise inexperienced dog or one with more enthusiasm than discretion may grasp the bitch and thrust wildly. The bitch, though apparently prepared to accept his advances, may not be prepared to stand and quietly assist his efforts, in which case the stud dog owner and you may need to take a hand. The bitch should be gently restrained, preferably by her owner, while the stud dog is encouraged to mount once more and his efforts manually directed. Sometimes, if there is a disparity in height between the two, adjusting their relative heights is all that is needed to improve accuracy and facilitate penetration. If this is not achieved within about fifteen minutes, it is wise to separate the two in order to prevent the dog from wearing himself out, prevent premature ejaculation and for absence to make the heart grow fonder. Put the bitch back in the car while the dog rests in his kennel. Now is the time for what may well be the first of several cups of tea.

After twenty minutes or so, the attempt can be resumed with the dog and bitch refreshed by their rest and perhaps more likely to achieve success. Occasionally, after several such attempts, it becomes apparent that a mating is not going to be achieved. You may then be offered the opportunity to use a different dog, in which case you will have to make a quick decision, and all your prior research and study will be invaluable. If it seems that the bitch is not ready, you may be given an opportunity to return on the following day or, if she is past the optimum time, at the next season. It might even be suggested that you leave the bitch in the kennel for a few days. If you are satisfied that she will then be mated to the dog of your choice and is likely to accept the stay without undue stress, this may seem to be a suitable way out of your difficulty. There is seldom reason not to trust the owner of a stud dog to respect your choice of dog and, in any case, with the advent of genetic fingerprinting, reliable means now exist to verify the parenthood of puppies.

The entire process is one which is based on mutual trust. Just as you might have to trust the stud dog owner not to use another dog when your back is turned, so you are trusted not to mate your bitch to another inferior dog and claim the better one as the sire of the puppies. Indeed, how can the stud dog owner know, except on trust, that the puppies you will eventually register are, in fact, the product of the mating with his or her dog? Trust is an essential component of the entire enterprise.

Eventually, a mating should be achieved. The dog will mount and penetrate the bitch and will remain in this position for a few moments. A maiden bitch may now feel some discomfort, even pain, as his penis becomes enlarged and she may make determined attempts to escape. It is important that she should be quietly restrained in order to prevent damage to herself or to the dog, whose career at stud could easily be terminated by a strong bitch determined to escape his attentions.

As penetration takes place, the dog can be kept in place by means of a strategically placed knee on his rear. The contortions of an experienced stud dog handler at this time can be quite unexpected and demand unsuspected flexibility. Once the dog has penetrated the bitch, the ring of tissue at the end of his penis, the *bulbus glandis*, will swell and will be gripped by a corresponding ring of muscle inside the vulva. The dog and bitch will now be locked together in the beginnings of the classic tie which is a characteristic part of the mating of all canids, wild as well as domestic. However, it must be stressed that while the tie should be regarded as a normal part of the mating process, it is not a prerequisite to conception, nor is it something which is necessarily dependent only on the dog. Some successful stud dogs never tie with any bitch, some bitches do not tie with any dog and, from time to time, exceptions occur to what may have come to be regarded as invariable. Once the two are locked together the dog will attempt to turn by going through a complex contortion which involves placing his front legs on one side of the bitch and lifting one leg over her back so that the two end up facing in opposite directions. Once this position has been achieved, the pair will become quiet and almost sleepy, the only sign of activity being the strong pulse under the dog's tail which indicates a continued ejaculation. In order to be in a position to exert control, if required, the two tails can be held in one hand, but otherwise what is now needed is more patience.

Zoologists have puzzled for years about the reason for getting into this apparently vulnerable position. It has been suggested that a prolonged mating with a heavy dog resting on a bitch's back would impose an undue strain on the bitch and that a prolonged mating helps to cement the relationship between wild canids. This latter suggestion may have some validity among wild canids which lead a social life and in which both parents help to rear the offspring, but in such as foxes it has no validity whatsoever. Others suggest that the tie, vulnerable though it may appear, places the dogs in a position whereby they are able to defend both ends, but anyone who has seen a pair of foxes tied will realise that the unco-ordinated movements when they are threatened make such an explanation untenable. On the other hand, if the tie achieves no useful purpose why is it continued and if it is necessary only to prolong the union in order to achieve conception why has a quicker method of mating not evolved in dogs as it has in other mammals?

Whatever the reason, the fact remains that dogs tie and sometimes, usually in our experience during cold or wet weather, for long periods. Ten minutes to half an hour is not unusual and two hours is not unknown. During this time the dog's three-part ejaculate takes place. The first, lasting for less than a minute, consists of a clear and spermless fluid. This acts as a lubricant or medium for the second stage, lasting perhaps less than two minutes which, in a thick, opaque, white fluid contains, in a healthy dog, about 1,250 million sperm. Thus, perhaps less than two minutes after the tie the bitch has been fertilised. What then happens is that a third and copious ejaculate of prostatic fluid takes place and washes the sperm further into the bitch's reproductive tract. It is this final phase which occupies the greater part of the time when the owner of dog and bitch are able to exchange their life stories and catch up with all the canine gossip.

Eventually the two will separate. The dog will clean himself and should be returned to the quiet of his kennel, preferably with a refreshing drink and his delayed evening meal, since a dog is less likely to have amorous intent on a full stomach. The bitch should be returned to her box. Some owners believe that it assists conception to upend the bitch and massage the stomach. If that is what they

163

believe, there is no harm in going through the ritual but it is doubtful if it has any significant effect. Others believe that a bitch which urinates straight after mating will expel all the sperm. Again, this is most unlikely but if it comforts the owner to take steps to prevent this, no harm is done.

Supposing, though, that there are reasons which prevent a natural mating, what can be done to achieve the desired result? Artificial insemination (AI) is the obvious answer but here problems arise. The Kennel Club, in order to prevent AI from being used as a means to achieve matings between dogs which are too unsound or too savage to mate naturally which should not be bred from at all, will register puppies which result from the use of AI only if it has given permission prior to the mating taking place. Permission will only be granted if both the dog and the bitch have previously produced registered progeny by natural means and for insemination which utilises fresh semen. In other words, the Kennel Club, unlike a growing number of other kennel clubs in different parts of the world, will not accept the use of stored semen. The use of stored semen would enable a dog to produce puppies after its death, could facilitate the international exchange of the semen of the best dogs and could extend the influence of outstanding dogs. On the other hand, its unwise use could so deplete an existing gene pool that, should unexpected problems occur, there would be no avenue of escape. However, controlling the use of stored semen is one thing but attempting to control the use of AI is another. The techniques are so simple that, in the words of the Canadian Kennel Club, 'the very best practitioners are experienced breeders who use a milk-shake straw and a plastic cup'. But let us not expose ourselves to the risk of being accused of encouraging forbidden practices.

All that is now left is for the paper work to be completed. You should receive a copy of the dog's pedigree and a Kennel Club registration form, signed by the owner of the stud dog, giving his name and registration number, the date of the mating and the date when puppies are expected, and you will pay the required fee and receive a receipt.

Pregnancy

Once the bitch has been mated, you will need to wait for about sixty-three days before the pups are born. During the early part of her pregnancy she needs nothing which is different from her normal routine except that she must be strictly kept away from all other suitors for the entire time she is in season. You may well be surprised at the efforts both she and they make to get together but if all your planning and efforts are not to be totally wasted you must ensure that they are kept apart. As time passes, your impatience will increase but may be assuaged by the early signs of a developing

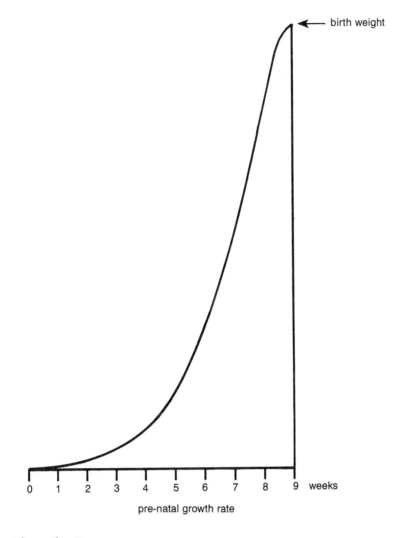

Pre-natal growth rate.

165

pregnancy: the swollen vulva, swollen teats, a slight corpulence and, perhaps, even in a Parson Jack Russell bitch, a tendency to take things easy. When the pregnancy is advanced about three weeks, it is sometimes possible to feel the developing embryos and the use of ultra-sound scanners can be used to verify the existence of puppies. There is sometimes an inclination to borrow from human experience and rush to the vet for a pre-natal check. By doing so you will expose your bitch to unnecessary stress and to the possibility of exposure to infection in the vet's waiting room. You will part with a fee and all you can hope for is a more or less tentative confirmation of your own suspicions. At worst, you will have exposed your bitch to stress or infection which will make her reabsorb the developing embryos or, more distressing for you, make her abort them. Better to curb your impatience.

As the pregnancy progresses you should protect the bitch from hard exercise, while ensuring that she remains fit. Her diet can be changed to take account of her growing burden by substituting more nutritious food for her normal diet and by splitting her daily intake into two or three meals. You might, particularly if she is in contact with dogs which may carry infestations of parasites, ensure that she has been properly wormed but you must only do so by using a vermifuge which can safely be used during pregnancy; it is wise to seek advice from your vet.

Preparation for Birth

The nine-week wait between mating and birth may pass slowly but you can usefully fill some of this time by ensuring that all is in readiness for the birth. Is your bitch to whelp indoors or in her kennel? Can you supervise what could be a prolonged birth if she is outside and can heat be provided for the puppies? If both these conditions can be met, there is really little to choose between indoors and out. A bitch in a kennel may have to tolerate less disturbance than one in the house and so may devote all her attention to the job in hand. One indoors can be more closely watched so that any incipient problems are quickly noticed and, as they grow, the puppies will become accustomed to the sights and sounds of a busy household. Indoors or out, you will need to provide the bitch with a comfortable bed which is big enough for her and her litter. A simple wooden box with one side which allows very young puppies to leave and regain entry is ideal. A covered box retains heat better than one with an open top and one which is lacquered or painted is more easily and thoroughly cleaned. For bedding, newspapers or the synthetic fur fabrics, marketed as dog bedding, are ideal. Outdoors heat is most easily, cheaply and safely provided by means of an infra-red heater, providing that an electricity supply is available. Ensure, however, that the lamp is not suspended over the puppies in such a way that they are at risk of being either cooked or frozen.

You might also collect all the equipment which might be needed during the birth. Clean towels, sterilised scissors and perhaps even something with which to celebrate the birth or assuage the disappointment might all be useful. You must also consider the possibility that you may not wish to keep all the puppies born. More may be born than the bitch can rear well, one or more may be deformed or in some other way below the standard you would wish to rear. Such things are most unlikely, especially if you have chosen your bitch and her mate well, but from time to time breeders must face up to the unpleasant task of destroying unwanted puppies. The euphemism is 'culling' but this neither makes the task less unpleasant nor the responsibility less onerous. It is not for us to lecture you about what your decision should be, but you must consider the quality of life which all the puppies you rear might expect and you must also consider the possibility that they may be bred from. If Parson Jack Russell Terriers are to maintain their present high quality, they can only be bred out of sound and typical stock, and you, as a breeder, have a responsibility to do your bit to ensure that this is the case.

Many breed and kennel clubs throughout the world impose on their members and those who use their services codes of ethics which are intended to ensure that all breeders conform to high standards. Caring and responsible breeders will have no difficulty in complying with these codes; uncaring and irresponsible breeders will find it impossible. It is for you to decide to which category you would prefer to belong.

11

Whelping and Rearing

It is not easy to know where to begin a chapter intended to deal with just some of the problems which might be encountered during the birth and early life of a litter of puppies. It is not even easy to decide just when the process of rearing a litter begins. Certainly, it does not begin only with the birth of the puppies because by that time they will have been individual, if parasitic, beings for almost nine weeks and will have flourished according, among other things, to how well or how indifferently their dam has been cared for. Even before the dam was mated, the fate of her puppies will have been, within certain broad limits, affected by her health and vigour and that will be, to some extent, dependent on how well she herself was reared.

Three main factors tend to reduce survival rates and produce weakly puppies. They are low birth weight, multiple births and low antibody levels, all of which are to some extent interrelated. Neonates with low birth weights may be produced by a dam which has been kept on an inadequate diet during her pregnancy or was in poor condition when she was mated and has needed to improve her own condition. Small neonates may also be produced by a dam which has been kept on a diet so rich or a dam which was so overweight that during her pregnancy her diet has been reduced, either by her voluntary action or by the decision of the breeder. Small puppies are also often found in litters with higher than average numbers.

Small puppies tend to have a reduced chance of survival because, due to competition from more vigorous siblings, they may be unable to suck while colostrum is present in the bitch's milk. As a consequence, they will have low antibody levels and a reduced resistance to infection. Access to the best teats is denied to them and they are unable to occupy the warmest places in the nest. They are continually at a disadvantage which tends to increase, as stronger puppies grow more quickly.

The lessons are obvious. Bitches which are intended for breeding must themselves have been well reared and be in good condition

168

when they are mated. They must be kept on a good, but not excessively good, diet throughout their pregnancy. All puppies must be allowed to suckle as soon as possible after their birth while colostrum, which contains the antibodies necessary to protect them from infection, are present in the bitch's milk. Any small puppies, particularly those in a large litter, should be given some preferential treatment if they are to be reared and a careful watch must be maintained on the development of all the puppies.

Early growth rates are of less economic importance to dog breeders than they are to farmers but they are important to the ultimate quality of the animal itself. The maintenance of good rates of growth is a necessary prerequisite to the production of a quality adult. No animal has achieved its ultimate size by the time it is born. During the post-natal period, the nutritional needs of a growing puppy are dependent on a complex and interrelated series of factors which make rearing a litter so that each puppy will achieve its full potential a fascinating and demanding process. It would be depressing if we were to realise just how many potentially outstanding puppies are ruined by indifferent care before they leave the breeder. It is equally depressing for breeders to watch well-reared puppies being ruined by indifferent care after they have gone to their new owners.

The growth rate of a puppy of any breed is quite prodigious when compared with that of a human infant. A puppy may double its birth weight in the first nine days of its life and by the time it is three weeks old it may be – indeed should be – four times as heavy as it was at birth. A human baby does not double its birth weight until it is about five months old and may not quadruple it until it is well over two years old. This is one of many reasons why food intended for human babies is unsuitable for puppies. It is designed for an omnivorous infant which grows at a leisurely pace and is inadequate for a carnivore which must grow very much faster.

Farm animals kept on a high nutritional plane will achieve their carcase weight far more quickly than those which are obliged to survive on a less good diet. That is obvious, but carcase weight is of no interest to dog breeders. What is important is the way in which growth occurs: brain first, then bone, then muscle and finally fat. Thus, intelligence, body size and conformation are, to an extent, within the control of the breeder. Good conformation is dependent upon good skeletal development and so can mar or realise the potential which careful breeding has given a puppy.

Whelping

Nine weeks after your bitch has been mated she should, all being well, present you with a litter of healthy puppies. This is the time when the nerves and confidence of even the most experienced breeders are stretched almost to their limit and for the new breeder it can be a traumatic experience. You will, of course, have done everything in your power to prepare for the event and to ensure that the birth is trouble free, but until you have been through the process you cannot expect to be other than apprehensive and nervous. It is at this time that things can go wrong, sometimes tragically so, but, fortunately, Parson Jack Russell Terriers are not one of the breeds in which whelping problems are to be expected. Nevertheless, problems can and do occur sometimes. Every whelping is different and none is free from minor dramas. Breeders of any livestock realise that the more they breed the more problems they are likely to encounter. They do not expect them but they know that all sorts of problems are just waiting to happen; the trick is to arrange matters so that problems are given as little chance as possible to occur. Even then, they will contrive to outwit even the best-laid plans.

During the sixty-three days of her pregnancy you should have kept the bitch away from shows and any other place where she might pick up some infection. You will not have expected her to do any work and will have been especially careful that she does not go off on any illicit hunting trips. Her exercise will have become more sedate though will have been maintained at a sufficient level to keep her fit. Nothing in our opinion, contributes more to whelping problems than poor physical condition and trauma during pregnancy. You will have increased the bitch's nutritional intake by giving more nutritious food in two or three smaller meals and you will, either before she was mated, or early in her pregnancy, have made sure that booster vaccinations are up to date and that she was well wormed. You will also have made arrangements to provide a suitable nursery for the pups. (*See* Chapter 10, page 166 for advice on a whelping box.)

Eventually, after what will seem to have been an interminable wait, the day will arrive when the puppies are due to be born. Do not, however, expect the full period for pregnancy to be strictly observed. Some bitches will habitually whelp after sixty-one days; others may tend to go slightly beyond the appointed time but, providing that the divergence from what is regarded as normal is not too great, there is no need for concern. The signs of impending birth are easily noticed. The bitch will become restless, exploring places in which she might consider giving birth, tearing up her bed, eating her food and then regurgitating it, and generally demonstrating her increasing lack of ease. This may all happen days or just hours before birth takes place. A more reliable indication is a reduction in the bitch's body temperature from the normal 101.5°F to about 98°F (38.6–36.7°C), though obviously in order to get this information you will need a clinical thermometer and the ability to use it.

Once the temperature has fallen, the next stage of birth can be expected to begin within twenty-four hours. The bitch will become even more restless, almost frantically arranging and rearranging her bedding, panting, sleeping intermittently, refusing her food and licking her vulva to remove the sticky, mucous discharge which will now be becoming copious. This stage may last for forty-eight hours or may be over almost before you are aware that it is taking place. Something between six and twelve hours is usual, but though birth follows a strictly defined pattern there is room for great variation within the pattern. While you must not expect things to proceed to a strict schedule and must not be panicked by normal variation, you must not ignore signs that things are not progressing according to the basic inexorable pattern.

Only when the birth passages are fully dilated can the next stage begin and the puppies be pushed out by their mother's muscular contractions. Panting and restlessness will cease and strong abdominal muscular contractions will become increasingly apparent. A bag of what appears to be black liquid will appear before probably disappearing and reappearing. Within a short time the bag will be followed by the puppy and the first birth will be complete.

Prior to their birth, the puppies have existed in an environment which is maintained at a constant temperature of 101.5°F (38.6°C). In order to prepare them for what is to come, their own temperature at birth is several degrees lower than this. The puppy will emerge into a world of which it has no knowledge and no experience, will be wet, tired and sore and, for the first time, must find its own food. The process of drying and getting its first vital feed will further drain already depleted stores of energy and the puppy's body temperature can fall quickly. Even in a temperature as high as 79°F (26°C), an isolated new-born puppy can quickly become hypothermic. As it becomes colder it will complain pitifully and will search frantically for warmth, but as hypothermia progresses it will cease to complain and will become torpid, its motor activities having become atrophied. At this stage, it can be revived by warmth but beyond this stage revival becomes progressively more difficult. Tolerance of low temperatures increases rapidly as the puppy grows and, by the time it is ten days old, a temperature as low as 60°F (15.6°C) is necessary to produce hypothermia. Therefore, puppies must be born into a temperature in which they can survive and they must not become isolated from their dam, the most effective and important source of heat and nourishment.

The arrival of the first puppy may seem to come as a bigger shock to the bitch than it does to you, in which case the puppy will need assistance. Carefully open and remove the membrane in which it may still be enclosed, gently massaging the umbilica towards the puppy and cut it, about an inch (2.5cm) from the puppy, with sterilised scissors. Clean and dry the puppy with a clean towel and return it to the bitch who, by now, should be eager to continue the compulsive cleaning and licking which will stimulate the puppy into independent life. At the same time, another puppy may be being born, then another and another. Parson Jack Russell Terrier bitches can have surprisingly large litters, sixes, sevens and even eights being not uncommon.

Perhaps the most worrying stage for a concerned breeder is the interval between the birth of one puppy and the next. Sometimes this may be a matter of minutes, while at other times, particularly as the bitch grows tired, it may be a couple of hours. A careful watch should be kept on the bitch. If she is straining without apparent result it is time to warn your vet that you may need his help. Once more, the breeder must tread the line between the need for urgent action and waiting a little longer. If the bitch rests quietly between births all should be well, but if she is straining without effect the need for help is indicated. Skilful manipulation may relieve the problem or there may be need for surgery. With a large litter or a poorly conditioned bitch, sheer exhaustion may produce a need for surgery, though this should be a very unusual occurrence for any Parson Jack Russell Terrier breeder. A more common problem may result from inertia, the bitch's inability to produce the contractions required to expel her puppies. Inertia may precede the birth of any puppies or may intervene part-way through the birth. It is probably the cause of the greatest number of puppy deaths at birth and is best avoided by ensuring that bitches are in good physical condition, but may be relieved by a stimulating injection given by your vet.

Not all births go smoothly; indeed, it is rare, even with such a relatively trouble-free breed as Parson Jack Russell Terriers, for any birth to be completely without its heart-stopping or pulse-racing moments. Whelping a bitch is not an experience for the faint-hearted or for those given to bouts of panic. There are times, infrequent though they may be, when decisive action is called for in order to relieve some problem. In some abnormally shaped breeds the angle or size of the pelvis may present an obstacle which unborn puppies cannot negotiate. There is then no alternative but for surgical delivery. Parson Jack Russell Terriers are unlikely to encounter this particular problem. However, puppies, especially in a breed which shows great variation of breed type, may vary considerably in size and the largest may be too large to get through the pelvic aperture. In this case, surgical delivery is again necessary. On the whole, though, such problems as are likely to be encountered can usually be solved by a knowledgeable breeder with or without veterinary assistance.

A bitch may be reluctant to move into the third stage of labour. She may not have developed normal maternal instincts as a result of an unusual lifestyle or her owners may be so strongly imprinted on her as to have suppressed her maternal instincts. If the first stage is unusually protracted or she is not in good physical condition, progress may be terminated. It may also be terminated if she has not been properly familiarised with the quarters in which she is to give birth or has been made apprehensive as a result of some disturbance by another dog, inquisitive strangers, thunder or some such. An echolic injection may be all that is required to stimulate progress. Well-conditioned bitches with normal instincts, carefully provided with familiar whelping quarters, respect for privacy coupled with unobtrusive supervision all help to avoid the nervous inhibition of labour. Delays may also be experienced as a result of uterine inertia.

The journey from uterus to the outside world is assisted not just by muscular contractions but also by the shape and size of the puppy itself, more especially of the first puppy in a litter. One which makes the journey head-first will assist the birth passages to open, provides the right sort of hydraulic assistance, and is less likely to present problems as its legs meet unyielding obstructions. However, many puppies are born feet first without difficulty and both presentations can be regarded as normal. If a puppy's hind legs appear first it should be eased out gently. There will be no time to summon a vet if the puppy is to survive. Thoroughly scrubbed hands, a sterile towel, some sound knowledge sympathetically applied and a dash of courage are required.

By inserting the finger into the vulva it is often possible to discover the nature of the obstruction – a leg folded back, the head in an awkward position, more rarely the puppy on its back or, in a breech birth, the hind legs resisting further forward movement. Gentle manipulation can then release the obstruction and, by grasping the part of the puppy which protrudes from the vulva with a clean towel, and easing it gently, in time with further contractions, the puppy can be freed. If it cannot be freed, the vet, who you will have already warned about a likely problem, should be summoned without further delay.

If, as is most often the case, the puppy can be freed, its delayed and difficult birth may have drained it of all energy. It may appear to be dead, but hope remains. Once the umbilical cord has been cleanly severed about an inch (2.5cm) from the puppy, it should be stimulated by being gently massaged with the towel in much the same way that a bitch's vigorous licking will stimulate a new-born puppy. Its mouth should be cleaned out to ensure that nothing is obstructing its breathing. Open its mouth and gently, very gently, blow air into it. Hold the puppy securely and swing it so that any obstruction to breathing is forced from its throat and chest. If, after half an hour or so, there is still no response you must accept that the puppy is dead but it is surprising how many apparently dead puppies can be revived by timely attention. While all this has been going on, it is likely that other puppies will have been born. One which has its delivery delayed tends to have a queue form behind it and its slow journey puts these puppies at risk. Once the passage is clear, these puppies may well be born with great speed.

Care of the Bitch and Puppies

Once all the puppies are born, a weary breeder and a more justifiably weary bitch will require rest and quiet. The bitch should be given a warm drink of water, perhaps laced with glucose, but before the breeder can rest it is necessary to ensure that all the puppies are taking nourishment. Puppies which do not suck very early in their life do not get sufficient colostrum, and so have a reduced expectancy of survival and an increased likelihood of infection. Eberhard Trumler recorded the development of puppies in relation to the time

174

taken between birth and reaching a teat. He found that puppies which took the longest time subsequently achieved the poorest level of development and grew into the least vigorous adults. He used this rating to help him to decide which of a very large litter should be reared and so based a process of artificial selection closely on what would have been the result of natural selection.

All the puppies should be carefully checked for deformities or other problems which might indicate that they should not be reared. Destroying young puppies is a horrible task but it is a task which the conscientious breeder will not shirk. Rearing weakly or deformed puppies may seem humane but is likely to result in the production of still more weakly or deformed puppies if these are ever bred from, as some surely will be. Culling is neither easy nor pleasant but is necessary if the breed and your reputation as a breeder are to be kept in good health.

Some breeders keep detailed records about their puppies which can form the basis for a document offering a mass of valuable information and which, in any case, adds to the fun of rearing a litter and is a means to recall the fun at some future time. The record will begin with the order in which puppies were born, the precise time of their birth, their weight and other details such as whether they were breach or assisted births, and will continue with the pups' weights being recorded on a daily basis, which, even if it does nothing else, accustoms the puppies to being regularly handled. In fact, growth rates can provide a very valuable means of checking a pup's progress. One which does not match the growth of the others can be given supplementary food or can have its health checked to ensure that there is no intractable problem.

The first few days after whelping may produce yet more problems. You will have seen the placentas, the afterbirths, which have supported the puppies prior to their birth and will perhaps have been surprised at the relish with which the bitch eats these unappetising pieces of dark flesh. Let her do so, however, because the placenta contains a substance which helps to stimulate milk production. You may try to match the number of placentas with the number of puppies, taking account of any twins – puppies which are attached to the same placenta – though these do not occur often. If the number does not match and one or more has been retained, watch during the next few days, for the development of a dark or even black vaginal discharge. If the bitch seems out of sorts, has no appetite, is not interested in her puppies, seems unusually thirsty and is running a temperature she will need an injection to release the afterbirth, and antibiotics to control any infection.

The breeder now faces some weeks of constant but enjoyable and rewarding work as well as of appreciable expense. During the post-natal development of the litter there are points at which changes take place and which herald a need for changed management. Immediately after birth, a healthy pup will quickly seek a nipple and will suckle vigorously, its stomach becoming noticeably more rounded. Even so, for the first twenty-four hours of its life the pup may lose weight, but in a warm and dry atmosphere and with a healthy bitch which is content in familiar surroundings lost weight will soon be regained and the pup will begin to grow.

For the first three days after giving birth it was customary to keep the bitch on a bland diet of white meats, fish or eggs but nowadays it is possible to buy food which is specially formulated for nursing bitches. This is more convenient for the owner and cuts out the uncertainty which is attendant on any home-concocted diet. During the first three or four days the puppies will change considerably. It is almost as though their journey down the birth passages somehow squeezed them out of shape and only after a few days does their normal shape begin to reassert itself. They will spend most of their time either suckling or sleeping. A nest of contented puppies chirruping quietly to themselves or sleeping in a tangle against a contented and proud bitch is a pleasant sight and is a very different picture from frantically squeaking and ill at ease puppies, cold, hungry or unwell. The random movement in an unhappy litter cannot be confused with the eager scrum which forms against the bitch when feeding time comes round or with the rotund and contented creatures which have just finished a satisfying meal.

During these early days a careful watch should be kept on every puppy to ensure that it is thriving, that the bitch is cleaning them up well and that umbilical cords are healing properly. The bitch too should be carefully checked to ensure that any slight discharge which remains does not indicate a problem. If the discharge is slight, dark red or brown all can be assumed to be well. If it is green or smelly it is time to summon a vet, and we mean summon. No vet worth his salt would expect a bitch with a litter a few days old to be subjected to the trauma and possibility of infection which a visit to his surgery would involve. The bitch's teats should also be carefully examined to ensure that all are functioning well, none is blocked and that there are no other untoward problems.

Before the puppies' eyes open, usually at about the tenth day, operations to dock their tails or remove dew-claws must, if they are going to be done at all, be carried out. Some Parson Jack Russell Terrier bitches produce puppies with dew-claws on their hind legs as well as on the front, which is more usual. Those on the hind legs must be removed; those on the front legs are usually removed, not just for the cosmetic advantage of producing a cleaner outline but because dew-claws torn while a dog is working create a fearful injury and because, if neglected, they can cause discomfort for a pet dog. Snipping them off close to the leg with a pair of sharp, sterilised scissors is a simple matter which seems to produce not more than momentary discomfort for the puppy. Docking is, when carried out by experienced hands, no more troublesome but, because some vets and some breeders argue that there is no practical justification for the operation, public opinion is increasingly being persuaded, often by inaccurate and sensational reports, that docking is cruel. Nowadays, few vets will carry out the operation and those who do may charge exorbitant fees to salve their consciences. Furthermore, few vets have the experience of the breed which is necessary to produce the desired length of tail in an adult, they cut far too short or not short enough. The operation is simple to perform, though not one to be undertaken by inexperienced hands. You will need to find someone, preferably an experienced breeder, to carry out the operation and to supervise your first efforts.

During the first fortnight of their lives the puppies' needs, other than cleanliness and, perhaps, warmth, can be supplied by a well-fed, healthy bitch. They should grow at a prodigious rate and be quiet and content. In order to provide for their needs, the bitch should, after a day or so, have her food increased to three or even four times her customary intake – its quality too should reflect the demands now being made on her. Bitches' milk is rich in protein and calcium – it follows, therefore, that her diet should be rich in both these substances. The tremendous growth rate caused by the bitch's milk imposes a considerable strain on her and may, if her diet is inadequate, so deplete her own reserves as to endanger her health or even her life. A loss of calcium and phosphorus, both substances which the puppies need in order to sustain skeletal development, can induce eclampsia (often referred to as milk fever) in the bitch. Unless the onset of symptoms are quickly recognised and treated they can prove fatal. The early stages of eclampsia are characterised by panting and trembling and as the deficiency progresses these are replaced by muscular tremors, unco-ordinated movement and hysterical behaviour. After this stage the bitch will lose consciousness and will die unless she is given an intravenous injection of the necessary minerals. Some bitches whose diet apparently contains adequate amounts of calcium and phosphorus may still require a preventative injection when they are nursing puppies but for most a diet rich in these substances is an adequate precaution against eclampsia. Not only will bone growth be properly sustained but nails, not being worn down on a soft bed, will also become long and sharp. These should be kept trimmed with a pair of sharp scissors or they will lacerate the bitch and reduce her enthusiasm for feeding her puppies. Keeping nails short at this stage also seems to make them easier to trim in later life and may, just may, help to encourage the development of round, tightly padded, cat-like feet.

When the puppies are about a fortnight to three weeks old they should be wormed, even though you have scrupulously wormed the bitch before she whelped and are convinced that the puppies harbour no worms. Worms, particularly roundworms, are especially active in nursing bitches and young puppies, and even a mild infestation can severely debilitate a young puppy and retard its development. Furthermore, roundworms are both dangerous and distasteful. It is as well to ensure that none are present when the pups go to their new homes. Worming, with a suitable vermifuge, should then be carried out at fortnightly intervals until the pups are twelve weeks old.

By the time the puppies are about three weeks old they will be exploring their nest and soon after will be giving every sign of being dissatisfied with their diet of mother's milk. In the bitch's absence give the puppies a bowl of puppy food and help them to suck from it. Some will get the idea immediately, others will take longer, but a growing appetite is an excellent stimulant to rapid learning. When the puppies have finished, allow the bitch to clean up the remains of the food which, by now, will be liberally distributed around the puppy run and all over the puppies. Within a day or two the puppies will be eating independently and should have the number of meals increased as their needs increase and the bitch's ability to satisfy them decreases. Do not be tempted by apparent economies to feed out-of-date human baby foods. They may provide all the nourishment needed for a slow-growing and relatively inactive omnivore but they do not provide what is necessary to rear rapidly growing and very active carnivores. Nor should cows' milk be regarded as an adequate substitute for bitches' milk. Bitches' milk is over twice as rich in protein, fat, calcium and phosphorus as is cows' milk.

Use a puppy food mixed in strict accordance with the manufacturer's instructions, produced by a reputable specialist firm. At this stage, little and often is the rule. Four, five or even six small meals a day are far better than a couple of larger ones. Make sure that every puppy is getting its share and that none is being bullied by stronger siblings. By the time they are five weeks old the puppies should be having four or even five meals a day and the bitch will be spending little time with them. They will effectively be weaned. Let the puppies themselves decide how much they will eat. Give them a generous dish and allow them to feed until repletion, ensuring that all get their proper share. Take the remains of the food away and wait until the next feed time. They will develop rapidly, each becoming a distinct individual with its own individual responses to new sights, sounds and experiences.

In this hygiene-conscious age it might be taken amiss if we were to suggest that preoccupation with standards of hygiene poses a threat to the proper development of puppies. Let us, therefore, insist with all the force at our disposal that puppies and dogs should be kept in scrupulously clean conditions throughout their lives. Keeping a well-fed litter of puppies, confined to a puppy pen, clean is a never-ending and not always pleasant task, which will produce mountains of soiled newspaper, the best lining for a puppy pen, to be disposed of. The pen itself should be impervious to wet and stain and should be kept thoroughly clean. There are good disinfectants on the market which not only eradicate unpleasant odours but do not replace them with another which is equally unpleasant. Some of these are formulated for kennel use and have the very valuable property of destroying parvovirus. Puppy pens can, with hard work, be kept clean, sweet and germ free. There is, therefore, nothing incompatible between rearing a litter in the house and good standards of hygiene.

It is important that, during the first few weeks of life puppies are exposed to new sights and sounds. If, at this stage, they are reared in isolation, perhaps seeing people only briefly when they are fed they will not get the sort of experience which will enable them to develop into well-adjusted, well-socialised puppies. These are the sort of conditions in which puppies produced by puppy farms are often reared and it is strange that they are precisely the sort of conditions which inspectors may regard as ideal. In fact, though tradition is often disparaging of so-called 'kitchen sink' breeders, there are no better places for rearing puppies than in the midst of a busy household. There they will constantly be exposed to all manner of new sights and sounds, will be handled frequently and will enjoy constant supervision. Their presence, of course, will interrupt the normal routine. Growing puppies are great time wasters, as their antics and needs divert attention away from more routine, and less enjoyable, matters. But then rearing puppies, hard work though it is, should also be fun. There are enormous advantages to be gained from rearing puppies in the house. At this stage, the puppies' development has an enormous influence on the sort of adults they will become. An inadequate diet and an environment which offers no opportunity to extend experience will produce weakly and shy puppies which, once they have passed the age of about eight or ten weeks are set on a predetermined course which can only produce weakly and shy adults. Weakly and shy adults are themselves likely to produce weakly and shy puppies. The process of rearing a litter of puppies is one which will have an effect on subsequent generations.

Puppies which are deprived of human contact and a wide range of experience for the first few weeks of their lives are unlikely to make satisfactory pets, may be difficult or even impossible to train and will lack the ability to make a close attachment either with human beings or their own kind. The term applied to the process of gaining the experience which will enable puppies to grow into well-adjusted adults is 'socialisation'.

The period between five and twelve weeks of age is critical for puppies. In human beings the same critical period of development occurs between twelve and fifty-two weeks. Deprived of social contact they will grow up to be emotionally isolated, shy, anti-social, possibly aggressive and unhappy, but given an overprotective environment they will lack independence, will be maladjusted and emotionally inadequate. Puppies which are reared during these critical weeks entirely by people will lack the ability to make normal relationships with other dogs, they may become aggressive or fearful and might be useless for work, show or even breeding. Given a stimulating environment and the company of other dogs they will have the opportunity to develop normally.

Good breeders are instinctively aware of the critical nature of this short period. They spend a lot of time with their puppies. They ensure that they meet other dogs and any other animals which share

180

Young puppies need to be exposed to new experiences and allowed to extend their range of activities.

their home. They are exposed to all the sights and sounds of a busy household and learn to associate people with a pleasant experience. The lessons learned during this period will never be forgotten and will determine their behaviour as adults.

There is a commonly held fallacy among many breeders that puppies should not be overfed so that they grow fat. The theory is that the excessive weight of such puppies will bend their young bones and deform their joints and will, therefore, result in deformed puppies. In addition, they will grow to enormous proportions, far bigger than a Parson Jack Russell Terrier should be. Not only are such theories almost total nonsense but they are, to a large extent, often the opposite of the truth. Of course, puppies should not be fed quite like Strasbourg geese but neither should they be starved in a misguided attempt to reduce the load on their developing frames or to restrict their growth. Unless growing puppies have an adequate diet which will properly fuel all their growth, they are very likely to grow into adults with skeletal and other problems which are a direct

181

result of their early inadequate diet. Furthermore, though an inadequate diet may slow their early rate of growth it will not have any effect on their ultimate size, unless they are to be maintained on a starvation diet throughout their lives – a regime which is hardly likely to produce a quality animal of any sort. Bones and joints are more likely to become distorted because of rickets, caused by a dietary deficiency of vitamin D, or because of an inadequate supply of calcium and phosphorus or a genetic propensity to such characteristics. In general terms, a puppy up to about three or four months of age needs about twice as many calories per pound body weight as does an adult and no one should be surprised or alarmed if a vigorous puppy consumes more than this.

By the time the puppies are five or six weeks old they should be fully weaned; if the bitch sees them at all, her visits should be brief. Doubtless the puppies will still take an interest in her teats but the previously copious milk supply will, by now, have all but disappeared. You should recognise this by slowly reducing her diet, though if she is kept on the highly nutritious diet on which she has reared her puppies the depletions caused by her maternal duties will be rectified the more quickly. It is not at all unusual for bitches to be back in the ring and winning about eight or ten weeks after producing puppies. However, if they are taken to shows care should be taken to ensure that they or other dogs do not bring any unwelcome infections or parasites home with them.

There is a great deal of debate about how frequently bitches can be bred from. Normally they come into season every six months and producing a litter seems to have little effect on the cycle. They can, therefore, be bred from every six months and some are. They spend their lives producing puppies and are discarded when their fertility begins to wane. One of the advantages of Kennel Club recognition will be that registration details will provide information about how many puppies every bitch has had prior to those which are currently being registered. Those who over-use their bitches will have to face public exposure or avoid this by breeding unregistered stock.

Bitches tend to produce more and better puppies with less difficulty if they are bred from when they themselves are still in the full vigour of early adulthood. Many good breeders will take two litters at successive seasons from a young bitch before giving her a twelvemonth, or longer, rest from maternal duties. But it is impossible to lay down hard and fast rules. Breeders must decide for themselves according to their own standards.

If your first litter produces a puppy as promising as this well-reared young chap, you have every reason to be well satisfied with your efforts.

If puppies are born during the spring and summer months they can be put outside in a secure run when they are five or six weeks old. We use a movable pen, about six foot (1.8m) square and two feet (61cm) high, which gives the puppies room to run and play but is not too heavy to move onto unsoiled ground or too cumbersome to store. If the puppies are to spend any length of time in the run, make sure they have protection from wind, wet and sun and are not at risk from wandering dogs, cats or predatory birds. Even carrion crows are not averse to taking a sly peck or two at a young puppy.

By this time you will be thinking about letting the puppies go to their new homes, but you should on no account let them go before they are eight weeks old and, if they are going to new homes in winter, which contain young chldren or which have no prior experience of owning a dog, it pays to wait a couple of weeks longer. You will be able to supply the new owners with a neatly and accurately written pedigree, a diet sheet, some basic advice on care and whatever other advice you think necessary. You may also have begun the course of injections which will offer protection against the handful of dangerous diseases to which all dogs are prone. This, however, will depend on your vet's advice. Puppies of this age may retain some maternal immunity which can reduce the effect of injections and it may be better to delay injections for a couple of weeks, if they can be protected from any likely source of infection. On the other hand, any local outbreak of infection or a trip to somewhere which may harbour infection may make it advisable to begin the injections without delay.

Once the puppies have gone to their new homes make sure that the whelping and puppy pen are well cleaned and disinfected, repaired and repainted if appropriate and stored away in clean conditions to await your next need of them. You will have learned a great deal and had a lot of fun, mixed with hard work and some anxiety. Breeding and rearing a litter of good puppies can be a rewarding experience though your bank manager may not think so. At the end of the experience you are likely to be out of pocket but does that matter if you have produced some good puppies and have a good prospect or two in your own kennel?

12

Showing

Showing dogs is fun, or should be. If you don't think that you would find it enjoyable or, after trying it, discover that you would rather find your fun elsewhere, do not belittle yourself by disparaging those who do find dog shows a source of enormous enjoyment. We all find our fun in different activities, many of which provide an easy butt for cheap jokes or ill-informed comment; showing dogs is neither better nor worse than any other competitive activity. It is, however, different from many in that it relies, at shows run under Kennel Club rules, on the opinion of a single judge, and very occasionally, at hunt and working terrier shows, on two, three or even four judges. A number of sports, such as ice-skating, diving, synchronised swimming, trampolining and gymnastics, rely on the opinion of a panel of judges in order to decide the winner. Even sports such as boxing, wrestling and judo, from time to time, require the opinion of several judges. Apparently, panels of judges or a multiplicity of judges are deemed necessary in these sports in order to provide protection against the possibility of biased decisions, though it seems that they do not always achieve their objective. At dog shows run under Kennel Club rules it is not ever considered necessary to use more than one judge, except where the size of an entry is greater than one judge can comfortably handle. In this case, a breed may have different judges for each sex who together decide which is Best of Breed from their respective winners. Should they fail to agree, the opinion of a referee is sought but that referee acts alone, not as part of a panel of three. Some working terrier show organisers seem to feel that there is strength in numbers and make use of panels of judges though the end result can then easily be an unsatisfactory compromise between strongly held conflicting opinions or nothing more than the opinion of the strongest judge on the panel.

In the excitement of competition, the importance of a judge's decision may be inflated in the mind of an exhibitor. Dr Johnson put the matter in perspective when he said, 'A fly, sir, may sting a stately

185

horse, and make him wince; but one is still but an insect, and the other is a horse still.' A judge's decision, whether laudatory or not, makes absolutely no difference to the quality of the dog on which the opinion is passed. Decisions vary, sometimes for good reason and at other times in a baffling way. If they did not, there would be no point in having more than one dog show under the same judge every couple of years or so. We all have a right to our opinion and judges are appointed because it is felt that their opinion will be of interest to exhibitors. The extent of that interest can be gauged by the size of their entry.

It was Alexander Pope who said that:

> 'tis with our judgements as our watches, none
> Go just alike, yet each believes his own.

Every exhibitor is entitled to his or her own opinion and it is possible, even likely, that this will differ from that of the appointed judge. There are three things to be remembered in such a situation. The first is that the judge on the day has had an opportunity to examine every dog and so is in the best position to assess the quality of each. Disagreements with the judge's decision are always based on less than complete evidence. Secondly, the exhibitors have willingly submitted their dogs for the judge's opinion. They did so having exercised their own judgement of how that judge might perform. If they subsequently disagree with the judge all they are really doing is exposing their own lack of judgement, and if they also find it necessary to advertise their disagreement they are merely compounding their lack of judgement with a lack of sportsmanship. Thirdly, as we have already said, win or lose, the judge's opinion does not alter the quality of any dog. An undeserved win or an unwarranted defeat at one show will invariably be put into more accurate perspective at subsequent events where judges have less eccentric opinions. Moaning about a judge's decision is stupid, unsporting and destructive, not only of the complainant's enjoyment but of that of other, probably more successful, exhibitors. We all have a right to our opinion but none has a right to destroy another's enjoyment or moment of glory, no matter how undeserved. It is as well for the exhibitors of Parson Jack Russell Terriers to remember that their breed is far from stupid, is very sporting and is adept at enjoying life. It sets them an example which should not be ignored.

The earliest dog shows, which probably began during the

eighteenth century, were intended as a means for enthusiasts to meet in order to share and extend their interest. At this time, there were enthusiasts such as John Warde, the father of British fox-hunting, who was running hound shows at his home at Squerries in Kent. They could, by comparing their favourite dogs, gain the sort of information which would enable them to select the sort of mates which would, in subsequent generations, eliminate their faults and improve their virtues. Showing dogs was, and largely still is, an extension of an interest in breeding dogs.

During the early days of dog shows the competitive element was not pronounced. Dog shows were regarded largely as exhibitions which, as well as providing a meeting place for enthusiasts, gave an opportunity to the public to see and admire good specimens of a variety of breeds. Inevitably, however, the competitive element quickly assumed greater importance. We now go to dog shows not just to compare one dog with another and to meet our friends but to try to win. Competition has now taken on a far greater importance.

There are very few activities which provide similar opportunities for competition between young and old, rich and poor or which are so cosmopolitan. Dog showing attracts people of all ages and from all walks of life; people, in fact, just like you and us. We can think of no other popular, competitive activity which is accompanied by so few problems of any sort. The Kennel Club, which exercises control over all the shows it licenses, deals with a mere handful of disciplinary cases each year, and only a small proportion of these arise out of unacceptable behaviour at any of the seven thousand or so licensed events run each year under its jurisdiction, the largest of which will receive well over twenty thousand entries. Even at the four hundred or so smaller working terrier shows which take place outside Kennel Club authority and which do not enjoy the benefit of a disciplinary body, trouble is more a remarkable exception than a customary rule. Dog shows and exhibitors have a great deal in which they can take pride.

For many years, indeed since well before the Kennel Club was founded in 1873, the owners of working terriers have enjoyed access to a loosely knit system of shows, providing them with the means to meet in order to share experiences and enthusiasm, to compare their terriers and to enjoy friendly competition. Without these shows it would have been difficult, if not impossible, for breeders to gain the knowledge which is necessary if they are to breed better dogs. Some might argue that the Parson managed to do so but, in fact, he did not.

Showing dogs is not a hobby confined to a narrow age group. Here, a group of youngsters demonstrate their expertise in a class for Junior Handlers.

Not only did he judge at shows all over the country but he also frequently stayed with his hunting, Kennel Club and Fox Terrier cronies and they with him and so would be very well informed about what was happening in other breeder's kennels. Those who do not enjoy the Parson's wide circle of friends, who want to breed Parson Jack Russell Terriers but who have no wish to attend dog shows must find other means to extend their knowledge and exercise their enthusiasm. Shows may not be a vital part of dog breeding but they are certainly of immense value to dog breeders in their efforts to breed better dogs. Indeed, it is true to say that very few dog breeders who neither compete at shows nor attend them regularly, produce quality dogs. Showing is not a cheap pastime and so those who are breeding simply for profit are unlikely to appreciate an activity which will dissipate their profits.

Types of Show

The shows which, for many years, have provided an opportunity for the breeders of Parson Jack Russell Terriers to meet are mainly organised by hunts or their supporters' clubs, by some agricultural societies and game fairs, and, more recently, by the breed clubs. The breed's immense popularity meant that many of these shows received large and profitable entries and, as a result, other organisations, with a less obvious interest in the breed, or the sport in which it was involved, began to promote shows. By 1988 there were about four hundred shows to choose from, though they varied in both size and quality.

The best of these shows offered advantages not to be found at Kennel Club events. For many of them it is not necessary to make a prior entry. An intending exhibitor can rise on the day of the show, assess the weather, the state of the dogs and the pull of other attractions and only then make a final decision about attending the show. It is also quite acceptable to take dogs to these shows which are not to be among the exhibits or which, because of their breed, could not be. Only dogs which are entered at the show are allowed

Not all terrier shows are as relaxed or set in such grand surroundings as this one. The judge is examining a terrier on the ground rather than making use of a table.

David Hunt's Barney with his array of trophies, having won Best in Show under judge Bill Gillott.

into shows run under Kennel Club rules. Furthermore, because the working terrier shows usually cater only for three or, at most, four working terrier breeds and, sometimes, also for lurchers and, very occasionally for other sporting breeds, they do not need to start judging at 10 a.m. or even earlier in order to complete the judging by early evening, as do some Kennel Club shows. A leisurely start in the early afternoon is the order of the day. In addition, the absence of a

190

need to produce schedules, produce and process entry forms, finally produce a catalogue and even to make use of a venue which provides adequate space and a certain level of basic facilities means that shows are very much cheaper to run outside the Kennel Club system than within it. Some may be more basic but this does not necessarily make them less enjoyable.

In the absence of any central authority the quality of these shows is entirely dependent on the competence of the organisers and the honesty of judges and exhibitors. Most are good, conscientious and imaginative; only a very few are more interested in counting the profit at the end of the day or in enhancing individual careers than in running the sort of show which can be enjoyed by exhibitors and spectators. It also has to be said that the absence of enforceable authority enables petty dishonesty to take place with impunity. Dogs may be shown in puppy classes well after they have passed their first and even second birthdays, dogs recently owned, or even still owned, by the judge may be submitted for his opinion, exhibitors may arrive and depart – often laden with valuable prizes – with the judge. All of which is obvious to any discerning spectator but cannot be prevented because of the absence of any disciplinary body able to formulate and enforce rules which seek to ensure and protect fair and honest competition. Much of what takes place at some of these shows must be very similar to what took place at shows before the Kennel Club was formed. It is like going through a time warp but, for those who are determined not to be unduly upset by the occasional petty dishonesty, working terrier shows can offer a thoroughly enjoyable and valuable experience.

Terrier shows are, or should be, very much cheaper to enter than are Kennel Club shows which enjoy none of their freedoms. On the other hand, the absence, in most cases, of prior notification of who is to judge means that a long journey might be undertaken only to discover that the judge is the very one who so disliked your terriers at the last show. Another drawback of these shows also arises out of the absence of a method of recording previous wins or even an agreed procedure for arriving at the status of champion. Classes are arranged according to the age of the dogs, though there is no way, if dogs are not registered with the breed club, that the age of exhibits can be checked. They are further subdivided according to the type of terrier. A good classification might offer classes for puppies of either sex and for adults, again split between sexes. The classes might be split still further by discriminating between smooth and rough coats.

191

Once all the possible permutations of age, sex, height and coat type have been exhausted, a more varied classification must be dependent on the introduction of classes not confined to Parson Jack Russell Terriers. For example, for supporters of the local or adjacent hunts, or for entered (using the word in its working sense) or unentered dogs. This inevitably means that newcomers find that they are thrust into the deep end to sink or swim with seasoned exhibitors whose reputations may already be well established.

These hunt terrier shows are great fun; the best offer access to the honest and valuable opinion of judges who have spent their lives among working terriers, the worst offer something very different. For as long as hunting is legally allowed to continue, they will exist to provide for the needs of working terrier exhibitors. The Kennel Club has long recognised this need and has been content to allow Border Terriers and any other recognised terrier breed which has pretensions to work to make use of these unrecognised shows in order to gain the opinion of judges with a practical experience of working terriers and to compare their dogs with other, perhaps unregistered, working terriers of different breeds. There is, as far as we are aware, no suggestion that recognition of the Parson Jack Russell Terrier will, in any way, alter the Kennel Club's understanding attitude. Recognition will not in any way affect what the owners of unregistered terriers have for so long enjoyed and to which they, rightly, attach great importance. It will, however, open another avenue for the owners of Kennel Club registered terriers.

The problem is that the continued existence of many of these shows relies on the continued existence of field sports. There have already been a number of attempts made in Parliament to abolish some, if not all, field sports and, as we write this, attempts are being made within the European Community to outlaw a number of activities which are deemed to involve cruelty. If fox-hunting were to be abolished, as seems increasingly probable, the system of shows on which working terriers rely would completely vanish or at best be decimated, overnight. A handful of club shows and a few run by agricultural societies might be all that is left to cater for the enthusiasm of the breed's very many supporters. If recognition does nothing else it will at least provide an alternative career for Parson Jack Russell Terriers just as it has for Otterhounds and a number of other sporting breeds whose original activities are no longer possible.

Inevitably, the system of shows over which the Kennel Club exerts

Lountwood Sam was Best in Show at the last Parson Jack Russell Terrier Show held, in 1989, prior to recognition. Sam, a replica of Carlisle Tack, was bred and owned by Gerald Shaw, the Quorn's earthstopper.

control is more constrained than are those which cater exclusively for working terriers. It is available only to dogs which have been registered with the Kennel Club, and registration is, in usual circumstances, available only to the progeny of registered parents. Some weeks before the event, shows produce schedules which list the classification, the entry fee, the name of the judge, the method of entry and other relevant details. Entries must be made by a specified date well before the event takes place. The classification for a breed as popular as the Parson Jack Russell Terrier might vary from about four classes at a small open show to sixteen or even more at a large championship show. The classes may be arranged by age, with classes for minor puppies, six to nine months old; puppies, six to twelve months old; juniors, six to eighteen months old; and sometimes yearlings, six to twenty-four months old. In addition, a hierarchy of classes from maiden, tyro, special beginners and novice (intended to cater for newcomers to the show scene and from which established winners are excluded) to higher classes, postgraduate, limit and open (intended to provide for seasoned exhibitors but which are also available to beginners with aspirations to fly higher) may be available. All help to provide competition which is appropriate to the needs and ambitions of different exhibitors. A breed club show might well offer even more classes which provide still further subdivisions to cater for different levels of ambition and which also provide classes for brace, team, progeny and, of course, for dogs which have earned a working certificate.

A catalogue is produced and is available at the show which gives the age, ownership and breeding of every exhibit. It thus acts as an additional and very effective brake on false representation as well as a valuable source of future reference for anyone interested in the show scene or in breeding. After the show it is customary for judges to write critiques which explain the reasons for their decisions. These critiques are published in one or both of the two weekly dog papers and often reappear in Breed Club publications. They act as a means by which exhibitors are provided with further information as well as a topic for further detailed discussion and analysis.

Kennel Club shows are themselves organised in a hierarchy to cater for differing needs and aspirations. The recently introduced and, as yet, not well-supported primary show is intended as an introductory event. Above this are sanction and limit shows from which dogs which have previously won at certain levels are excluded. Above these events are open shows which, as their name implies, are open to all. At these shows breed classes offer the opportunity to win points which count towards a Junior Warrant, which many regard as the equivalent of a junior champion title. At the highest level, the Kennel Club selects a few shows, the number being dependent on the level of entries in the breed over a three-year period, at which its Championship Certificates are available for competition. There are four shows: Cruft's, Birmingham National, one of the Scottish Kennel Club shows and the Welsh Kennel Club show, which have by right CCs for every breed which enjoys championship status. Others, scattered all over the country, have allocations of CCs according to the support achieved by the breed. These shows may cover all six groups, be confined to a single group or to a

A brace of workmanlike terriers shown on a terrier couple as is customary at working terrier shows. At Kennel Club events it is usual to put each terrier on a separate show slip, though there are no hard and fast rules which dictate what is appropriate.

single breed or varieties of a breed. In order to qualify for the title of Champion a dog must win three CCs under three different judges and one must be won after it has passed its first birthday. The title is one which is recognised throughout the world as being one of the hardest to win and, consequently, is highly prized. Dedicated breeders and exhibitors tend to regard breed club shows as the most important events in the show calendar, and success at these shows tends to be regarded as the pinnacle of achievement within the breed, despite the popular attention which shows such as Cruft's attract.

195

Obviously, the two systems are very different and each has its own advantages and disadvantages; it is a very fortunate breed indeed which is able to enjoy the benefits of both. As a consequence of recognition, Parson Jack Russell exhibitors are now enabled to compete within both systems. Recognition has extended opportunities for those who wish to avail themselves of them and has done nothing to reduce the opportunities available to those who oppose recognition. There seems to be no good reason why the two systems should not continue to exist amicably side by side for Parson Jack Russell Terrier breeders just as they do for Border Terrier exhibitors.

Preparation

Each system will make different demands on exhibitors. One of the attractions of the hunt terrier shows is their friendly informality. Many exhibitors seem to make no obvious effort to present their dogs in a way which is calculated to appeal to the judge and so to increase their chances of success. Indeed, some seem to go out of their way to make their dogs and themselves look as bucolic as possible, perhaps in the mistaken opinion that a scruffy appearance is indicative of working ability and the not always mistaken belief that some judges may well confuse one with the other. It is not unusual to see an exhibitor remove a perfectly smart and serviceable collar and lead from a terrier and replace it with something which is thought to be more appropriate, perhaps a piece of binder twine. It is hard to resist the thought that these exhibitors believe that their rural clothing and leads and not their dogs are being judged.

A few terriers arrive at working shows looking as though the liquid with which they have had the most recent encounter was sheep dip or worse. Some exhibitors even parade badly and recently scarred dogs in the mistaken impression that a knowledgeable working judge will be impressed. Of course, terriers do get injured during the course of their work but the place for a recently injured terrier is at home, certainly not at a show. Old scars are a different matter and most judges, in both systems, will overlook what are obviously, or seem to be, scars earned in the course of work. A reluctance to walk on a lead may also be regarded as an indication of working ability. Of course, it is nothing of the sort. Many a pampered pet will show precisely the same reluctance and lack of discipline.

In order to excuse, if not to defend, an apparent reluctance to groom their dogs or even to keep them clean, and to train them to walk on a lead, accusations of over-emphasis on hairdressing and characterless behaviour are made against those who show other breeds at Kennel Club events. It seems that some owners of allegedly working terriers believe that a layer of dirt enhances or proves a terrier's ability to work and that familiarity with a comb and brush will somehow detract from working ability. Tell that to the Master of any hunt whose Huntsman arrives at a meet unshaven, with a stained, creased coat, on an ungroomed horse and accompanied by dirty and malodorous hounds! Such a huntsman would not long remain in hunt service. The fallacy of the argument is too obvious to need comment but it cannot be denied that skilful handling and presentation sometimes seem to be more important than the quality of the dogs themselves at Kennel Club licensed shows. When skilful presentation, sometimes allied to the use of cosmetics, is employed to hide faults and enhance or even create virtues, the whole purpose of dog shows is put at risk. In fact, only a few breeds attach a far greater level of importance to glamour than it deserves and sometimes break the rules on presentation. One would expect Parson Jack Russell exhibitors to do nothing other than present clean, well-groomed, well-behaved dogs in tip-top condition for the judge's inspection no matter in what sort of show they were competing.

One of the ways in which differences between show Fox Terriers and those principally used for work first began to develop was in the way show dogs were groomed. Smooth Fox Terriers first became popular because of their smart outline and appearance but it was eventually realised that the coat of a Wire Fox Terrier provided opportunities to alter the outline and create a more glamorous appearance. Both the Kennel Club and, initially at least, the breed clubs sought to restrict methods of presentation to what was not calculated to deceive a judge. There were rules against cutting and singeing coats, against the use of cosmetic substances and cosmetic surgery which were intended to prevent what was regarded as faking. In the main, these rules, which still exist and of which every exhibitor should be aware, were respected, though from time to time some exhibitors would be found guilty of ignoring them and be banned from shows. Today the Kennel Club make unannounced spot checks at shows to ensure that dogs are being prepared for exhibition in accordance with the rules. Samples of coat are taken and submitted for forensic examination and woe betide the exhibitor whose dog's coat is found to contain foreign substances.

The profuse coat of a modern Wire Fox Terrier is skilfully trimmed to create a carefully sculpted outline.

It is interesting to read what Walter Glynn had to say on the subject in Robert Leighton's *New Book of the Dog*, first published in 1907, especially so because he describes, though incidentally, the way a Parson Jack Russell should be prepared for the ring.

There is a real difference between legitimate trimming, and what is called 'faking'. All dogs with long or wire-hair or rough coats require more attention, and more grooming than those with short smooth coats. For the purposes of health and cleanliness it is absolutely necessary that such animals should be frequently well groomed. There is no necessity, given a wire-hair with a good and proper coat, to use anything but an ordinary close toothed comb, a good hard brush, and an occasional removal of long old hairs on the head, ears, neck, legs and belly, with the finger and thumb. The Kennel Club regulations for the preparation of dogs for exhibition are perfectly clear on this subject, and are worded most properly.

198

They say that a dog 'shall be disqualified if any part of his coat or hair has been cut, clipped, singed, or rasped down by any substance, or if any new or fast coat has been removed by pulling or plucking in any manner'. There is no law, therefore, against the removal of old coat by finger and thumb.

There are very few breeds, especially rough coated breeds, whose preparation for show would comply with this old regulation. The regulations have been progressively relaxed since 1907 but Parson Jack Russell Terrier exhibitors have no need of these relaxed conditions as they are well able, and prefer to abide by the 1907 regulations.

Skilled presentation, within amended rules, has allowed the exhibitors of Wire Fox Terriers and, to a somewhat lesser extent, of Smooths to place increasing emphasis on presentation. Features are

Clean, smart and untrimmed, Mr and Mrs Lodge's owner-bred Ryemill Fudge presents a picture which would have gladdened the Parson's heart.

enhanced, outlines altered and appearance modified with the aid of skilled grooming techniques. To see the effect of these techniques, it is necessary only to look at a pet Fox Terrier given basic grooming and one which is ready to enter the show ring. Some of the skills employed are so sophisticated as to be beyond the reach of novice exhibitors, so the professional handler, whose skill often transcends what even the most experienced amateur can achieve and may sometimes appear to make a mockery even of existing relaxed rules, is to be seen in the rings of trimmed breeds. We neither criticise nor condone the effect of these techniques, we merely record their existence. Parson Jack Russell Terrier exhibitors have chosen an entirely different course. For some this means little grooming and even little attention to cleanliness but for the majority cleanliness, the removal of dead coat and a terrier in fit and hard condition are necessary prerequisites for entry to the show ring and to proper pride in the smart appearance of one's companion.

At the Show

The differences between shows stem, in part, from variations in the way they are administered, and a few, relatively minor differences in tradition and practice, size and number. Both unlicensed and Kennel Club licensed events share the same basic routine. Exhibitors arrive well before judging is due to begin in order that they and their dogs can familiarise themselves with the layout of the show. Terriers which have travelled to the show in a box or cage (by far the safest way for any dog to travel in a car) will be exercised. If the show is benched, which is customary at the larger Kennel Club licensed shows, the bench, numbered according to the pass which is sent to every exhibitor prior to the show, will need to be found and the dog fastened on it with a collar and chain or placed on the bench in its cage. The rules say that a dog may only be away from its bench when it is being exercised, prepared for exhibition or while the breed is being judged. This may sound unduly restrictive but, in fact, allows considerable freedom. The breed's benches often form a very convivial meeting place at larger shows and it is not unknown for impromptu parties to spring up or for parties to be organised to celebrate some particular occasion. Benches also allow exhibitors to wander round a large show while their dog is safely confined to its bench. Once a dog is benched or if the show is unbenched it is wise, before judging starts, to find a good vantage point at the ringside. Assess when you are likely to be called into the ring and make sure that you and your dog are ready in good time, looking smart and on your toes.

The judge (called 'he' here for simplicity's sake) will usually be assisted by one or two stewards whose task it is to deal with administrative procedures, such as issuing ring numbers by which each dog is identified, and generally to assist the judge according to his needs and instructions. Eventually, exhibitors will be called into the first class, their numbers issued and checked and they will be marshalled into order by the stewards. At the start of each class most judges will ask all the exhibitors to walk their dogs once or twice around the ring. This allows the dogs to be settled and the judge to make a quick preliminary assessment. His initial impression may have a considerable bearing on eventual decisions and so it is important to ensure that when your dog is moved in front of the judge it is looking its best, moving smartly and not interfering with or being interfered with by another exhibit. A table is usually placed at one end of the ring on which the judge will examine the dogs. A few judges prefer not to use a table, but if each dog of a large entry is to be thoroughly examined it takes a judge with a very strong and flexible back to examine each exhibit thoroughly on the ground. You should, therefore, ensure that your dog is prepared to be examined either on a table or on the ground. You may be asked the age of your dog but should refrain from addressing any other remarks to the judge while he is examining your dog. He is not interested that it won at the last show, that its scars were caused by a fox or that it has recently visited the vet and may be a bit resentful of inspection. Injudicious remarks, especially those calculated to influence the judge, may well require a subsequent explanation to the Kennel Club and are in any case likely to do more harm than good to your chance of success.

Each dog will be examined in turn, either in numerical order according to their ring numbers or simply according to how they happen to be arranged in the ring. As soon as the judge has examined the dog in front of you and asked to see it move, put your dog on the table and get it standing quietly and smartly before the judge turns to begin his examination. Once more, first impressions may be important and so, when he turns round, you want your dog to be looking its best. If the judge is an experienced one, he will have a well-tried, almost automatic routine for examining each dog. He

Lountwood Sam, bred and owned by Mr G. Shaw, stands alert and four-square in a way which would be sure to catch the judge's eye.

may stand a few feet from the table to examine its outline and overall balance. He will then, usually starting at the head, examine the dog quite quickly but in greater detail than you might realise. Having done so, he will ask you to move your dog across the ring so that he can assess its movements from both front and rear and, usually, from the side as well. If the dog is not willing to walk on a lead in a reasonably civilised manner, he cannot do so and so cannot be expected to be impressed. You then join the dogs already seen and wait until he has seen the rest of the class. Once this is completed, the judge will have a fair idea of the dogs likely to be among his winners. He will probably go down the line once more, perhaps to make some final detailed comparisons or just to finalise his choice. At this stage, your ability to show your dog to best advantage may enable you to beat a dog of similar merit which is not looking its best, but the judge has probably already made his basic decisions. Having confirmed these with a last look, he will indicate his winners from first to fourth, or even sixth, depending on how generous the show is with its prizes, and you will know your fate.

The basic routine is much the same at both Kennel Club and working terrier shows. Each class is judged and its winners selected. Eventually all unbeaten exhibits, perhaps divided by sex, will be called again into the ring and the judge will begin the task of deciding which is to be the Best of Breed. He may go through the entire judging process once more but, since he has already examined each one and should be able to recall its salient points, he is more likely to rely on refreshing his memory about some aspect of one or two dogs. Eventually, perhaps having selected a best dog and reserve, and correspondingly a best bitch and reserve, the Best of Breed winner will be chosen. At a breed club show this will automatically be Best in Show but at working terrier shows it may then proceed to compete with the other Best of Breed winners – the Best Border, Lakeland and Fell Terriers, for example – for Best in Show. At Kennel Club licensed shows the system is slightly more complex because of the larger number of breeds involved. Even if the show is confined to the terrier group there may be two dozen other Best of Breed winners to contend with. If the show includes all breeds it is customary for each of the six group winners to be selected before the final six dogs, including the Best Terrier which may or may not be the Parson Jack Russell Terrier, are paraded before the judge who will decide which is to be Best in Show.

To someone who does not like dogs or appreciate shows, the entire process, repeated in class after class, is tedious in the extreme but there are subtleties and nuances, as in any sport, which only the knowledgeable devotee is likely to notice or appreciate. Only real devotees are likely to get a full measure of interest, excitement, and enjoyment. If you find the whole thing pointless and boring try to remember that dog shows have been growing in popularity for the last two hundred years and that millions of people all over the world derive a great deal of enjoyment out of showing their dogs. It is not likely that they are all wrong.

We have concentrated our attention on hunt and working terrier shows and on shows run under Kennel Club rules because these are the events at which decisions of importance to the breed and to its future are made, but we must not give the impression that these are the only events at which the owners of Parson Jack Russell Terriers can have fun. There are a great many shows called exemption shows, because they are exempted from Kennel Club rules, which are open to all dogs whether registered or not. These shows are usually run to raise funds for some charity and so are worthwhile as well as enjoyable. The judges may be very experienced and knowledgeable or may have neither knowledge or experience but they do offer an opportunity for new exhibitors to enter the shallow end of the dog show world.

Terrier racing is not an activity for those who appreciate tranquillity or, indeed, for those who do not enjoy noise and excitement.

Run in conjunction with many hunt and working terrier shows are terrier races, perhaps the most exciting events and certainly the noisiest, in which Parson Jack Russell Terriers may take part. Races are run over a short course, flat or with small jumps, and chase a fox's brush or rabbit skin pulled on a string attached to a bicycle or small engine, depending on the energy and resources available. The races are started in small traps or by dogs being released by their owners on a given signal. Rules are minimal, variable or nonexistent. The fun is fast and, if terriers dispute ownership of the 'quarry', can be furious. Some owners take their racing very seriously and train their dogs to come out of traps quickly and to chase with determination. Some are inspired simply by enthusiasm and a competitive nature, others by the hope of profit to be made from betting on the result. Terrier racing is great fun but not for those with a weak heart!

Finally, there are opportunities not related to shows or to anything competitive to take well-behaved Parson Jack Russell Terriers into institutions, hospitals, old people's homes, prisons and the like, where the presence of a dog might help to ease the burden of the lonely, confused, rejected and lost of our society. Your dog can offer help and affection to others who are less fortunate than yourself.

13

Judging

During the previous chapter, reference has been made to the process of judging as seen from the viewpoint of an exhibitor but almost as inevitably as puppies grow into adults so, it often seems, exhibitors develop an ambition to grow into judges. Indeed, this ambition may even develop long before an exhibitor has much experience or has achieved any significant success in the show ring. In the past, Parson Jack Russell Terriers have tended to be judged by people who have, or who profess to have, some expertise about working terriers. With Kennel Club recognition the breed must now face up to the fact that, at Kennel Club licensed events, it may often now be judged by people whose experience of working terriers is, to say the least, very limited and who are not themselves owners of Parson Jack Russell Terriers. Such judges are referred to as all-rounders, though in truth, only the best who have developed a genuine interest in, experience of and considerable knowledge about a number of breeds from a secure basis of success as breeders and exhibitors in one or more breeds, have any real right to be regarded as all-rounders. These all-rounders may not have the detailed knowledge of the breed specialist, though the extent of their knowledge should never be underestimated, but the best are able to bring to their judging a breadth of experience which, taken alongside the specialist's often narrower view, can be of immense value.

Let us assume that you rather like the idea of standing in the middle of the ring and delivering your opinion about other people's dogs. If we may, once more, make use of the good Dr Johnson's wisdom we would remind you that he believed that every man had a right to an opinion and that every other man had an equal right to knock him down for it. It is, of course, very unlikely that delivery of an unpopular opinion will result in you being physically knocked down, though there may be times when it will be a close-run thing, but you must accept that not even the best judge can expect to please every exhibitor and that a dishonest, biased, inexplicable or incompetent opinion will certainly go a long way towards knocking down your hard-won reputation.

You will need four things if you are not to make an ass of yourself. The first being integrity and the ability to preserve that integrity against all manner of pressures, some subtle, some blatant, some unintentional, some applied by others and some self-induced. You will need the ability to organise a ring and to deliver your decision without hesitation so that you, the exhibitors and the spectactors are clear as to your intentions and are satisfied that those intentions are unequivocal. You will need a considerable knowledge, preferably gathered during several years of success as a breeder and exhibitor, of the breed itself. Those whose knowledge, worn conspicuously, is nothing more than a veneer are quickly exposed by their own decisions and by their subsequent attempts to justify those decisions. You should also have an ability to retain something better than the common standards of courtesy and to conduct yourself in a civilised manner under all manner of provocation. Judging is not an activity for those who lack self-discipline, integrity, knowledge and competence. It is something into which only the unwise and unreasonably ambitious will rush. Others advance more cautiously.

Initially, judging appointments stem from an invitation issued by a show society. Some, though not nearly enough, go to the trouble of consulting breed club judging lists before they issue invitations and so it pays to do whatever is necessary to satisfy the conditions which the club imposes on its listed judges. These are not usually onerous or unreasonable. Evidence of an interest in the breed, some knowledge of it and evidence of a desire to increase that knowledge are usually all that is required. These may be subjected to formal tests but in the main tend to rely on nothing more than the good opinion of the club committee or members. Whether or not you entertain any ambition to judge you will, of course, do all in your power to learn as much as you can about the breed. You may supplement this specialist knowledge by formal courses of study on more general canine topics and will slowly improve your fitness to judge as experience and knowledge continue to grow. Judging, however, is not an activity which relies solely on a knowledge of dogs. It also involves specialist skills which should be mastered before you even consider accepting an invitation. Far too many people, often knowledgeable and experienced people, make their début as judges without even being aware of the skills required or of the procedures, both formal and informal, which are involved. They expose themselves to a situation from which they may well emerge with their reputation in tatters and their standing in the breed very considerably diminished. Whatever may be the strength of your ambition, beware of exposing your limitations by appearing in the centre of the ring in the guise of a judge until you are confident that you are fully prepared for the experience. The centre of a ring is a lonely place in which a judge's inadequacies can be mercilessly exposed.

Let us suppose you have received an invitation to judge and let us further suppose you would like to accept the invitation. From your experience as an exhibitor you will already be familiar with the mechanics of judging but are you sure that you are aware of the less obvious requirements? Perhaps the best approach might be to go through just some of the things you will need to consider when you step into the ring. The first thing you will need is a thorough knowledge of the breed you are about to judge. We will again stress that this is best acquired by owning, breeding and showing that breed. Learning from books and seminars, even those run by breed clubs, is a poor substitute for practical experience and should be regarded more as a supplement rather than as a basic educational diet. This is not to say that you should not take any and every opportunity to increase your knowledge and widen your experience. Education is never wasted and never ended.

When you first receive an invitation to judge make quite sure that, if you decide to accept, you will be able to fulfil the appointment. At shows run under Kennel Club licence you will enter into a contract with the show, a contract which places obligations on both sides. If you fail to honour your obligations you may find yourself called upon to explain matters to the Kennel Club and could, should your explanation be unsatisfactory, be banned for some time from further judging. Working terrier shows can exert no such discipline but your obligations are not thereby reduced.

It is probable that you will be expected to make your début as a judge in an honorary capacity, though you should always expect to receive some contribution towards your out-of-pocket expenses, which it is wise to agree and have confirmed in writing before you finally accept the invitation. As your career develops and you come to judge larger shows or if you are to judge a number of breeds you should also expect a judging fee, the size of which will depend on your own and the show's assessment of your worth. Judging is a difficult task and a competent and conscientious labourer should be regarded as worthy of his hire. It is also important to find out precisely what you are expected to judge. Show secretaries can be very vague and you may be encumbered with a task for which you are ill-equipped or in which you have little interest. Ensure that you have all the details agreed before you accept the invitation. Having done so, all that remains is to await the date of the show, probably with increasing nervousness as your début comes ever closer.

Give some thought to what you will need to wear. You will want something comfortable but smart and appropriate – high heels, cocktail dresses and scarlet finger-nails are as inappropriate for lady judges for Parson Jack Russells as they are for their male counter-parts. If the show is indoors, something smart on which white dog hairs will not be too obvious is suitable for your début and, if it is outdoors, something which is appropriate to whatever the weather may decide. Some shows, particularly those run under Kennel Club rules, may offer a choice of outdoor and indoor accommodation. Delicate breeds, with correspondingly delicate exhibitors and judges will invariably choose to remain indoors. Parson Jack Russells will usually prefer to be judged out of doors even if that means spending a day out in the wind and rain. Remember that judging provides a service to exhibitors and should, as far as is reasonable and possible, provide what exhibitors prefer.

As the fateful day approaches make sure you know precisely how to get to the show, what time judging is due to start and that you can get there in good time. Reread the Breed Standard, not just to refresh your memory but to focus your mind on its requirements. On the night before the show do your best to get a good night's sleep. You may even succeed!

Most judges begin their career by judging a match, the smallest and simplest of canine competitions. These are normally organised by breed clubs expressly for the purpose of giving experience to new judges and exhibitors. They consist of up to sixty-four dogs which compete in pairs, usually selected by lot, and judging proceeds on a knock-out principle. The judge is, therefore, required to make decisions about the relative merits of only two dogs at a time but, during the course of a match, may make sixty-two such decisions before arriving at an overall winner. There are no opportunities to make reversals, that is to place a dog in one class below a dog which it had beaten in a previous class, and few opportunities for an inexperienced judge to go drastically astray. Matches are an excellent way for new judges to dabble their toes in the shallow water at the edge of a very big pool.

The next stage might be to judge up to half a dozen classes of the breed either at a working terrier show – if you are satisfied that your knowledge of the essential qualities of working terriers is up to the task and are convinced that you can convince others of your knowledge – or at a show under Kennel Club rules (not that a knowledge of what Parson Jack Russell Terriers are for is, or should be, an unnecessary part of shows under KC rules). It does not much matter whether you make your début at a sanction, limited or open show. In some ways the better quality of dogs which might be expected to appear at an open show may make that task the easier one. Judging mediocre dogs is much harder than judging good ones. No matter what you do, your winner will be mediocre and it is so easily forgotten by critics, of which all judges can expect to have more than their fair share, that all the others were even worse.

You will, first of all, need to get your stewards to arrange the ring so that you will have the best light behind you, illuminating the dogs rather than shining in your eyes. You will need to place your table so that the dogs are moved across the most level piece of available ground. If you are indoors the floor may be slippery, in which case you need to have any mats arranged in such a way as to enable you to assess the movement in the best way possible. You will need to let your stewards know where you want unseen dogs to stand and where dogs should stand after you have examined them. Having got your ring organised to your liking, take whatever precautions are necessary to ensure that you will have no need to leave the ring until your task is complete. Nothing looks worse than a judge who repeatedly leaves exhibitors waiting while he vacates the ring. Such excursions can give rise to all manner of speculation which might easily turn into firm belief.

The first class can then be called into the ring. While your stewards are getting the first class sorted out, take a look at your judging book, in which is marked the number of every exhibit in the class. Refresh your memory about the order in which classes appear and of their number. You should then be able to calculate at what speed you will need to proceed in order to remain within the allocated time. Make a note, too, of any classes which are in any way unusual and of any special awards which you should bear in mind as judging progresses. Judging books differ slightly depending on the supplier, but all, using the allotted ring numbers, which are the only means you have of identifying the individual dogs before you, will tell you what new dogs are entered in each class and which reappear from previous classes. There will be a space for your notes, on which you will base your critique for the canine press. More importantly, there will also be tear-off slips on which your winners as well as any absentees must be marked. One you will keep, another goes to the show secretary and the third is intended for the Kennel Club. Both of these will carry your signature verifying their accuracy, and their accuracy is your responsibility. If stewards fill in the details make sure that you carefully check every entry before you sign the slips. Never sign them until you are sure that all the details are correct. Should your judging give rise to complaint or doubt, these slips will be carefully examined and you may be called upon to explain the story they tell.

Having familiarised yourself with your secretarial duties the time has come for you to turn your attention to the dogs which by now your stewards should have arranged according to your previous instructions. Good stewards are of immense help to a judge: they get dogs into the ring and in their right place quickly, and they then seem to have the knack of disappearing until next needed. Good stewards are neither seen nor heard; they do their job unobtrusively and without fuss. They leave you free to devote all your attention to the job in hand and make your task both easier and pleasanter. Not all stewards are good; some seem to think that they are in the ring merely as ornaments, while others feel it necessary to try to influence the judge. Remember that what happens in the ring is your responsibility; you are, within what the rules require, in total charge. Anything that goes wrong is your fault and it is no good trying to blame an incompetent steward.

Take a look at each dog as they all stand before you and make a mental note of any obvious good or bad points. Move them round the ring to make an initial assessment of movement and temperament. Make a mental note of anything to which you will need to pay particular attention when you examine each on the table. Having now completed the second stage of your examination, indicate that the leading dog in the parade can be placed on the table or, in the absence of a table, in some suitable spot in the ring.

In the sort of entry which a good judge of Parson Jack Russell Terriers can reasonably expect to achieve at large shows, with a dozen or more classes for the breed, you will be faced with the prospect of examining about 150 or even more dogs. If you spend one minute on each and allowing for the time taken for the change-over between classes, distributing ring numbers, handing out prizes,

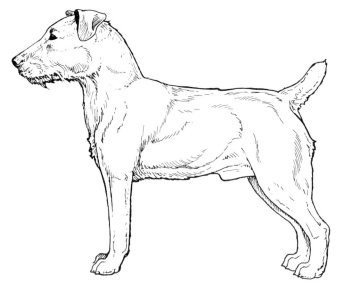

This terrier has a short upper arm and upright shoulder which might give a superficially smart appearance but would impede movement.

A squirrel tail – the 'gay stern' so abominated by hound men – is equally disliked by working terrier people.

A high-set ear offers little protection to the inner ear of a terrier working rough cover or below ground.

for your general assessment at the beginning and end of each class and for the inevitable minor delays, you can expect to be in the ring for well over three hours. If you allow yourself an extra thirty seconds on each dog, you might be in the ring for five hours. Any judge, no matter what his final decisions may be, who spends an inordinate length of time arriving at decisions will, rightly, be regarded as a boring ditherer and may not remain in ignorance of the impression he has created. He will find exhibitors drifting away before the end of the show and should not be surprised if further invitations to judge are as slow in coming as he is in judging. Efficiency rather than haste is needed because every exhibit, no matter how obviously good or bad it may appear to you, has a right to precisely the same consideration as every other.

Allow each exhibitor time to set their dog up on the table. Examine its outline and balance, assess its size and condition and then move to the head to begin your detailed examination. Is the skull flat and reasonably broad, the stop shallow and the muzzle strong? Are the master muscles strong and well attached but without being cheeky? Are the ears the right size and shape, do they hang correctly and naturally? Are the eyes dark and well shaped, are they the right size? Is there any evidence of disease? Is the nose black with open nostrils? Are the teeth strong, evenly spaced and in correct alignment? Do the

213

lips fit well or are they loose and fleshy? By the time you have completed your examination of the head you will have made decisions about thirty or more different things and you still have the rest of the dog to examine. You must then retain, in your memory, the aspects of your examination which are going to be relevant to your decisions. By the time you have completed your examination you will have taken about two hundred points into consideration and you might still have more than a hundred dogs to see.

After you have examined each dog in the class in turn, not forgetting to reappraise any which have appeared from a previous class, you should be fairly close to making your final decisions and will have noted the half dozen or so dogs which will be in your final line-up. If you have a big class before you, after another quick look along the line you can then ask those from which your final selection is to be made to place themselves in the centre of the ring. Make sure they know that you have not yet finalised your choice and that they are not being pulled out in any particular order. Once this is done, the rest can be courteously asked to leave the ring, thus giving you more room to work. Take another quick look at your short-listed

This terrier has a long hock which exaggerates the bend of stifle and would reduce the ability to gallop. Even worse is the deep brisket which would impede the terrier below ground.

Stilted movement is often the product of an upright shoulder; it might look smart but suggests an inability to gallop freely.

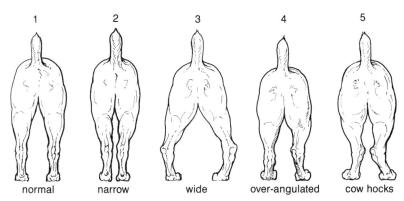

Seen from the rear, hocks should be parallel and firm (1); narrow back ends (2) tend to be weak; wide legs (3) are not acceptable; over-angulation (4) restricts the ability to gallop freely, while cow hocks (5) are acceptable only on cows.

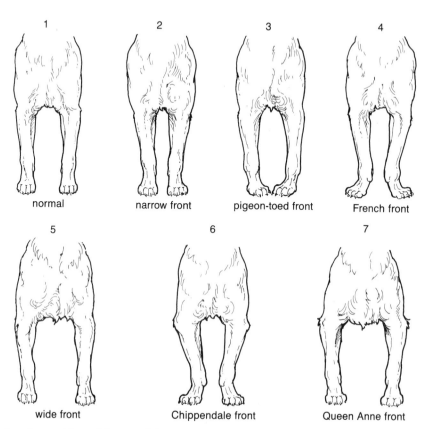

A clean front with straight, parallel, well-boned legs (1) is easily distinguished from the sort of tied-in front (2) which is the product of faulty shoulder construction, and from one which is pigeon-toed (3). A front which is narrow and weak in pastern (4) would not carry a terrier over rough ground, while a wide front (5) is often the product of barrel ribs which would prevent a terrier from working in tight places. A front which is out at elbow (6) is also the product of poor shoulders, while the deformed Queen Anne front (7) is most often found on short-legged terriers.

dogs, perhaps with them moving round the ring, perhaps with them standing, depending on what you want to look at again. Unless you have totally forgotten about some particular point, you should resist the temptation to handle any dog again, it not only wastes time but suggests either that you did not look properly the first time or that the particular dog is questionable on that particular point. If you do feel a need to check something, then check all the remaining dogs.

The muzzle and skull of Tasha of Redwood, bred by Mr M. Brinkley, demonstrate strength without coarseness. The expression, too, is defiant without being mean.

Get the final order in which you want the dogs placed firmly in your mind before quickly and decisively indicating your decision. Nothing looks worse than a judge who pulls one out in the first place, then dithers about his choice of second and then, in a later class, places what seemed to be a decisive winner well down the line. Anyway, your job is to place the winners in order, not to demonstrate your notion of the distance which separates them. Once your line-up is in place, a final check and you can indicate to your stewards that the decisions are made. Mark the results in your judging book, make a note or two about the leading dogs before they leave the ring and return to the table to await the next class.

Within the space available it is not possible to consider all the many things which might go wrong – the way some exhibitors may, deliberately or by accident, misconstrue even the clearest instructions to try to gain a higher place for themselves, what happens when a dog appears in a class for bitches, how to deal with a dog which arrives in the class when all other exhibits have been seen, how to deal with dogs which refuse to be handled and all the other, thousand and one problems which a competent judge must be ready to take in in his unhurried but efficient stride. Going through the motions of judging is easy but to do the job well demands knowledge, concentration, efficiency and stamina.

14

At Work,
Then and Now

Heinemann was very disparaging about the lady who regarded a successful excursion in pursuit of moles as evidence of working ability. Goodness knows what his reaction might have been to those who regard a propensity to dig holes in the rose bed or a reluctance to allow starlings on the lawn as evidence of working ability. It is doubtful if his reaction would have been printable or one to be expected of a man who once contemplated a career in the church, but we are not born with a knowledge of terrier work and not everyone is able to live the sort of life in which a knowledge of terrier work is part and parcel. Our often urban lives tend to divorce us from such matters but they do not, and should not, prevent us from learning about terrier work. Indeed, a knowledge of terrier work and the demands which it makes is essential, we believe, to the proper appreciation of any working terrier breed. We accept that not every terrier owner will want to become involved in work and that some may be actively opposed to it, though trying to separate Parson Jack Russell Terriers from their sporting roots seems to us to be a bit like trying to persuade Eskimos to become vegetarians. At best, it is a pointless exercise and at worst it could lead to the destruction of the race.

Terriers have their origins among the small dogs used well over 1,000 years ago to drive deer or birds out of the thickets in which they had spent the night. Parson Jack Russell bred his terriers to work with Foxhounds; his terriers ran with hounds and were to hand whenever a fox took refuge below ground. William Carrick used terriers, bred from Jack Russell's stock, to do precisely the same job with Otterhounds. Arthur Heinemann, though for a short time Master of a pack of Otterhounds, was more interested in badger digging and used terriers to draw badgers from their setts. Since those days, Parson Jack Russell Terriers have been used to hunt all manner of other quarry. They have been used on coypu and mink in Britain, racoon and chipmunk in America and equally exotic quarry in other parts of the world. Parson Jack Russell Terriers have proved themselves to be one of the most versatile of working terriers. This versatility, however, is sometimes inclined to obscure the fact that their real purpose is to work fox. Rats and rabbits are mere, and almost unworthy, side issues while, of course, work to otter and badger is now illegal in Britain, though that, regrettably, has not deterred a few owners from regularly allowing their terriers to taste this forbidden fruit.

It is possible that, given a concerted drive by anti-field sports organisations or a slight shift in the favoured political hue, all field sports might be banned by law. Already Parliament has been faced with Bills put forward by well-meaning but ill-informed MPs which would have gone so far as to make it illegal for a terrier, or any other dog, to kill a rat and there have been several which have sought to ban coursing and hunting. These are often based on an ill-informed, emotive or ideological reaction to field sports. Field sports are regarded by some as the preserve of the rich and privileged (which is not true) and must, therefore, be banned. They are seen as the cause of cruelty, though the cruelty which would arise as a result of a ban as guns, traps, gas and poison are pressed into service as alternative means of control, is blithely ignored. There are even those who would ban field sports because of a desire to impose their own reluctance to kill any living thing except, often, their fellow creatures, on all others. Together, these opponents of field sports form a strong, if motley, force which might someday prevail.

It is vital that, for as long as the law allows, Parson Jack Russell Terriers are used for the purpose for which the Parson bred them. Once a breed, any breed, loses contact with the purpose for which it was bred it becomes very difficult for breeders to remain faithful to the old type. Preserving the old type then relies on the ability of breeders to resist the inexorable tendency to change and changing demands, imposed by transient fashions, without thought or care for function. Show ring success, which might be achieved as a result of change and so encourages change, then becomes the arbiter of quality or, worse, popular appeal, and is used as the basis on which the breed is assessed.

We have discussed the way in which the Parson used his terriers and, perhaps, before we go on to look at some of the ways they might be used today, we should retrace our steps to examine briefly how terriers were used before the Parson's time. Edmund Langley had a very low opinion of foxes as worthwhile quarry. The fox, he said, is a 'fals beest and as malicious as a woolf' which is too feeble to provide a good run for hounds and which often prefers to stay in coverts, where they hide under briars and have to be ejected by terriers before hounds can have their chance. Only with apparent reluctance does Langley concede that a fox sometimes 'gooth to the earth wher he may next eny finds, which he knoweth wel, and then may men digger hym out and take hym so that he be in esy digging but not amonge roches'. The tools and perhaps the inclination to undertake an arduous dig were not available in Langley's time, but perhaps more significant is the way in which Langley accepts terriers as a means by which foxes could be pushed out of cover but not as a means to persuade them to leave an underground retreat.

In 1570, Johannes Caius produced his *De Canibus Anglicas* and six years later this was translated into English, though in a rather imaginative and liberal fashion, by Abraham Fleming and published as *Of English Dogges*. It contains a description of the work of terriers which, after over 400 years remains as accurate as it is succinct.

> Another sorte there is which hunteth the Foxe and the Badger or Greye onely, whom we call Terrars, because they (after the manner and custom of ferrets in searching for Connyes) creepe into the grounde, and by that means make afrayde, nyppe, and byte the Foxe and Badger in such sort, that they teare them in pieces with theyr teeth beyng in the bosome of the earth, or else hayle and pull them perforce out of their lurking angles, dark dongeons, and close caves, or at the least through coceud feare, drive them out of their hollow harbours, in so much that they are compelled to prepare flight, and being desirous of the next (albeit not the safest) refuge, are otherwise taken and entrapped with snares and nettes layde over holes to the same purpose. But these be the least of that kind called Sagax. [Sagax, derived from the Latin for having keen senses, was the smaller type of terrier then in use.]

In 1581, George Turberville's *Noble Arte of Venerie* even went so far as to discuss the different sorts of terrier and the way in which they should be introduced to their tasks.

> Now to speake of Fox houndes and Terryers, and how you should enter them to take the Foxe, the Badgerd, and suche like vermine –

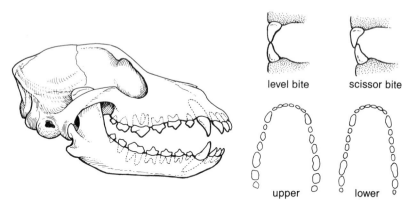

A working terrier without a full complement of large, strong, evenly spaced teeth would have its useful working life shortened as teeth were prematurely lost.

you muste understand that there are sundrie sortes of Terriers, whereof wee hold opinion that one sorte came out of Flaunders or the Low countries, as Artoys and thereabouts, and they have cooked legges, and are short heared moste commonly. Another sorte there is which are shagged and streyght legged – those with the crooked legges will take earth better than the other and are better for the Badgerd, bycause they will lye longer at a vermine – but the others with streyght legges do serve for twoo purposes for they wyll Hunte above grounde as well as other houndes, and enter the earth with more furie than the others – but they will not abide so long, bycause they are too eagre in fight, and therefore are consteyned to come out to take ayre – there are both good and bad of bothe sortes. And because it is a good pastime, and brave fight, without great payne and travayle to the huntsman, therefore I have thought good to set downe here some precepts for the entrying of terriers, and for the better fleshyng and encouraging of them.

You should beginne to enter them as soone as they be eyght or tenne months old – for if you enter not a terrier before he be a yeare old, you shall hardly ever make him take the earthe. And you must take good heede that you encourage them, and rebuke them not at firste – nor that the Foxe or Badgerd do hurt them within the earth, for then they will never love the earthe agayne. And therefore never enter a young Terryer in an earth where there is an olde Foxe or Badgerd – but firste lette them be well entered, and be a yeare olde full or more. You shall

221

do well also to put in an old terryer before them which may abide and endure the furie of the Fox or Badgerd. You may enter them and fleshe them sundrie ways. First when Foxes and Badgerds have yong cubbes, take all your olde Terryers and put them into ground – and when they beginne to baye (which in the earth is called yearnyng), you muste hold your yong terryers every one of them at a sundrie hole of some angle or mouth of the earth, that they may herken and heare theyre fellowes yearne. And when you have taken the olde Foxes and Badgerdes, and that there is nothing left in the earth but the yong Cubbes, take out then all your old Terryers and couple them up – then put in your yong Terryers and encourage them, crying, To him, To him, To him; and if they take any young Cubbe lette them take theyr pleasure of him, and kill him within the ground and beware that the earth fall not downe upon them and smother them. That done, take all the rest of the Cubbes and Badgerds pigges home with you, and frie theyr livers and theyr blood with cheese, and some of theyr own greace, and thereof make your Terryers a reward, shewyng them always the heads and skinnes to encourage them. When they have bene rewarded or rather before, washe them with sope and warme water to get out the clay which shall be clodded in theyr heare – or els then will soone become mangie – and that would be hard to be cured.

Obviously the details of entering a terrier to fox or badger are not what would be acceptable today but the basics remain unchanged. Puppies should not be entered when they are too young but neither should their education be delayed too long. They should be given a gentle introduction to work, watching and listening to older terriers and being encouraged rather than being forced to go to ground. Care should be taken to ensure that the earth is not likely to collapse and when they emerge they should be cleaned, inspected for injury and rewarded. It seems to us that Turberville, unlike many authors, then and now, gives every evidence of having a first-hand knowledge of his subject even to the extent of advising that 'he that will be present at such pastimes, may do well to be booted. For I have lente a Foxe or Badgerd ere nowe, a piece of my hose, and the skin and fleshe for companie, which he never restored again.'

After Turberville came, in 1590, Sir Thomas Cockaine's *Short Treatise on Hunting, compyled for the delight of Noblemen and Gentlemen*, and short it was, being only thirty-two pages long. Its owner recommended his efforts as 'a very good note for any yong gentleman who will breed hounds to hunt the foxe'. Apparently, in

222

those halcyon days hunting was, unlike today, the preserve of gentlemen. Mixed with sound advice about entering hounds is a reference to the need for two couple of terriers which Cockaine says are indispensable to any pack of Foxhounds. In order to get them working it is best to 'take two or three quicke cubbes to make your terriers withall' and that entering your whelps should begin a fortnight or three weeks before Batholomew Day and continued until the Feast of All Saints – in other words, from the end of August until the beginning of November, a period which coincides with the time now set aside for cubbing before the season proper begins on 1 November.

It is apparent that nearly 400 years ago the value of terriers was much appreciated and the way to introduce them to their tasks was already well worked out. Even the way in which they were used alongside hounds followed much the same pattern as that adopted by the Parson. Turberville explains what happens after two couple of the slowest hounds had been used to push a fox out of cover: 'One couple of the best terriers . . . which must bee kept to follow the huntsman his heeles . . . the other couple of your terriers should bee used to hunt with the rest of the hounds.'

What has not changed during the last four centuries is the job for which Parson Jack Russell bred his terriers. A Parson Jack Russell Terrier which has the speed and stamina to run with hounds, the intelligence to find its way across country and be at hand when a fox goes to ground, which will work amicably among hounds, farm animals and other terriers, is capable of going to ground wherever a fox may have taken refuge and has the courage to persuade that fox to leave its refuge, cannot be other than a good working terrier and that, first and foremost, is what the Parson Jack Russell Terrier must be.

However, we must be realistic. Very few people have the opportunity to work their terriers legitimately to fox and even fewer have the opportunity to run them with hounds. Fewer still can run them over the sort of country which the Parson hunted. This situation is not going to improve and it is inevitable that it will slowly become more difficult even if fox hunting is not banned completely. We would strongly advise everyone who has an interest in the breed to ensure, while opportunity remains, that they have at the very least, seen terriers working with Foxhounds and that they understand the job they do and the demands it imposes. Without such an understanding it is impossible fully to appreciate the breed.

Bred in the Eskdale Hunt by Mr E. Parker, Eskdale Lizzie of Clystlands is another terrier which is very similar to the Parson's first.

Fortunately for the breed, some will not be deterred by increasing difficulties and will want to see their terriers working. The first step is to get yourself known at the local hunt kennels as a person who is keen, sensible and helpful and who has good terriers. Go out with the hunt whenever you can, involve yourself in their out of season activities and with any fox control work they may be asked to undertake. Make it known that you are ready to help should any terrier get into difficulties underground but do so only if you are able to help. Terrier work, especially when it is necessary to rescue a trapped terrier, involves a great deal of digging, usually in foul weather and on an exposed site. There is no room for people who are unable to contribute fully to the enterprise and to take their turn with a spade, crowbar or mattock. The days when a digging party could summon up a gang of hired labourers while the terrier owners sipped their whisky and chatted with the ladies are long gone.

However, you must realise precisely what you are exposing your terrier to before you accept such an invitation. Working terriers get hurt, sometimes very badly. They may get killed, either by their quarry or as a result of becoming trapped underground. When you give your terrier the opportunity to work you are exposing it to the risk of serious injury or death. You must, therefore, never expect your terrier to go to ground unless you are equipped and able to give it assistance should assistance be required. Blithely watching a terrier disappear down an earth in the course of a Sunday afternoon stroll is the act of a thoughtless and uncaring person. Equally, those who allow their terriers to wander to look for their own sport – and country dwellers seem every bit as guilty of this as town dwellers – should, in our opinion, be banned from keeping any dog. If a terrier goes to ground and becomes trapped and you are not equipped to render assistance or even do not know where it is, time will pass before anything can be done and during that time your terrier may die.

If you still want to test your terrier at the job for which he was intended, you must await an invitation to do so with all the patience that you can muster. Do not let your enthusiasm lead you into an excursion to test your terrier on your own. That might easily make you unpopular with local landowners or with the hunt and place you on the wrong side of the law. Worse still, your inexperience may mean that your terrier is exposed to needless danger. It is best to be patient and to avoid any needless risks.

Your terrier will probably first be given a chance to enter alone and, if your early training has been right, will probably do so after only slight hesitation. Parson Jack Russell Terriers tend to enter early and keenly, even to the point of foolhardiness. Their precosity is often a source of great pride to their owners and a source of embarrassment to the owners of other terriers which, though they make excellent workers, may be initially hesitant about going to ground. If your terrier is reluctant – and remember that nothing can force a terrier to work – it might be given the opportunity to follow a reliable worker into the earth. Such a course, though, in our experience, too often results in the leading terrier being needlessly injured as the beginner, suddenly finding a desire to get at the fox, drives the leading terrier into a position in which he cannot defend himself. If all goes well, you have at least made a start but you should not think that your terrier is a genuine worker until it has a great deal more experience. Certainly, you should not expect a début, no matter how successful or impressive, to qualify a terrier for a working certificate. Some Masters and huntsmen may be ready to sign any slip of paper testifying to your terrier's worth, especially if you are regarded as a good supporter of the hunt. If a piece of paper to enable you to enter classes for entered terriers is all you want, you could probably get

The narrow, clean front on Mrs S. Atter's owner-bred smooth Parson Jack Russell Terrier Ridley Redstart would allow the terrier to gain access to the most restricted earths.

An intelligent terrier with all its sporting instinct intact will, given the opportunity, quickly learn to hunt.

one without making your terrier venture below ground at all but the paper would be worthless no matter how many cups your terrier wins.

However, you should not expect a terrier to make his working début against fox. Some introductory lessons and experience are necessary to learn something of what the job is about. Obviously, before you expect your terrier to face a fox fighting for his life, you will ensure that it is mature, fit and strong. A terrier which is not accustomed to hard exercise will tire quickly and either be severely punished by a far stronger adversary or will be unable to return to the surface. We will assume that you will ensure that your terrier is fit, and that you are capable of wielding a spade to good effect.

Possibly the best and certainly the easiest introduction to sport is provided by rats. Remember, though, that rats carry leptospirosis and ensure that your terrier's protective vaccines are up to date before you undertake any excursion in search of rats. In the course of an evening stroll along the hedgerows or along a stream you will, if you are observant, notice signs of the presence of rats. Encourage

227

your terrier to take an interest in these signs and it will not be long before he is pointing them out to you. He will begin hunting on his own account and it is only a matter of time before he catches a rat unawares. When he catches a rat he should kill it quickly and efficiently and then drop it. Walking around carrying a dead rat may seem cute and increase your pride, but it means that he is unnecessarily mouthing a possibly contagious animal and is not ready to deal with the next one. Encourage him to drop the carcase quickly and praise his efforts before moving on.

Similar excursions around farm buildings, especially where poultry are housed or grain is stored, will probably be more fruitful and the day may well come when you have an opportunity to be present when a farm building is being disturbed for cleaning or change of occupants. This disturbance will result in rats running in all directions and provide an excellent test for your terrier and especially so as there is likely to be a number of terriers present. Poultry houses seem to have replaced the old rick yards as the places in which rats are to be sometimes found in huge numbers; catches running into hundreds are not uncommon, and will test both you and your terrier. Rats, however, are not found only in rural localities. One of us enjoyed childhood sport in the cotton warehouses of Lancashire mills. These were warm and dry and teemed with rats, especially after a new delivery of cotton had disturbed their familiar runs. We have recently watched rats playing round the shrubbery of a town-centre supermarket and suspect that urban ratting offers just as many opportunities as does rural ratting.

Of course, during your rural strolls you will not only disturb rats. You will come across rabbits, which are becoming more numerous now that the obscenity of myxomatosis is beginning to lose its virulence, and again offer enjoyable sport which has the added advantage of providing something tasty for the pot. However, hunting rabbits with a terrier is not a matter to be entered lightly. If your terrier is intended to work fox he will need to be reliable to fox. Neither you nor he will be popular if he shows great interest in an earth which later proves to contain no more than a rabbit. Some terriers will behave slightly differently depending on their quarry; if your terrier is one of these and you are able to correctly interpret the often subtle indications, all might be well but if your terrier does not discriminate between different quarry or you are unaware of slightly different behaviour you might well be wise to choose between hunting rabbits or working fox.

When you come across rabbits they will, inevitably, run and your terrier will chase. You and your dog should learn how best to approach them unawares – how to make use of whatever cover is available and the prevailing wind. You will both have a lot to learn and it may well be that your terrier will learn more quickly than you do. He will learn to curb impetuosity and to think for himself, and will begin to hunt properly, investigating likely spots quietly and being quick off the mark when he finds. If he has an older, reliable terrier to learn from, then so much the better and, if rabbiting is going to be a regular activity, a small lurcher or a whippet will help to improve sport. You might then get into the fascinating world of ferreting, though not until your terrier can be relied upon not to kill ferrets. Ferrets killed by unreliable terriers tend to be very expensive indeed. Not only must your terrier be trained to ignore ferrets but it must also be sensible enough to keep quiet when the ferrets are below ground and to stay strategically well away from the bury, waiting quietly until a rabbit bolts. Incidentally, the same considerations also apply to you.

Once your terrier – and you – know a thing or two about hunting and is reliable among other terriers you might like to become more ambitious. Two or three couple of good-nosed, sensible terriers working along a river bank might well put up a mink or two, since mink seem always to operate in pairs. Then you will begin to see just what your terrier is made of. Mink do not offer the same challenges as do fox but they are streets ahead of rats or rabbits. Hunting mink offers an excellent test of your terrier and also provides great sport, helping to keep this destructive immigrant under some sort of control. Perhaps it might be possible, as has been possible with the much less destructive and less successful coypu, to rid the country-side of this pest. Nowadays, there are a number of packs of mink hounds in operation. Mink hounds are often Otterhounds, pure or partly bred, with a sprinkling of superannuated Foxhounds. They are often informally constituted enterprises which offer great enjoy-ment. They also offer, to the right sort of terrier, an opportunity to run with hounds much in the way the Parson's might have done, though, of course, not over the same distance or similar country. Mink tend to inhabit the watersides rather than the open country and do not offer the sort of runs which fox-hunters enjoy most. Nevertheless, an opportunity to work alongside hounds provides something very much closer to what the Parson expected of his terriers than does the sort of hunting in which they are decanted from a warm van within yards of the earth and after hounds have been removed to a respectful distance.

Hunting rats, rabbits and mink may offer sport of a sort but never forget that Parson Jack Russell Terriers are intended to work fox. Other creatures may provide them and you with sport but only fox can provide real work. But there are very few opportunities for terriers to be worked in the way in which the Parson worked them and for which they were bred. The sort of work which has forged their make and shape, their temperaments and characters is nowadays available only to the very fortunate few. Those who live in the moorland counties of the south-west and the north may still have such opportunities but the rest of us must be satisfied with something very different. However, a proper appreciation of the breed demands an appreciation of what was involved in the way in which the Parson worked his terriers and for this we must rely on contemporary descriptions. Heinemann himself provided just such a description:

Perhaps the prettiest part of moorland fox-hunting is to see hounds drag up to their fox through heather or sedge, or rush on some open plateau along the steep hill-side of some Devonshire combe.

Disturbed frequently by harriers and stag-hounds, and collie-dogs, these moorland foxes lie tightly, and seldom wait to be found, stealing away at the first strange sound, so that when drawing in the open the huntsman of a moorland pack must have his hounds handy as ladies' maids, ready to spread out and draw at a wave from his hand, or come across some valley quickly to his low whistle of 'Leu, leu,' or 'Tsst, tsst.' No chattering should there be among the little ladies of the field, whose shrill voices carry far in the rarified air of the moorland, and no blowing of the fragrant weed on the part of the male members of the hunt, if one would find a moorland fox handsomely in the open.

Between hounds and the field lies the great gulf of an impassable combe, which has to be coasted, and by the time that has been done hounds have gained such a start as may not soon be overtaken. Surely, it is true that a fox well found is a fox half killed; yet how many huntsmen one sees drawing some thick gorse like men in a dream, their hounds following the line of least resistance at their horses' heels. There is, indeed, a time for everything; and just as there is a time to practise the silent system, so equally is there a time when voice and horn should galvanize into life both hound and horse and fox. Digging foxes is, perhaps, the dullest part of moorland fox-hunting, where earth-stopping is seldom practised or practicable, but it is a

Exaggerated movement is inefficient; a terrier moving like this might look impressive crossing a show ring but would soon tire in the field.

necessary evil if one would ask the rather bloodthirsty hill-farmers to preserve foxes for the hunt.

Yet even on Exmoor some system of putting-to main-earths might well be devised with but little expenditure. Terriers are, of course, a necessary adjunct of moorland packs, and it is wonderful how they soon contrive to turn up when hounds have earthed their fox. I remember running a fox to ground once in Curr Cleave, which one of my terriers had bolted an hour before, and, as no terrier turned up, we began to dig. But when we reached our fox, there was the same terrier in grips with him, and I only just saw his hind pad in time to save him from the pack, which I had let in to draw what was apparently their fox. Another day, a bad-scenting one, I saw another of mine – Toby by name – leading the pack all along the fringe of the big Horner woodlands, throwing his shrill treble tongue with the best of them. But wet and weather play sad havoc with terriers, who fare but ill on kennel-food, and it is best to station them in charge of a runner or second-horseman at various likely farmhouses in the day's draw.

Dartmoor foxes and Exmoor foxes are stout and strong, and fleet of foot, having long distances to go for good or fellowship, and being real creatures of the wild.

231

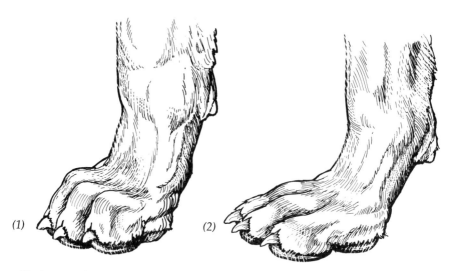

No foot – no hound. A well-arched and padded, tight foot (1) will carry a dog all day over the roughest ground, whereas a thin and open foot (2) is easily damaged.

There have been at least three major technological advances which have had or are likely to have their effect on terriers. The first, which happened so long ago that its effect is now difficult to assess, was the production of tempered steel spades which made digging easier than hitherto had been the case. The second was the production of motorised transport capable of carrying a terrier to within a few yards of the place where it was required to go to ground. We have seen how this contributed to the production of short-legged terriers incapable of running with hounds. Much more recently, the production of radio transmitters small enough to attach to a terrier's collar, enabling a receiver to pin-point a terrier's position below ground, has taken much of the guesswork out of terrier work. Undoubtedly, this equipment can save much futile digging, can speed up the operation and can, therefore, save undue wear and tear on both terrier and owner. However, breeders who are concerned with preserving a terrier as it was over a hundred years ago must consider the possible effect of these transmitters and be prepared to resist changes which might thereby come about, just as they have refused to breed short-legged terriers simply because motorised transport is available.

One of the worst faults a terrier could have was to work mute. A terrier which did not speak when he was up to his quarry not only gave no signal as to his position to diggers but could also only persuade his quarry to vacate the earth by violent means which a hunt may not appreciate. Such a terrier was, therefore, of very limited use especially for work with Foxhounds. Of course, a terrier which half murders his fox before persuading it to move is still unwelcome to a hunt, but for those who are engaged in clearance work this may be no problem, and if the use of transmitter and receiver reduces the amount of digging necessary, then the implement is unlikely to be ignored. What the owners of Parson Jack Russell Terriers must guard against is the acceptance of mute terriers which can only work with the aid of a transmitter; such terriers would have been discarded by the Parson and must be faulted by those who respect and maintain the standards and traditions to which he subscribed.

15

Some, Hopefully Uncommon, Ailments

Parson Jack Russell Terriers usually enjoy what might be described as rude health. They tend to live long lives and enjoy their renowned vigour until they are well into old age. They are not one of the breeds on which veterinary surgeons rely for their new car or the foreign holiday. They will survive and even thrive in conditions in which many other, less hardy, breeds would perish and as a result are sometimes expected to live in just such conditions. A life locked in a tiny box, hardly big enough for a rabbit, or chained to a barrel in some draughty corner of a cold, damp yard can hardly be worth living. Let us not forget that one of the Parson's priorities when he moved from Swymbridge to Black Torrington was to build a new and substantial stable to house his two remaining hunters and some of his terriers. The rest shared his home and made themselves comfortable on his rather eccentric furniture. In addition to excellent home comforts he gave them good food and adequate exercise. Today's terriers deserve conditions which are at least as good, and they will repay their owners by remaining remarkably free from illness.

While we do not advocate that every dog owner should rush along to their vet at the first sign of trouble, neither do we think it wise that they should place too great a faith in their own diagnostic skills or ability to treat illness. Nevertheless, the ability to recognise the first signs that something is amiss and to take the necessary action promptly which will prevent the condition from worsening and the dog from unnecessary suffering are abilities which all dog owners should have. In addition, they should ensure that they have access to a vet whose knowledge is up to date and whose service is first rate. Breeders, in particular, are wise to ensure that they have a vet who is sympathetic to their aims who will offer advice and help to enable those aims to be achieved. Vets, like breeders, vary in quality and it pays to find the best in your particular area. Do so by seeking advice from other, more experienced breeders. When your puppy has its injections take the opportunity to assess the service you are likely to be offered, see how helpful the receptionist is, how well equipped the surgery is and what the vet's attitude is like. If you are going to work your terrier it is best to find a vet who is not opposed to field sports. If you are going to show, find one who understands your ambitions. If you are going to breed, find a vet who does not think that all breeders are part of the great unwashed. A good vet will, in time, become a friend and even a partner in your endeavours, providing guidance, support, encouragement and a reliable service. A less good one will do nothing but the necessary minimum and may not do that very well.

It may surprise caring and thoughtful owners that there are health problems to which all dogs seem prone and which are the direct result of the actions of their owners. Perhaps it could be said that some accidents fall into this category, but these are not accidents, they result from deliberate actions of dog owners. The first of these is obesity, the result of a fond owner giving a dog too much unsuitable food and too little exercise. Vets have said that obesity is the cause of many of the health problems they are called upon to treat. Surveys have shown that more than one third of British dogs are overweight. The condition is more likely to be found in bitches than dogs and is twice as common in neutered than entire animals. Obesity makes dogs more prone to disease, especially to heart, lung and locomotive problems. Their ability to enjoy life is reduced and their expectation of life is shortened. Anyone who deliberately does that to a dog cannot be regarded as other than cruel. The problem is now so great that dog-food manufacturers actually produce obesity diets to be given under prescription by vets. The situation is ridiculous. A fifteen-pound (6.8kg) Parson Jack Russell Terrier getting an average amount of exercise needs about 500 calories per day. More, whether part of its normal diet, or in the form of scavenged food or given as titbits, will tend to make the dog fat. Caring owners will avoid getting their dogs fat.

How will you know when your dog is ill and what is the best course of action? All illness, no matter how trivial, is a departure from normality, and normality should be regarded as good health. So, let us assume that your dog, puppy or adult, has been in good health for some time. A pattern of behaviour will have been established which can be regarded as normal for your dog. Any departure from this normal pattern should be treated with suspicion as should any departure from its normal appearance, and, unless there is some obvious and innocent explanation such as having eaten the remains of last night's curry or enjoyed unusually demanding exercise, your suspicions should remain until a sound explanation is available.

If the unusual behaviour is prolonged or the dog appears to be in any discomfort your vet should be consulted at the first available moment. Vets learn to tolerate the unreasonable behaviour of some of their clients but that does not mean that they welcome it. Do not try to ring your vet at midnight in expectation of a full and sympathetic discussion about a condition which may have been present for some days. Vets are adept at getting information which their patients themselves cannot provide and out of fearful and worried clients, but you will help your vet as well as your dog if you make the effort to observe your dog's condition with care and accurately report your findings to your vet. Veterinary advice does not come free and can be very expensive, except in terms of your peace of mind when it consists of nothing more than an assurance that the dog is in good health. Even worse is the situation which could arise as a result of your disregard of a deteriorating condition or inability to describe the salient features of the problem. Prompt action and an accurate report will help the vet towards a correct diagnosis and speedy and effective treatment. It pays, therefore, to know at least a little about some of the conditions which may become a threat to customary good health. Most books refer to these as common ailments; in our experience and in every dog owner's hopes, no ailments are common, and hopefully they are all very uncommon, especially so among Parson Jack Russell Terriers.

Suspicions of illness might be aroused by any departure from what has come to be regarded as normal behaviour. It is also indicated by a temperature raised from the normal 101.5°F (38.6°C) the most obvious sign of which will be a tendency to drink more and to seek cool places. Illness, in dogs as in people, is also often indicated by the presence of pain but they also have a far higher threshhold of pain than do we, so that even injuries which cannot do other than cause pain may produce few indications of that pain. It is a salutary experience to watch a bitch who, just minutes previously, has had puppies surgically delivered, totally ignoring her own discomfort in her concern for her family. Watch the enthusiasm with which a dog will eat its dinner just after having teeth removed. Consider the way in which a working terrier will make light of serious injury in its eagerness to carry on with its job. Most terriers, certainly all those which work for a living, at times seem almost impervious to pain. So how do we know when they might be in pain unless they have suffered some obvious injury which is an obvious and inevitable cause of pain?

Look for half-closed eyes, a distant expression and for an increased desire for gentle human attention. If a dog devotes particular attention to some part of its body try and discover what, if anything, is amiss. Pawing the eyes, scratching the ears, licking feet, nibbling at the stomach or pawing, scratching, licking or nibbling at any other part of the body should all arouse suspicion. If the pain is in the mouth or throat the dog may drool excessively or hold its head in an unusual position. If it is deep seated it may seek ease by lying or sitting in an unusual position and will give signs of being uneasy. Pain in a joint, leg or foot may cause lameness but it takes a certain amount of skill to decide, from a particular form of lameness, precisely where the problem may be. Indeed, spinal pain can result in lameness and initially, at least, might seem to indicate problems elsewhere. Spinal problems, however tend also to be associated with an arched back, trembling and, if the condition is not new, some wasting of the muscles of the hindlegs.

Pain can also alter a dog's attitude to life. A normally boisterous dog may be reluctant to take exercise. A friendly one may come to resent the approaches of other dogs or people and a quiet dog may become noisy, especially if it is touched. Any behaviour which is an unexplained departure from the normal should be watched with care in case it is the first indication of a loss of health.

Dogs are capable of regurgitating food either for their young or themselves. Consider a wild dog which must eat as much of a limited supply of food as it can in order to survive and to feed its young. It must do so quickly and in competition with other pack members. The food will be swallowed in large pieces and then either carried to the nest where partly digested food can be supplied to puppies or taken to a secluded place where regurgitated food can be eaten without competition. Domestic dogs may do precisely the same things. Once more, there is no reason for alarm but if regurgitation becomes a habit try feeding in a secluded place with finely minced or otherwise easily digested food.

A sick dog or one which is beginning to feel out of sorts may lose its appetite but so might a dog which is suddenly placed in a strange situation, which is disturbed by the presence of other dogs or which

237

is very tired. Overfed dogs too may, sensibly, decide not to eat for a while and their owners show similar sense by not seeking to persuade them to do so. Except in the case of a young puppy, a lactating bitch, a dog which is already ill or an old dog, loss of appetite need cause no immediate alarm though thought should be given to the likely cause.

The amount of liquid that a Parson Jack Russell Terrier needs is fairly constant. It is affected by the weather and by the amount of exercise given but, such variables apart, will remain fairly constant while the dog is in good health. What may seem to be a change in a dog's drinking habits may often be no more than a reflection of some change in its diet. Thus, some dogs which are fed on well-soaked food may drink very little whereas if the diet is changed to a dry one they will need to drink a lot in order to compensate for the lost liquid intake. Remember that drinking is not the only means of taking in liquid. Food itself can contain all the liquid which a dog may normally need or it may contain none at all. So, bearing these matters in mind, an increased thirst and the consequent frequent urination may well indicate a health problem which calls for veterinary diagnosis.

Illness and Disease in Puppies

Perhaps we might proceed to more specific matters by looking at the problems which a puppy might be born with or which it is most likely to acquire during the first days or weeks of its life. We have already discussed diseases of genetic origin (*see* Chapter 9, page 141) and will do no more than again stress that no species of animal, domestic or wild, anywhere on earth is free of hereditary disease. Most puppies derive immunity from their mother to some of the major infectious diseases which used to plague dogs. This maternal immunity, however, is of varied strength and durability. It begins to decline as the process of weaning progresses and is likely to have disappeared altogether by the time puppies go to their new homes. This leaves puppies in a vulnerable state, facing stress which increases their vulnerability and the prospect of meeting infections to which they may have little resistance. Those most worthy of note are distemper or hard pad, as it is still sometimes called; hepatitis which is also sometimes called Rubarth's Disease; the two forms of leptospirosis – the impossibly named icterohaemorrhagiae and canicola; the relatively recent arrival on the scene, parvovirus, in both its forms; and the troublesome but usually less severe tacheobronchitis or kennel cough. Unless politicians resist ideological and short-sighted economic pressures to lower British defences against rabies, it might soon be necessary to include rabies in this list but Britain is now free from rabies, thanks to our strictly applied quarantine regulations. All these are highly infectious or easily transmittable and potentially deadly but, fortunately, all can be avoided by the timely use of protective vaccines with almost 100 per cent certainty.

Canine Distemper

Canine distemper is a viral disease which is often complicated by bacterial infection. It is readily transmitted by infected animals and has an incubation period of about twenty-one days. Signs of what may appear to be a cold, runny nose and eyes, high temperature, bronchial breathing, lethargy, diarrhoea and vomiting herald the onset of distemper. As the disease progresses the dog may develop fits or become partially paralysed, and these symptoms may persist even if the dog recovers. The pads of the feet may become hard and thickened, hence the name hard pad. Throughout the dog is highly infectious and should be kept in strict isolation. Prevention is far better than cure and any dog which has received the necessary protective vaccines, given, depending on the type used and the particular circumstances, at from six to twelve weeks of age and periodically boosted thereafter, can be expected to be fully protected.

Infectious Canine Hepatitis

Infectious canine hepatitis is another highly infectious viral disease, with an incubation period of about six days, which rapidly extends its hold over infected dogs. Early signs might consist of loss of appetite, fever, vomiting, diarrhoea, pale gums, stomach pains and a jaundiced tinge to the eyes. Dogs which recover from the disease may remain infectious for some months and, in some cases, for life. Once more, protection is provided by timely vaccinatioin, preferably carried out at the earliest possible age.

Leptospirosis Canicola

Leptospirosis canicola, also called Stuttgart Disease, is transmitted by contact, direct or indirect, with infected or carrier animals including humans. The incubation period may be as short as five days or as long as a fortnight. Early signs include high temperature, severe thirst, stomach pains, bloody diarrhoea and vomiting. Dogs which recover may have incurred kidney damage which will create problems in later life.

Leptospirosis Icterohaemorrhagiae

Leptospirosis icterohaemorrhagiae, also, and more conveniently, called Weils Disease when it infects humans (as is nowadays more frequent with the increased popularity of water sports), is transmitted by the urine of infected rats. Contaminated food or drinking water, or sporting excursions which bring the dog into direct contact with rats are the major sources of infection. Symptoms are similar to those of leptospirosis canicola except that jaundice may be more pronounced. In both cases early vaccination and regular boosters provide good protection.

Canine Parvovirus Infection

Canine parvovirus infection (CPV) is a disease which in the late 1970s extended its range to include dogs. Having no natural immunity to this new threat and no protective vaccine being available, they succumbed in their thousands. Infection may be direct or indirect, often being transmitted on the clothing of those who come into contact with infected animals. The incubation period lasts about five days. Myocarditis is a form of parvovirus which attacks the hearts of young and apparently previously healthy puppies which, as maternal immunity declines and they become more active, may suddenly collapse and die. If any puppies in a litter die in this way the entire litter should be treated as suspect and be examined for cardiac damage by a vet before any are sold. Fortunately, this form of the disease seems to be becoming less frequently met with.

The form of parvovirus which attacks the intestines, producing a thin, watery but blood-infused, almost explosive diarrhoea, is capable of killing a young puppy within hours but can be effectively treated, though patients may remain stunted and infectious. Vaccination of breeding bitches may help to maintain maternal immunity and early vaccination of puppies should provide adequate protection. If this is allied to strict kennel hygiene, preferably using one of the newly developed parvocides (unlike less specific disinfectants these will kill the virus), and the isolation of young nursing mothers and young puppies from any members of the kennel which, at exercise or, more particularly, at shows may have been in contact with infection, the problem can be kept at bay.

Kennel Cough

Kennel cough is a disease or, more accurately, a group of diseases, which show themselves in the form of a troublesome, persistent and highly infectious cough. This can be very debilitating to young puppies, old dogs or those which are not otherwise in good health. Its prevalence from late spring to early winter coincides, perhaps significantly, with the most intense part of the show season. A vaccine is available which offers protection against some of the agents which cause the disease and offers worthwhile protection for a dog which is likely to come into close contact with many others.

Early vaccination along with strict attention to hygiene, avoidance of likely sources of infection, scrupulous disinfection after visits to shows or veterinary surgeries and constant vigilance will help to ensure that none of these diseases can carry out their ever-present threats. However, should they occur, veterinary treatment should be sought without delay. Some can kill in a matter of hours, as we have said, while others leave permanent damage which timely treatment may prevent.

A dog which is suffering from or has been in contact with any infectious diseases should not be taken to dog shows or to any other places where dogs are likely to congregate. Every exhibitor at shows run under Kennel Club rules signs a declaration which says that 'the dogs entered have not contracted or been knowingly exposed to any infectious or contagious disease during the six weeks prior to exhibition and I will not exhibit them if they incur such risks between now and the day of the Show'. Failure to comply with the terms of the declaration could lead to an exhibitor being banned from shows.

Parasites

Other problems which a young puppy may face result from parasite infestation, and, once more, good kennel management will usually provide adequate protection. Parasites can be subdivided into those which live within their host, endoparasites, and those which live on it, ectoparasites. The latter will seldom be a problem until puppies leave the protection provided by a clean and well-run kennel but endoparasites, in their many forms, can easily be imported into even very well-run establishments. In recent years a number of endoparasites new to Britain have made their appearance to create problems for dog owners. Although those most likely to be encountered are still roundworms and tapeworms, we must now also be aware of hookworms, whipworms and lungworms. The subject of roundworm infection, the notorious *Toxocara* and *Toxascaris*, receives regular and, usually, sensational press attention. It seems to us to be not without significance that the very few reports of damage resulting from *Toxocara* seem invariably to occur among new dog owners while those who share their homes with a dog and spend their lives among dogs seem not to incur damage. The discovery that a quarter of samples of soil taken from London parks were found to contain roundworm eggs or larvae caused a considerable furore. The fact that all of the samples taken from beaches were infected with various strains of salmonella, some of them virulent strains, provides a telling comparison in attitudes and priorities. It is a simple fact that salmonella poisoning represents a far greater threat to health than do roundworms which, in any case, are not present in well-cared-for dogs.

Toxocara canis A round, creamy white worm from 3 to 6 inches (7.5–15cm) long which is especially active in pregnant and nursing bitches and young puppies. Worms can be picked up from infested dogs or from the excreta of infested dogs. Severe infestations in young puppies can be debilitating and may even result in fits and death. A typically pot-bellied appearance, a harsh, poorly conditioned coat, bad breath, diarrhoea, a peculiar straddling movement and a general debility are all signs of roundworm infestation. Breeding bitches should and can be kept free of worms by means of a regular worming routine with one of the many, and constantly improving, vermifuges. Puppies, which can be born with infestations, should be wormed first at a fortnight old, at fortnightly intervals until they are three months old and at six-monthly intervals for the rest of their lives. Such a regime, using the best of the modern products, will ensure that roundworm is not a problem. Beware, though, of importing infestation on second-hand equipment, by giving hospitality to infested dogs or by contact with infested dogs outside the kennel. Routine worming, scrupulous attention to hygiene and sensible quarantine precautions for any new animal introduced to the kennel will keep risks at a minimum.

Toxascaris leonina Similar in appearance to *Toxocara canis* but seldom transmitted from bitch to puppies. Owners need not concern themelves about the difference between the two because control of *Toxocara canis* will also effectively control *Toxascaris leonina*.

Dipylidium caninum This is a tapeworm which can measure as much as 20 inches (50cm) but is most often seen in excreta in the form of small segments which appear almost as grains of rice. General debility, poor condition, slow growth rate in puppies and suscepti- bility to infection are the major problems resulting from infestation. The worm is passed on by fleas which carry tapeworm eggs. Control of fleas is, therefore, essential to the elimination of tapeworm. In- fested individuals should be treated with an appropriate vermifuge. *Dipylidium* is also to be found in our own species who can, therefore, infect and be infected by dogs.

Taenia This is a tapeworm which can grow to 10 feet (3m) in length, deriving from eating infected meat, usually offal. Control consists of the avoidance of infected food and regular worming.

Echinococcus granulosus A small tapeworm derived from eating infected meat, usually the uncooked offal of sheep or deer. Infestation eventually produces hydatid cysts in its hosts, including man, which can be life threatening. Any dog which is exercised over land on which sheep or deer graze should be wormed regularly. Sheep or deer meat should be well cooked before being fed to dogs.

Hookworms These worms were first noticed in Britain in Grey- hound kennels. Diarrhoea and anaemia and often dermatitis on the feet, especially between the toes, are indications of possible infes- tation. Treatment with an appropriate vermifuge and strict attention to hygiene offer effective means of control and elimination.

Whipworms   These are about 2¾ inches (7cm) long with a narrow fore end and a bulbous rear. There are no obvious signs of whipworm infestation other than occasional dark diarrhoea. Again, Greyhounds seen to be the most frequently affected breed. Treatment is problematical.

Lungworms   Minute worms which produce a harsh, dry cough and subsequent loss of condition. There are no effective vermifuges, and surgery may be necessary to remove severe infestations.

The list may seem long and awe-inspiring but, apart from a rare exception, all endoparasites and fungal growths are easily controlled by means of careful attention to hygiene and regular treatment with the appropriate vermifuges. Do not expect to see worms if you use the more modern treatments; no longer do they merely kill worms, they also digest them and the time is probably not far off when the best vermifuges will be capable of killing larvae and eggs and providing residual toxicity which will prevent reinfestation.

Skin Diseases

Skin diseases, which come in a multitude of forms, are perhaps the most common health problem encountered by dog owners. Incidence will be considerably reduced by vigilance, regular grooming, cleanliness and correct diet but even then it is possible to import a problem from another kennel, show, exercise or work. One common characteristic of many skin problems is that they itch and the dog, by scratching to relieve the itch, may actually cause more damage than the problem itself. Some of them also regard man as a desirable environment. It is not uncommon to refer to skin conditions which are characterised by a patch of red, wet and often hairless skin as eczema. Properly speaking, the word describes a symptom, or rather a group of symptoms, and not a disease. Eczema may be produced by any one of several causes, including friction, perhaps from a collar, bandage or licking, parasites, allergies, infections and wounds.

Allergies

Allergies seem to be on the increase, perhaps because we nowadays make use of far more possible irritants in order to keep our homes clean. The widespread use of cleansing agents which are spread on carpets has resulted in an increase in allergic conditions. Dogs, like people, may be allergic to almost anything. Some plants, fleas and a wide variety of other things may result in allergic reactions which produce itching, consequent scratching, skin lesions and, so, eczema. Identification and avoidance of the allergen is, if possible, the best treatment.

Calluses

Calluses are pressure sores resulting from continual contact with some inhospitable surface, such as concrete. They usually appear on hips, stifle or hock joints and are a sure sign of an ill-kept dog. Older dogs, given insufficient bedding and not inclined to move for long periods, may develop calluses. Adequate bedding and friendly surfaces will avoid the problem. Treat by cleansing and the use of a lotion to soften the skin.

Cheyletiella

Cheyletiella, rabbit fur mite, is a parasite which looks rather like moving dandruff and causes mild itching, reddening of the skin, usually of the head, neck and back. It can be picked up from infested animals, domestic and wild, and equipment. Treatment by appropriate washes is simple and effective.

Demodectic Mange

Demodectic mange is also caused by a mite but one which is normally present on all animals, including ourselves, without causing problems. Some dogs, however, seem allergic to the mite's presence. Non-irritant skin lesions on the head and legs are usually the first signs of a problem. The lesions can spread rapidly and once generalised the prognosis is not good. Treatment, though improving, is problematical. The condition seems to be particularly prevalent in some breeds and within some strains of those breeds. It is possible that the lack of immunity to the presence of *Demodex folliculorum* is inherited, so dogs which have a problem should not be bred from without careful thought.

Dermanyssus Gallinae

Dermanyssus gallinae, red mite, often to be found on and picked up from poultry, causes intense itching. Heavy infestations can result in anaemia. Washes and disinfection of kennels, bedding and all contact surfaces solve the problem.

Hay Mites

Hay mites, *Trombicula autumnalis*, may be picked up, usually in autumn, from infested soil, vegetation or from hay or straw used as bedding. The mites are visible as red, pin-head-sized spots, usually between the toes and on the ears. Appropriate washes and attention to kennel hygiene readily control the problem.

Lick Sores

Lick sores are produced, as the name implies, by a dog's excessive licking of one part of its anatomy. The licking may be a pathological response to a life of boredom, to efforts to relieve soreness resulting from a wound or infection, or to some deeper-seated pain.

Sarcoptic Mange

Sarcoptic mange, also called scabies, causes intense irritation, usually of the soft areas of skin on the inside of thighs and under the belly. The resultant scratching often causes more damage than the mites themselves. Veterinary treatment to kill the mites should be supported by destruction of bedding and thorough cleansing of kennelling. Sarcoptic mange is easily transmitted from dog to dog and from foxes to dogs which come into close contact with foxes or the places they inhabit. In the past, hunting has been suspended in some countries, because of outbreaks of mange among foxes and consequent outbreaks among hounds and terriers. Any terrier worked regularly to fox should be washed regularly in a lotion which will deter infestation.

Ringworm

Ringworm is not a worm at all but a fungal growth which is characterised by roughly circular patches of scaly skin and hair loss. The condition can be picked up from other infected animals, including wild and farm animals, and can be transmitted to or by man. Topical treatment is usually effective but care should be taken to cleanse thoroughly any places in the home or kennel which may harbour residual spores capable of causing reinfection.

Once more the list may seem awe and itch inspiring, but in practice, most infestations, given regular grooming, vigilance, timely treatment and cleanliness, are seldom a major problem.

Hair loss may also be caused by non-irritative disorders resulting from hormone imbalance. Some bitches are inclined to shed, partially or wholly, a small patch of coat over their kidneys when they have recently been in season. The problem usually clears up without treatment as hormone balance is restored.

Thyroid deficiency results in poor, scanty and brittle coat. The skin may become thickened, darker than normal and less flexible. Thyroid deficiency is also associated with obesity, general dullness and irregular heat cycles resulting in a loss of fertility. The condition is familial and may be inherited. Treatment consists of hormone therapy.

Eye Problems

The eyes are not only one of the most delicate organs of the body but are also one of the most exposed and vulnerable. Since the eyelids are essential to the proper functioning of the eye, though not actually part of the eye itself, we will include them in this section.

Distichiansis

Distichiansis is a congenital condition produced by the growth of an extra row of lashes which abrase and irritate the cornea. Surgery is needed to remove the superfluous growth.

Entropion and Ectropion

These are two conditions produced by defective eyelids. In entropion, the eyelid is rolled inwards and causes the lashes to abrase and irritate the cornea. Ectropion results in the eyelids rolling outwards to expose haw, the mucous membranes of the eye. Both conditions can be corrected by surgery and are inherited. Dogs which have had surgery to correct these conditions may not be shown and should not be bred from.

Conjunctivitis

Conjunctivitis, commonly called pink eye because of the characteristic red and inflamed condition of the lining membrane, may be caused by infection or irritation. Dogs working in loose, dry sand may develop pink eye unless their eyes are well cleaned afterwards. A dog allowed to stick its head out of the window while a car is in motion may also develop conjunctivitis. Eye lotions and washes suitable for human use will cleanse the eye and relieve irritation. In severe cases veterinary advice should be sought.

Sometimes a puppy may not open its eyes at the usual time. This may be the result of a type of conjunctivitis, which can be relieved by gentle bathing with a suitable lotion.

It is essential that the eyes are continually lubricated by secretions from the tear ducts. Occasionally, especially in older dogs, these become blocked. *Keratoconjunctivitis sicca* causes the eyes to become dry or produce a thick mucous discharge. Without continual lubrication, conjunctivitis will quickly develop. Bathe the eye with an appropriate lotion and, if the condition persists, minor surgery to restore the flow from the tear ducts may be necessary.

Epiphora

What may be regarded as the contrary condition is epiphora or watery eye which is the product of a blockage in the ducts which drain the eyes. This may result from infection or a congenital condition. Flushing of the ducts or minor corrective surgery may be necessary.

Keratitis

The cornea is the clear, central part of the eye and may be assailed by a variety of problems. Keratitis is an inflammation of the cornea and may result from a variety of causes. The cornea first becomes dull and then, as the condition progresses, opaque. Superficial keratitis may be the result of injury. The eye will be painful and will react against light. Infectious keratitis is the result of infection. Both conditions require veterinary treatment. Blue eye, another form of keratitis, is frequently a symptom of hepatitis infection which often clears spontaneously. Vascular keratitis is caused by degeneration of the blood vessels in or growth of pigment over the eye, often caused by chronic irritation. Removal of the irritant usually clears this up.

There are also a number of diseases, some of which are inherited, associated with the inner eye. Cataracts which reduce, perhaps totally, the transparency of the lens and so cause blindness, are seen as a milky haze behind the pupil. Hereditary cataracts have been found in Fox Terriers and in some dogs described as Jack Russell Terriers. Cataracts resulting from degeneration caused by age can be surgically removed and at least some sight restored. Other diseases of the inner eye include Progressive Retinal Atrophy (PRA) in which the cells of the retina are subject to progressive degeneration leading first to a loss of vision in subdued light. Hence the name 'night blindness'. The disease may not appear until the dog is five or six years old by which time it may have produced affected offspring. Central Progressive Retinal Atrophy (CPRA) is closely related to PRA but tends to affect vision of stationary objects. All hereditary eye conditions can be controlled only by regular screening to identify sufferers and possible carriers. Withdrawal from breeding of all infected and carrier stock will control the incidence of the disease.

Ear Disorders

In discussing ear problems, which thankfully seem both less numerous and less serious than eye problems, we will again ignore anatomical exactitude and deal with the ear flap and the inner ear as a single entity. As with any other health problem, prevention is preferable to cure. Do not forget to inspect the ears as you groom your dog. Remove any hair or foreign material which is likely to

*An effective Elizabethan collar to prevent a dog from scratching a
damaged ear or eye can easily be made out of a plastic carton.*

cause irritation. Clean any dirt or excessive wax out with some soft,
clean material but do not be over-zealous. A coating of wax helps to
keep the ear in good condition. Bacterial and fungal infections, as
well as infestations of ear mites, may all be treated with proprietary
medicines. Carefully place a small drop in the entrance to the ear
canal and by means of gentle massage encourage further penetration. Without this, the dog will rid itself of most of the lotion as it will
shake vigorously as soon as the treatment is complete.

The ear flap is thin, and vulnerable to violent encounters with
thorns or strong undergrowth or a dispute with a fox or another dog
may result in a tear which requires stitching or a smaller problem
which needs no more than basic first aid. If the wound becomes infected, as a result of inadequate cleansing or because a foreign body
is lodged in the flap, a Haematoma, the classic thick ear, may
develop. Veterinary attention to drain and clean the swelling is
recommended. In order to allow healing it may be necessary to make
use of an Elizabethan collar, useful also to prevent a dog from
scratching any part of the head.

Deafness may, in dogs as in people, result from the degenerative process of age but the condition seems more often to be encountered in white breeds than others. A puppy which is born deaf will obviously not respond to sound stimulus but it may be some time before this is noticed. The breeder is then faced with a decision as to whether the puppy should be culled or placed in a home where its disability is given sympathetic understanding. The pattern of inheritance seems not to have been studied and care should be taken to avoid breeding from dogs which have produced deaf puppies.

Nose Disorders

The nose and the air passages to which it gives access are not often a source of problems in Jack Russell Terriers. The breed is, as elsewhere, constructed normally and so avoids the breathing problems which are associated with abnormally short-faced breeds. Very occasionally, a puppy, particularly one which has been born before full term, may be born with the opening between the hard palate and the nasal cavity not totally closed. After suckling there will be a discharge of milk from the nose and the puppy may breathe noisily. Usually the condition rights itself within a few days. If it does not, a minor operation will correct matters. Sometimes the same condition may be created when a dog, through age or injury, loses its canine teeth or has a major injury to its mouth. Once more, surgery is the necessary corrective. Irritants in the nose may induce a bout of sneezing but generally dogs do not suffer from minor colds and snuffles. A runny nose is often a symptom of some major health problem, distemper or a similar illness, and should be a cause for real concern.

Teeth, Mouth and Jaw Problems

Occasionally, milk teeth may be retained beyond their proper time and can then push the permanent teeth into faulty alignment. When this occurs the milk teeth should be removed by a vet. A complete adult mouth contains six incisors in the upper jaw (these are the small teeth at the front of the mouth) flanked by a pair of canine teeth. Behind each canine are four premolars and, behind them, two molars. In the lower jaw there are again six incisors and a pair of canine teeth, four premolars on each side and three molars. Given normal wear and tear, the cusps of the middle incisors will show signs of wear by the time a dog is about eighteen months old. At two and half years they will be worn flat, after another year the cusps on the middle incisors will also be worn flat and at four and a half years the cusps of the intermediate incisors will be worn flat. By the time the dog is six years old the canines will begin to show signs of wear.

In Chapter 8 we have stressed the importance of regular inspections of the mouth and teeth to ensure that all is in good health. Dogs' teeth, particularly those which chew bones or are called upon to work for a living, undergo considerable wear and tear. If the dog begins with a full set of well-placed, strong, large teeth it is more likely to escape problems than is one which has irregularly spaced or faultily aligned small teeth. Any indication of discomfort, drooling, pawing at the mouth or reluctance to eat, suggests that dental attention might be needed. The most common problems are singivitis, produced by food trapped between teeth which feeds bacterial growth and leads to a diseased gum, and periodontal disease in which, unless treated, abscesses may develop and the tooth may be lost.

Drooling from the mouth is often an indication of anxiety or anticipation but may also be a symptom of tooth or throat pain, poison or some other problem. Some dogs suffer from travel sickness and may drool or be sick when on a journey. They may also be inclined to drool if given tranquillisers to prevent sickness.

Mandibular osteopathy is a condition found in some of the Scottish terrier breeds in which excessive amounts of bone material are deposited on the lower jaw. It can be prevented but cannot be treated effectively. It appears to be familial and is likely to be inherited but has not, as far as we know, appeared in any Parson Jack Russell Terrier.

Digestive Disorders

The mouth and throat are the gateway and vestibule to the digestive tract which consists of the oesophagus, stomach, duodenum, small intestine, colon, rectum and anus. At various places along this complex chain the pancreas, gall bladder, kidneys and liver make their own contribution to the digestive process. The most obvious signs that something may be amiss with the digestive tract is a refusal to eat or, having eaten, consequent vomiting. Dogs vomit readily and so are often able to rid themselves of ingested material which may otherwise cause a greater problem. Once the stomach has been cleared of food a frothy liquid may be brought up. This is suggestive of gastritis. If a dog vomits sporadically and is listless and out of sorts it may be suffering from worm infestation, diabetes or some other cause of chronic gastritis.

If blood appears in the vomit, either fresh or in the form of dark congealed grains, there is reason for concern. Ingestion of anti-coagulant poisons may be indicated by bloody vomit. Fresh blood suggests a rupture of the lining between the mouth and the small bowel. The rupture may be caused by a foreign object, an ulcer or a tumour. If blood is partly digested it is more likely that the problem lies further down in the stomach or duodenum. Projectile vomiting is suggestive of a blockage in the upper gastrointestinal tract but may also be induced by brain injury or tumours. There should be no delay in seeking veterinary advice should any of these conditions appear.

Vomiting may also be induced by motion, as in car sickness, or by fear or excitement, perhaps at a thunder storm or some major disturbance in the home or surroundings. A vet might prescribe a mild tranquilliser but do not expect a dog which has been tranquillised for a car journey to give of its best at a show.

Gastric Dilation

Gastric dilation, commonly and descriptively known as bloat, is a condition usually associated with large dogs and, as far as we are aware, not recorded in Parson Jack Russell Terriers. However, since it results in death in a matter of hours, even if treated promptly and expertly at best it offers a gloomy prognosis. Bloat appears to be the product of rapid eating of too much or unsuitable food which produces gas in the stomach, leading to distention and twisting. Pain is extreme and the animal swells rapidly and visibly. Prompt veterinary treatment is imperative if the animal is to have a chance of survival. Apart from being associated with large and, often, deep-chested breeds, bloat tends to appear in dogs over two years old, is twice as common in males than females and is associated with the ingestion of dry foods, followed by exercise or drinking large amounts of water. There may be a prior history of digestive problems and some familial association. The lessons are obvious. Dogs which are greedy eaters or which have a history of digestive trouble should not be fed dry food and should not be exercised after meals.

Diarrhoea

Diarrhoea is the passage of frequent and soft motions, of which the causes are legion. Indications of the cause may be found in the colour, consistency, smell and frequency of motions. Yellow or green stools suggest a bowel problem, black stools may be produced by bleeding in the upper digestive tract, bloody stools by bleeding in the lower tract. Light colouration suggests liver disease and grey inadequate digestion. A watery stool suggests bowel irritation, possibly caused by poisons or infection. Foam suggests bacterial infection and a greasy stool suggests malabsorption. A stool which retains the smell of the original food is indicative of malabsorption or overfeeding. A putrid smell suggests intestinal infection. Frequent motions, two or three an hour, suggest inflammation of the large bowel, colitis, while two or three times a day suggests malabsorption, a small bowel disorder or overfeeding.

Diarrhoea is a symptom and not, in itself, a disease. Treatment consists of identifying the cause and taking appropriate action. The most common cause of diarrhoea in dogs, especially in puppies, is a change of diet or water. Change cannot always be avoided but, with care and planning, can be kept to a minimum. No anthropomorphic nonsense or commercial pressure should persuade a dog owner to vary a diet which is known to be satisfactory. Diarrhoea may also be caused by unsuitable food, toxic substances, food allergies, irritants and obstructions. In most cases, identification of the cause and its removal or future avoidance is all the treatment needed but if the cause cannot be readily identified or the diarrhoea is associated with other symptoms, as for example in parvovirus, veterinary advice and treatment should be sought.

Constipation

The opposite of diarrhoea, perhaps, constipation is the inability to pass motions. Constipation may be caused by a diet deficient in fibre or liquid or which is high in calcium. Once the cause has been identified, milk, a frequent cause of diarrhoea, or raw liver can be given as a laxative and the appropriate action taken to prevent recurrence of the problem. Impacted material can be relieved by use of an enema.

Coprophagia

It is normal for dams to eat their puppies' stools, and other dogs may take part in this delectable task if they are given the chance. Dogs may also eat stools passed by herbivores, from which they may acquire fibre or other material in which their diet is deficient. However, the term coprophagia is properly confined to eating their own or another dog's stools. Ideas vary as to the cause but we would tend to favour boredom as the most likely.

The digestive tract ends in the rectum and anus, both of which may become sore after protracted bouts of constipation or diarrhoea. Soreness may produce scooting, where a dog will rub its anus along the ground. Scooting is often said to be a sign of worm infestation and so it may be because worms cause anal irritation, but so do other things. Insect bites, soreness, anal infections should all be considered. The anal glands, which lie slightly below and on either side of the anus may become filled and infected, especially in dogs whose diet is deficient in fibre. Treatment is simple, if unpleasant. Take the tail (here is another reason for having a good hand hold) and lift the anus. Then pinch the anus from below and squeeze upwards towards the anus. The material in the anal sacs will then be projected through the anus and the task is complete.

The liver, which synthesises proteins and sugars, removes wastes and toxins from the blood and produces enzymes, is perhaps strictly not a part of the digestive tract but nevertheless can be dealt with as such. Malfunction of the liver causes jaundice which, in dogs, is seen as a yellowing of the eyes and gums and a darkening of the urine. Among the sources of liver problems are hepatitis. leptospirosis, poisons, deficiencies of vitamin B, cancers, cirrhosis or heartworm infestation. Treatment is dependent on veterinary diagnosis.

The pancreas, again perhaps not strictly part of the digestive tract, produces insulin and digestive enzymes. Symptoms of pancreatic problems are increased appetite and increased intake of water coupled with a marked loss of condition and weight. Advanced cases may result in loss of appetite, dehydration, laboured breathing, lethargy, coma and death. Malfunction may result in diabetes mellitus, sugar diabetes, which is treated by means of dietary control and injections of insulin. Diabetic dogs often also suffer from cataracts.

Respiratory Problems

Breathing is, obviously, necessary to sustaining life. Parson Jack Russell Terriers are not heir to any of the problems which are often visited upon the brachycephalic breeds and so avoid the worst breathing problems which are likely to arise. Such problems as do arise are likely to be the result of injury or obstruction or to be the symptom of some other ailment or the result of excessive heat.

Inhaling sand and debris while working below ground can cause irritation or blockage, resulting in noisy or difficult breathing or in irritation, causing a cough. Blockages must be removed quickly and expertly; minor problems can be treated with small quantities of children's cough medicine. Veterinary advice should be sought if the condition worsens or does not disappear quickly.

Coughing spasms, especially after exercise or at night, may indicate heart disease. A prolonged cough may suggest kennel cough (*see* page 241) which should be treated by a vet and can be prevented by the use of the appropriate vaccine. It is highly infectious, though not a life threatening condition, except to old dogs and puppies. Bronchial or lung infections which result in coughing require veterinary treatment.

Heart Problems

The normal pulse rate in dogs varies from about 70 per minute in very large dogs to about 80 per minute in small ones. The pulse is more rapid in young or unfit dogs than in older, fit ones. It is also more rapid after exercise and when the dog is under stress, whether pleasurable or not. The pulse can be taken by feeling the heartbeat just behind the left elbow or in the groin. A stethoscope will enable more accurate tests to be made, and a dog breeder can soon learn to differentiate between the sound made by a healthy heart and that made by one which is abnormal in some way. As with people, physical fitness plays a major part in the health of the heart. An obese dog or one which gets too little exercise is far more likely to get cardiac problems than one which leads a more frugal and vigorous life. Some heart problems are, however, familial and may be inherited. These certainly occur in working terrier breeds and there is no reason to suppose that the Parson Jack Russell Terrier is necessarily exempt. Skilful use of the stethoscope will reveal the existence of problems in puppies and appropriate action can then be taken.

Neurological Problems

Neurological problems are most likely to be the result of injury, illness or parasite infection. Fits, especially those associated with hysteria, were once a fairly common result of dietary deficiencies but need no longer be encountered. Fits with other causes remain to haunt us. In young puppies, heavy worm infestations are a likely cause while in older dogs poisons or head injuries may also cause fits.

Epilepsy produces recurrent fits of a characteristic type. At their mildest they may be seen as nothing more than champing or chewing and a dazed expression but at their worst may result in temporary paralysis or coma in which the limbs remain active. Epilepsy can be triggered by excitement. It is incurable but can be controlled by medication. The condition or a predisposition to it is probably inherited. Epileptic dogs should not be worked and must not be bred from.

The body is supported by the skeleton which itself is the potential source of a number of problems. In some terriers, erroneously described as 'Jack Russell' Terriers, there is a marked tendency for the bones of the limbs to be abnormally shortened and bowed. In extreme cases, the condition is associated with dwarfism in which the head is enlarged in relation to the rest of the body and the voice is shrill. No such dog can be regarded as a Parson Jack Russell Terrier.

16

Accidents Will Happen

Even Parson Jack Russell Terriers which are not called upon to work for a living may at some time in their lives meet with accidental injury. Just as the home is the most dangerous place for people to be, in terms of the frequency of injuries, so it is also a dangerous place for dogs. Care in storing and using materials which may injure a dog, supervision, and anticipation of its likely actions will all help to reduce the likelihood of accidents. A knowledge of basic first aid might be sufficient to treat a slightly injured dog or to prevent one which has been more seriously injured from becoming worse and so is a useful skill for caring dog owners to acquire. The sort of materials and equipment normally to be found in any reasonably well-equipped home first-aid kit are all that may be needed and these can, in an emergency, often be supplemented by things usually to be found in the home. If injuries are not obviously slight or are of unknown extent the first action should be to call or get to a vet. When a vet has been called, treatment to relieve suffering or prevent deterioration to the dog's condition can be applied.

Dogs which have been injured may seek to bite the source of the pain or those who try to treat them. A muzzle made from adhesive tape, or a tube made from a plastic bottle, fastened by tapes to the dog's collar or the foot of a stocking may serve the same purpose. A dog trapped in a painful situation may also attempt to bite. A coat slung over its head while release is achieved may prevent injury to the rescuers.

Dog Fights

Parson Jack Russell Terriers do not usually start fights, though they will not go to great lengths to avoid them and once involved may give every indication of having a jolly good time. There is a voluminous and imaginative literature about fighting dogs and a huge variety of recommended ways, mostly ineffective, of separating them. Lighted cigars placed on tender parts of the anatomy, pepper, snuff, fingers thrust into orifices, buckets of water, loud noises, ringing bells, the offer of food and many more – all have their various disciples. The Parson seems to have been a believer in choking the assailant and biting its paw, at least that was how he separated Jock and Tartar. Choking the assailants can be effective but anyone who puts their face close enough to a fighting dog in order to bite its paw would need to be every bit as rash as was the Parson.

Supposing that you have two fighting dogs, try to keep calm – the two dogs are already highly excited and any additional excitement or noise is only likely to increase their aggression. The next thing to do is to insist that any bystanders keep their distance. Spectators seem to arrive from nowhere when dogs fight and some seem to enjoy taking a hand, and indiscriminately belabour either or both with any weapon which happens to be at hand or by kicking them, under the pretext of separating them. Such actions are likely to cause more injury than the actual combatants and to increase the aggression of both. Do not attempt to pull fighting dogs apart; all you will then do is use your very considerable weight and strength to cause far greater injury than the dogs could, if left to their own devices. If they are well matched for size they are unlikely to cause one another great harm quickly. You have time to assess the situation and to decide on appropriate action. One traditional and usually effective method of separating fighting terriers is to hang the pair over a fence, wall or gate so that one is on each side. Without their feet on the ground they will be unable to release their holds, either to get a better grip or to take a breath, which last you can make more necessary by pinching the dogs' noses and thus closing their nostrils. Once they have fallen to the ground, your purpose is achieved, providing that you move quickly enough to prevent a resumption of hostilities. If no suitable place is at hand to hang the assailants over, ducking their heads in water may do the trick. Even fighting dogs have to breathe and to do so they must release their holds. Once parted you only have to move more quickly than they do in order to prevent a resumption of the fight.

Convenient walls or tubs or water may not always be readily available, in which case you must rely on your own resources. If the two dogs are wearing collars these can be twisted to choke the dogs and so achieve the same effect as immersion in water. If they do not have collars choking the pair with your hands, which requires a surprising amount of strength, will achieve the same result. If one dog is larger than the other you may need a foot over its neck to immobilise it and achieve the desired result. Vigilance and proper training will prevent most fights from even starting. Only very occasionally will two terriers harbour an intense dislike for one another and fight at any and every opportunity. Youngsters may sometimes try their strength against others in the kennel but, once they have established their place in the pack, will then desist from further fighting. Sometimes bitches coming into season will become quarrelsome and separation for the duration is the only course. Most fights, though, are caused by people who produce the conditions in which fights are liable to start by disturbing the pack's social hierarchy, through their own nervousness or inability to impose their will, creating jealousy and excitement.

Stings, Bites and Wounds

Dogs may also be bitten by other than their fellows or by their quarry. They may be bitten by insects, or by snakes. Bees are the only insects which leave their stings behind to continue to pump venom into the victim. They should be removed as quickly as possible, not by pulling them out, which simply and effectively injects all the remaining venom into the wound, but by scraping with a finger-nail or knife blade. Then, as with all insect bites, treat with a paste of baking powder, relieve swelling by the use of ice packs and use calamine lotion to relieve itching. Keep a watch for allergic reactions, increased swelling, rapid breathing and drowsiness. If these are seen veterinary help must be sought. In Britain, only the adder, among our few reptiles, poses any serious threat, though toads, if mouthed by a dog, may secrete an irritant substance which is mildly but not dangerously poisonous. A dog bitten by an adder may be in extreme pain; it must be restrained and the bite isolated by the use of a tourniquet. The wound should be opened by using a knife or razor blade and the blood sucked from the wound. The dog should then be quietly carried to a vet, who can inject a specific antidote.

It has been said, not without some justification, that a dog's tongue is its best medicine. Once minor cuts and grazes have been cleansed they will often be kept clean by the dog itself or even by a solicitous companion. Only if attention to the injury becomes excessive need the owner do more than maintain a close watch over the healing process. For deeper injuries something more is needed. Bites, particularly punctures as distinct from tears, can be difficult to cleanse thoroughly and, by healing from the surface may trap foreign material which later suppurates to cause infection. Any deep or extensive wound should be treated by a vet. Deep cleansing, a few stitches with the dog sedated and a shot of antibiotics can save a lot of subsequent problems and speed the healing process considerably. Get the dog to the vet as quickly as possible, having applied whatever bandaging is necessary to keep the wound clean and to staunch bleeding. During the course of a terrier's work it is very liable to get injured. Good terrier men carry a basic first-aid kit with them. A roll of bandage, adhesive tape, cotton wool and disinfectant carried in a sealed plastic bag do not take up much room but can be invaluable if a dig should go wrong.

Poisons

Apart from indications of pain, a dog may also show other signs which depart from normality. It may, for example, vomit. Dogs do not suffer from our own inhibitions and so are able to vomit readily. They may do so after grazing on herbage without the slightest cause for alarm, providing it is known that the plants were not covered with some toxic insecticide, herbicide or fertiliser. Nowadays we often tend to sprinkle poisons quite indiscriminately round our gardens and even our homes. Dog owners should give thought to what they or others put on plants to which their dogs may have access. A number of common garden, house and wild plants are, to some degree, poisonous and, although dogs usually have the good sense to avoid them, this is not invariably the case. Ivy, delphinium, daffodil, foxglove, larkspur, wisteria, horse chestnut, yew, privet, rhubarb, green potatoes, buttercup, some fungi, and numerous other plants and trees are all poisonous.

Dogs will often eat grass or other plants; we have one at the moment which is very fond of sedum, as was her mother. She seems to eat it for nothing more than enjoyment and, since we have long since decided that any ambition to maintain an immaculate garden is incompatible with keeping dogs, we accept the slight damage which her taste causes. Others seem to enjoy soft fruit, especially rasp-berries and blackberries in season. Again there seems to be no good reason to curb their enjoyment. More frequently, though, dogs may

261

Emergency Treatment for Poisoning

POISON	SOURCE	SYMPTOMS	EMERGENCY TREATMENT
Strychnine	Vermin poisons	Tremors, intense pain, seizure	Induce vomiting, avoid noise, veterinary treatment imperative
Metaldehyde	Slug bait	Excitement, drooling, tremors	Induce vomiting, treatment imperative
Warfarin	Rodent poisons	Blood in saliva or motions, etc.	Induce vomiting, intra-muscular vitamin K
Ethylene Glycol	Anti-freeze	Vomiting, debility, incoordination	Induce vomiting, give coating material, veterinary treatment to prevent kidney damage
Petrol	Fuels drunk or inhaled	Vomiting, gasping, tremors, coma	Vegetable oil by mouth, artificial respiration
Garbage		Diarrhoea, sickness	Induce vomiting, antibiotics
Toads		Drooling, sickness	Wash mouth, induce vomiting

graze grass. This gives rise to all manner of theories – a sign of worms or even an instinctive attempt to rectify some dietary deficiency. It is more likely that some dogs just enjoy eating grass but we might also remember that dogs are carnivores and that carnivores are not animals which eat meat, they eat other animals, usually grazing animals, and these carry quantities of partly digested herbage in their stomachs. Perhaps a dog which grazes a lot is simply doing its best to satisfy a taste and need for some vegetable matter in its diet. Perhaps they eat the grass in order to make themselves vomit in order to ease some digestive problem. The owner should address this by means of a changed diet or feeding regime. More roughage in the diet and more frequent, smaller meals seem to be indicated. It is not a matter which need cause alarm providing that the grass is un-polluted and that no toxic plants have been eaten.

However, dogs may also vomit in an effort to rid themselves of some unpleasant substance, to ease a blockage or as a symptom of some disease. The observant and thoughtful owner will recognise the difference and take appropriate action. If a dog has eaten any poison he must be made to vomit. A small piece of washing soda pushed down its throat will quickly do the trick. Then Milk of Magnesia, milk, egg whites or vegetable oil to coat the bowels, bind with the poison and induce evacuation further limit the effects of the poison.

Far more dangerous than naturally occurring poisons are those which we distribute about our homes and gardens. The metaldehyde and arsenic contained in slug pellets, sodium fluoroacetate and warfarin used for killing rodents, phosporus to be found in fireworks and outdoor candles, ethylene glycol found in anti-freeze, paint strippers, cleaners, fuels of many kinds – these are all poisons. The most dangerous ones are those which are deliberately made palatable and attractive to other creatures and those which are inherently attractive such as anti-freeze.

Foreign Objects

A foreign object stuck in the throat or stomach will often cause vomiting. Plastic toys or cooked bones, especially poultry bones, are perhaps the first thing which vets expect in such circumstances but all manner of things might be swallowed by accident or as a result of some neurotic compulsion. It seems only sensible to ensure that dogs are not given plastic toys or small bones or, indeed, anything else which can be swallowed and is indigestible.

Trapped in a Car – Dehydration

The other major problem induced by the actions of careless or thoughtless owners is caused by leaving dogs locked in cars or, less often, in other confined spaces or even in an unshaded concrete run. In recent years, car parks at summer events have been patrolled by welfare officers in order to ensure that dogs are not left locked in cars and some owners have faced prosecution for cruelty. Even in relatively cool weather a car standing in the sun can become uncomfortably warm for its canine prisoner. On anything like a warm day it can rapidly become dangerously warm and could, quite literally, cook the occupant alive. If a dog does get overheated it should be cooled by any means. Immersion in cold water, being sprayed with a hose pipe or the application of ice packs will all help to bring its temperature down. If the body temperature has not climbed beyond 104 °F (40 °C), at which stage breathing will be noisy and laboured, the tongue and mucous membranes suffused with blood, the saliva thick and glutinous and the dog liable to vomit, cold water applied externally may be adequate treatment. If the temperature has risen to or beyond 106 °F (41 °C), at which stage the dog will be unsteady on its feet, may be in a state of collapse, and may have produced blood-suffused diarrhoea, a cold water or ice enema is likely to be required to bring the temperature down before death intervenes. Prevention is far better than cure.

A dog confined in a warm run or kennel without water or in some other dry, warm situation or one which has been suffering from diarrhoea may have its body fluids reduced to the point at which it becomes dehydrated. The skin will lose elasticity (if the skin on the skull is pinched it will remain in a crease), and collapse will be followed by coma and death. Drinking water may be insufficient to restore bodily fluids, and it may be necessary for a vet to put the dog on a drip. Treatment for mild cases or in an emergency should consist of the offer of electrolyte solutions of salt and glucose. If these are refused they should be squirted into the mouth.

Trapped Underground – Hypothermia

A dog working underground, particularly in loose or sandy earth, may find itself buried by a fall of loose earth, as a result either of mischance or, more likely, enthusiastic but unwise digging operations. The dog may be unconscious before it is recovered and will die unless treated immediately. Find the pulse or heartbeat to ascertain that the dog is still alive. Remove any obstructions from the mouth and throat, clear away any secretions and then place the dog on a flat surface on its right side. Place both hands on the chest and press firmly but not too strongly. Release the pressure quickly and repeat the process about twelve to fifteen times a minute. You should be able to hear air being drawn into the lungs as pressure is released, and expelled when pressure is applied.

Alternatively, use mouth to nose resuscitation. This is less likely to injure ribs or aggravate already injured ribs. The dog may be laid on your knee, again with the right-hand side downwards, the mouth and throat cleared and the tongue pulled forward. Then close the mouth and keep the muzzle firmly closed while air is blown into the nose for two or three seconds. Wait for the air to be released and repeat. When the dog recovers consciousness it should be kept warm and quiet.

Working terriers do most of their work in winter and often in very cold, wet conditions. A dog which is trapped underground may become hypothermic as a result of a fall in its body temperature. Signs are violent shivering, lethargy and apathy, eventually collapse, coma and death. The dog should be wrapped in a warm coat, and one which contains residual heat by having been taken off someone's back is ideal. Reflective aluminium kitchen foil is a useful addition to an emergency kit. The dog should be dried and rubbed vigorously with a dry towel to promote circulation. If a lukewarm bath or lukewarm bottles, hair dryer or an electric blanket are available these too can be pressed into service to help restore normal body temperature. Reddened and swollen ears, toes and scrotum may indicate the presence of frostbite. The areas should be warmed gently, and an antibiotic cream applied. Once consciousness is restored, the dog may be given a stimulating, warm – but not hot – drink of glucose or honey and water.

Burns and Scalds

Burns and scalds are best treated first with ice packs to reduce the heat and relieve pain, then gently dried and covered with an impervious and sterile material to exclude air. Transparent kitchen film is ideal. This should be fastened in place, though care should be taken to ensure that fastenings do not aggravate the injury. Chemical burns should be washed as quickly as possible under running water. Acid burns may be neutralised by the use of a solution of baking powder and alkali burns by the use of well-diluted vinegar. The burn should then be dried, treated with antiseptic and protected from infection.

Hypoglycaemia

Some dogs may become hypoglycaemic as a result of violent exertion, especially those with a tendency, no matter how slight, towards being diabetic. The condition is most likely to be found in long dogs but we have seen it in terriers being raced on a hot afternoon as well as in terriers enjoying a day after rabbits. The dog may seem confused and disorientated, it may stagger and even collapse. If he is conscious sugar, candy or honey will quickly restore the dog to normality. If the dog is unconscious, solutions of glucose, honey or sugar dribbled down its throat will help restore the lost blood sugars. The dog should then be kept quiet and an early opportunity taken to see if it is diabetic.

17

Keeping it Legal

It may sometimes seem that the laws which impose restrictions on
dogs and their owners have all come into existence during the last
few years. In fact, there have been laws controlling dog ownership,
the type of dog which could be owned, and the use to which dogs
might be put and the places to which they might be taken, for at least
a thousand years in Britain. Nor can it be said that the recently
enacted laws are any more unreasonable than were some of the old
Forest Laws. Unreasonable some may well be but it has to be
appreciated that they often represent a response to the unreasonable
behaviour of a minority of dog owners.

The law relating to dogs and to dog ownership may not be an ass
but there may well be times when it appears to have unusually long
ears and others when it seems to be in a mess with a number of
different Government departments sharing different and sometimes
conflicting responsibilities. Some of these are of doubtful value and
efficiency; others, though, are of vital importance. The unnecessary
complexity of these laws makes them difficult for owners to understand and, therefore, to comply with. They are, as some feckless
owners, breeders and dealers have discovered to their cost, thus
made much less effective than is desirable but there are times when
they can be very effective indeed.

When purchasing a puppy or a dog the rule is *caveat emptor*, let the
buyer beware, but this does not mean that the buyer is without
substantial rights which are intended to protect all purchasers. A
buyer who purchases a dog for a particular purpose, for show or
work, may establish an implied warranty from the vendor that the
dog will be suitable for its intended purpose simply by stating
particular requirements. Nevertheless, the buyer should obtain a
written warranty that the dog is fit for that purpose. The vendor
must ensure that pride or some other less praiseworthy tendency
does not lead him or her into making exaggerated and unwarrantable
claims for the dog. It is, for example, impossible to say that an eight-

267

week-old puppy will become a champion, that it will even be fit to show or will work; all that can honestly be claimed at that age is that it is a healthy, well-bred puppy with potential to do these things. Equally, it is impossible to say that a dog will breed champions, even if it has done so in the past. All that can be said is that it has the potential to do so. Claims which expose the vendor to subsequent action at law may be made directly to the buyer or indirectly in advertisements. An advertisement which says that puppies 'will make excellent workers' or are 'sure to win' are ill advised for the vendor and should be treated with suspicion by the buyer. Under the 1979 Sale of Goods Act, protection for the purchaser is provided by requiring that the vendor has a right to sell the animal, that the animal is reasonably fit for the purpose which the buyer intends, and that the buyer reveals the existence of any charges or encumbrances at the time of sale. A buyer should be satisfied that all these require-ments have been met before parting with any money.

An inaccurate pedigree provided with the intention to deceive constitutes a criminal offence of obtaining money by false pretences and is thus a particularly serious offence. In the past, falsification of pedigrees was difficult, though not impossible, to prove. However, as a result of improved genetic knowledge, particularly in the realm of genetic finger-printing techniques, it is a simple matter to verify, with absolute certainty, the parentage of any puppy and so to provide evidence which is acceptable in court. Furthermore, court cases have, in the past, accepted the evidence of genetic experts that puppies of a certain colour could not have been produced by the alleged parents. Official recognition also means that Kennel Club records are available as a further check on malpractice, while the Kennel Club would itself proceed against anyone found to be falsifying pedigrees.

A few cases have already appeared before the courts in which breeders have been called upon to answer for the existence of hereditary disease in the dogs they have sold. The situation is not, as yet, absolutely clear but it does seem that if a breed is known to harbour some particular hereditary problem and a breeder does not take such reasonable steps as are available to check his breeding stock for the existence of that problem, he may be at risk if he sells a puppy which is shown to have inherited the condition. The breeder will remain at risk throughout the life of every dog he sells. It is even possible that a breeder who sells a potential show puppy which eventually turns out to have inherited a problem would be at risk of legal action if it were known that the puppy's parents had previously produced offspring with the same problem. The same principle applies to all inherited conditions, and even ignorance of the condition's previous existence might not provide an adequate defence if it could be shown that the breeder could and should have known of the condition.

The complexity of existing laws relating to the sale of goods, including dogs, and the various liabilities they impose on dog owners make it prudent for every dog breeder to ensure that they are covered by adequate insurance. Nowadays, a number of insurance companies offer special policies tailored to their particular needs which offer cover against the costs of illness for a period after the dog has been sold and against claims made by people to whom the dogs have been sold. Selling dogs without adequate insurance cover is most unwise.

What purport to be Parson Jack Russell Terrier puppies are sometimes offered for sale from the backs of cars and vans at working terrier shows. Only a very foolish person would ever consider buying a puppy from such a source and no show organiser with a genuine concern for animals would permit the practice but nevertheless the practice is not unknown. Under the 1951 Pet Animals Act it is an offence to offer animals for sale in a public place. If it was successfully argued in defence that the point of sale – the boot of a car in a show car park – was not a public place, there would be a need to demonstrate that the car boot complied in every respect with the conditions set out in the Act to control pet shops which in turn would produce a need to establish that the car boot was a properly licensed pet shop. Such a defence could not hope to succeed. Furthermore, a show organiser who allows such practices may find himself implicated and one who accepts a fee for allowing puppies to be sold in this manner would certainly be implicated.

Having bought your Parson Jack Russell Terrier, different laws and regulations become applicable. The responsibilities incumbent on any dog owner do not end with care for the dog itself or even for the breed as a whole. Responsibility, enforceable at law, extends very much further and it is as well that every owner is fully aware of all the legal responsibilities. Especially so, perhaps, for those who own a breed which can be of an independent nature and which is agile and active. If a Parson Jack Russell Terrier is of a mind to enjoy an independent expedition it takes a very good fence to deter it; yet the owner may remain responsible for its activities and depredations throughout this expedition, and these could turn out to have ruinously expensive consequences unless the owner is fully insured and has not, by careless behaviour, invalidated the terms of the insurance. There are a number of insurance companies which offer cover against all manner of difficulties into which a dog owner may fall. At their most basic these consist of third party insurance, often provided through a block policy held by the breed club, which should be regarded as a necessary minimum level of cover. It is possible also to get cover against vets' fees for illness or accident, death by illness or accident, the recovery of costs incurred should a dog be lost, the cost of caring for the dog should its owner be unable to as a result of illness, and legal costs, excluding fines, arising out of prosecutions under the Animal Act 1953 or the Dogs Act 1871.

At law a dog, being a domestic animal, is regarded in the same light as is any other possession. A dog may be regarded as being stolen if it is taken and held without the owner's consent. If a stolen dog is resold, offences such as obtaining property by deception and receiving stolen goods may have been committed.

The owner of the dog or its keeper as, for example, the owner of a boarding kennel, is strictly liable for any damage caused by the dog. Damage may include injury or death or any impairment of the physical or mental well-being of other animals, whether domestic or farm animals, as well as of people, whether resulting directly from the dog's actions, as in the case of a bite, or less directly as in the case of a car accident. An owner or authorised keeper must take *reasonable care* to prevent his or her dog from straying, though precisely what constitutes reasonable care may be the subject of argument in court. A dog which habitually strays cannot be said to be in the hands of an owner who takes reasonable care to prevent it from straying. One which had strayed previously may also expose its owner to action at law, unless the owner has taken steps to prevent it from doing so again.

If a dog does stray on to the roadway and is hit by a vehicle and injured, the driver of the vehicle must stop and any witness with reasonable grounds for doing so may require that the driver provides his name and address. In any case, the driver must, within twenty-four hours, report the accident to the police. Failure to do so will constitute an offence.

A dog may commit a trespass if it strays on to land without the owner's permission. If, while on that land, the dog injures or kills livestock which has a right to be there the dog's owner will be liable

Beware of the Dog – a warning or an admission?

and may be fined and have to pay compensation. The owner of livestock is entitled to shoot a dog which strays into enclosed land containing livestock which is at risk because of the presence of the dog. It is not necessary to show that the dog was attacking the livestock but only that its presence, as in running through a flock of pregnant sheep, was likely to cause loss or injury. If a dog is killed, the matter must be reported to the police within forty-eight hours. It should also be remembered that rural magistrates are more likely to be far more sympathetic to their fellow farmers than to the owners of stray dogs.

Liability extends even onto the owner's property so that anyone who keeps a dog which is known to bite, and a notice on the gate 'Beware of the Dog', may be argued to give indication of that knowledge. If the dog bites someone who enters the premises in the normal course of business, a postman for example, the owner may find himself or herself accountable at law.

Some owners of Parson Jack Russell Terriers may need to know the conditions in which game may be taken legally. Few, for example,

271

seem aware of the fact that a licence is required by anyone who uses a dog to search for, pursue or kill game. This includes rabbits and hare as well as various birds. They may also need to know something of the law which relates to trespass in search of game and to the illegal taking of game which does not involve trespass, in other word to poaching, particularly of rabbit, hare and fox. They may also need to be aware of the particular laws which relate to protected species such as badger and otter.

It is an offence, punishable by fine or imprisonment or both, to disturb, injure or kill any protected species and it is no defence, as some terrier owners have found to their cost, to claim that they thought they were in pursuit of fox or some other unprotected quarry. It is an offence, under the Game Acts, to take or kill hares on Sunday or on Christmas Day or at night whether with permission or not. Hares may only be taken by the owner of the land or with his written and witnessed permission. Rabbits may be taken by day or night, by the owner of the land or with his permission at any time. They may not be taken on heath or moorland except by or with the permission of those who may hold common rights. They may not be taken without permission at any time.

Anyone intent on taking game without permission should be aware that the 1971 Criminal Damage Act allows a dog to be killed, by someone other than its owner, if by doing so that person honestly believes that the game can thereby be protected. Hare would certainly be regarded as game in this context but the position of rabbit and fox is less certain. Dog owners should also be aware of the fact that some statutory and other bodies, such as the National Trust, the Forestry Commission and the National Parks may be in a position to enforce prohibitions, which override laws and bye-laws generally applicable, against disturbing, worrying or chasing animals whether game or not. The situation has recently become even more complicated as a result of terrier owners being fined for causing unnecessary cruelty to their dogs by working them to fox. Whether this case is likely to form a precedent for future prosecutions is not yet known. Dog owners should also be aware of a campaign which is intended to prevent dog owners from allowing their dogs to run freely over moorland on which ground-nesting birds may be disturbed.

From time to time the popular press make sensational, and usually inaccurate copy out of incidents in which dogs are alleged to have infected people or other dogs with disease. If your dog has an infectious or contagious disease you can certainly be held responsible for damage and injury if you allow the dog to come into contact, at a show or in boarding kennels for example, with others who may contract the disease. You will also be guilty of fraud if you knowingly sell a sick dog without revealing the existence of the disease. You should also take note of the fact that the declaration signed by all exhibitors at shows run under Kennel Club rules lays down conditions about showing dogs which have been in contact with infectious or contagious disease in the period prior to the show. No similar restriction is usually imposed by hunt or working terrier shows but this would not negate legal restrictions.

The 1973 Breeding of Dogs Act is, though perhaps one of the best intentioned, one of the least satisfactory of the laws which relate directly to dogs. It requires that the owner of any premises on which two or more bitches are kept with the intention of breeding puppies for sale should apply to the local authority for a licence for which the authority can charge an undefined fee and impose undefined conditions. However, since the Act does not give the licensing authority the right of entry, unless an application for a licence has been made, its effect is easily avoided. Dogs are of no interest to the Act, neither are bitches which are spayed or which are either too old or too young to be bred from. It could even be argued that an owner cannot be said to have the intention of breeding from a bitch until the bitch has been mated. Proving intent would otherwise be very difficult. It has also been argued, by some breeders, that their primary intention is to produce a puppy or puppies for themselves and that the sale of puppies is incidental to this main purpose. They cannot be said to be producing puppies for sale. The success of such a defence would depend on the scale of the operation. For example, someone with five bitches who bred a litter only every two or three years might use the argument with some confidence while another with two bitches which were bred from at every season would find it difficult to do so.

The absence of a national fee scale allows local authorities to set their own fee and this may not only be deliberately punitive but may also be associated with an inspection fee intended to add still further to the cost. Such authorities deliberately use the Act's inadequacies in order to prevent people from following a perfectly legitimate hobby. But perhaps the worst aspect of the Act is that it does not require that inspectors have the sort of knowledge which will enable them to make a proper assessment of the way in which dogs are being kept. Far too often Health Inspectors whose skills and preoccupations do not equip them to assess the suitability of kennels or kennel regimes are used in preference to veterinary surgeons. As a consequence, some breeders, having applied for a licence, find themselves having to comply with unnecessary, unreasonable and even eccentric conditions. They might also find that the issue of a licence is taken as evidence of the existence of a business, in which case the authority may invoke other powers to re-rate the premises as a business or to demand a planning application for change of use. The Breeding of Dogs Act has achieved little of its original and laudable purpose but has produced needless harm and concern.

Dog breeders should be very careful about providing accommodation for dogs belonging to other owners. To do so may bring them within the scope of the 1963 Animals Boarding Establishments Act even if boarding is not carried out as a business. The Act may apply if dogs not belonging to the owner of the premises are regularly provided with accommodation. What is regarded as regular may be subject to local variations. Those who may provide accommodation for dogs other than their own as, for example, bitches which may be visiting a stud dog or dogs which are to be shown, should, even if they do not charge for the service, beware the effect of the Animals Boarding Establishments Act. Those who intend to embark on a business which involves boarding dogs should take expert advice before they make any commitments.

It is not always easy for dog owners to appreciate that there are people who dislike dogs in any and every situation. Fond owners may even find it difficult to accept that their dogs may be the source of what the law would regard as a nuisance. Dogs may create nuisance by excessive or untimely barking, by offending standards of hygiene or by being out of control on land owned by private, national or local bodies. In order to prevent nuisance they may be banned from certain places, which nowadays include areas of beach, parks and premises to which their owners may wish to gain access. The proliferation of local bye-laws takes a succinct review of the current situation well beyond the scope of this book but it is well to remember that all these bye-laws respond to a nuisance which is, whether real or merely perceived, the product of the behaviour of irresponsible dog owners.

Finally, law-abiding owners of Parson Jack Russell Terriers may wish to be aware that it is an offence to wash a dog in any British Waterways Board Canal other than the Gloucester and Sharpness Canal.

Appendix 1

WHELPING TABLE

DATE OF SERVICE
DATE OF WHELPING

JAN 1 2 3 4 5 6 7   8   9 10 11 12 13 14 15 16 17 18 19 20 21 22 23 24 25 26 27 28 29 30 31
MAR 4 5 6 7 8 9 10 11 12 13 14 15 16 17 18 19 20 21 22 23 24 25 26 27 28 29 30 31 1 2 3   APR

FEB 1 2 3 4 5 6 7   8   9 10 11 12 13 14 15 16 17 18 19 20 21 22 23 24 25 26 27 28 - - -
APR 4 5 6 7 8 9 10 11 12 13 14 15 16 17 18 19 20 21 22 23 24 25 26 27 28 29 30 - - -

MAR 1 2 3 4 5 6 7 8 9 10 11 12 13 14 15 16 17 18 19 20 21 22 23 24 25 26 27 28 29 30 31
MAY 2 3 4 5 6 7 8 9 10 11 12 13 14 15 16 17 18 19 20 21 22 23 24 25 26 27 28 29 30 31 1   JUN

APR 1 2 3 4 5 6 7 8 9 10 11 12 13 14 15 16 17 18 19 20 21 22 23 24 25 26 27 28 29 30 -
JUN 2 3 4 5 6 7 8 9 10 11 12 13 14 15 16 17 18 19 20 21 22 23 24 25 26 27 28 29 30 1 -   JUL

MAY 1 2 3 4 5 6 7 8 9 10 11 12 13 14 15 16 17 18 19 20 21 22 23 24 25 26 27 28 29 30 31
JUL 2 3 4 5 6 7 8 9 10 11 12 13 14 15 16 17 18 19 20 21 22 23 24 25 26 27 28 29 30 31 1 AUG

JUN 1 2 3 4 5 6 7 8 9 10 11 12 13 14 15 16 17 18 19 20 21 22 23 24 25 26 27 28 29 30 -
AUG 2 3 4 5 6 7 8 9 10 11 12 13 14 15 16 17 18 19 20 21 22 23 24 25 26 27 28 29 30 31

JUL 1 2 3 4 5 6 7 8 9 10 11 12 13 14 15 16 17 18 19 20 21 22 23 24 25 26 27 28 29 30 31
SEP 1 2 3 4 5 6 7 8 9 10 11 12 13 14 15 16 17 18 19 20 21 22 23 24 25 26 27 28 29 30 1 OCT

AUG 1 2 3 4 5 6 7 8 9 10 11 12 13 14 15 16 17 18 19 20 21 22 23 24 25 26 27 28 29 30 31
OCT 2 3 4 5 6 7 8 9 10 11 12 13 14 15 16 17 18 19 20 21 22 23 24 25 26 27 28 29 30 31 1 NOV

SEP 1 2 3 4 5 6 7 8 9 10 11 12 13 14 15 16 17 18 19 20 21 22 23 24 25 26 27 28 29 30
NOV 2 3 4 5 6 7 8 9 10 11 12 13 14 15 16 17 18 19 20 21 22 23 24 25 26 27 28 29 30 1 DEC

OCT 1 2 3 4 5 6 7 8 9 10 11 12 13 14 15 16 17 18 19 20 21 22 23 24 25 26 27 28 29 30 31
DEC 2 3 4 5 6 7 8 9 10 11 12 13 14 15 16 17 18 19 20 21 22 23 24 25 26 27 28 29 30 31 1 JAN

NOV 1 2 3 4 5 6 7 8 9 10 11 12 13 14 15 16 17 18 19 20 21 22 23 24 25 26 27 28 29 30
JAN 2 3 4 5 6 7 8 9 10 11 12 13 14 15 16 17 18 19 20 21 22 23 24 25 26 27 28 29 30 31

DEC 1 2 3 4 5 6 7 8 9 10 11 12 13 14 15 16 17 18 19 20 21 22 23 24 25 26 27 28 29 30 31
FEB 1 2 3 4 5 6 7 8 9 10 11 12 13 14 15 16 17 18 19 20 21 22 23 24 25 26 27 28 1 2 3 MAR

Appendix 2

Club Submission to the Kennel Club

In its submission to the Kennel Club the Parson Jack Russell Terrier Club set out the arguments which, it was hoped, would persuade the Kennel Club that recognition should be granted. That document is now of historical as well as intrinsic interest. It is reproduced below.

The Parson Jack Russell: the Working Fox Terrier, unchanged in Type and Carefully Bred for over a Century

In the view of the Parson Jack Russell Terrier Club, recognition by the KC is in the best interest of the breed, for the following reasons:

1. The need for a central registry keeping accurate records.

Because the breed is not recognised officially, the name Jack Russell can be used with impunity. This has led to a situation in which many purchasers, in particular those from abroad, have paid high prices (£400–£500 is by no means uncommon) for small terriers which do not conform to the Breed Standard. This leads to a lack of trust in *all* breeders in this country.

2. Recognition of the breed in other countries.

One result of the dissatisfaction felt by enthusiasts in other countries is that breed clubs have been established which are actively seeking recognition from their own Kennel Clubs. Obviously such recognition could itself have repercussions in this country, if registered Parson Jack Russell Terriers were to be imported and permission requested for them to be exhibited at KC shows.

3. The need to control inherited disease.

The Parson Jack Russell Terrier is a healthy, long-lived breed with few problems. However, the 'Jack Russell type' comes high in the list of problem breeds with a great many inherited defects. By granting recognition to the Parson Jack Russell Terrier, the KC would in effect be endorsing a healthy breed, and discouraging the perpetuation of such faults. As part of its programme for responsible dog ownership the PJRTC already encourages all members to have their breeding stock checked for hereditary eye disease. It is perhaps worth noting that, although lens luxation is regarded as a very serious problem in the 'Jack Russell', every pure-bred Parson Jack Russell Terrier so far tested has been found to be clear of this condition. Whilst the breed is denied KC recognition, however, those terriers which have been tested cannot be recorded under the KC/BVA scheme, and there is thus no official certificate of such testing.

4. Proposals to ban fox-hunting represent a threat to the very existence of the breed.

Conformation, temperament and working ability are inextricably linked. If opportunities to work are lost, the only incentive to breed the correct type is success in the show ring. Kennel Club recognition would give breeders of the Parson Jack Russell Terriers the opportunity, denied to them at the present, to compete not only in breed classes, but also against other breeds.

5. Access to a recognised disciplinary procedure.

The lack of recognition of the breed has enabled some people to indulge in practices which are at best doubtful, at worst downright dishonest. The members of the PJRTC are united in their condemnation of those practices. Yet without access to a centralised registration system and a recognised disciplinary procedure it is impossible to prove unacceptable behaviour, let alone prevent it.

By refusing recognition to the Parson Jack Russell Terrier and thus denying breeders access to KC facilities, in respect of registration, exhibition and health schemes, the Kennel Club, far from promoting the improvement of a pure breed, seems to be encouraging the excessive production of mongrels, which with a modicum of respectability (given by the unjustified use of a well-respected name) do little for the canine world in general, but add greatly to the already enormous problems of those organisations dealing with unwanted and stray dogs.

The case against recognition has been argued on several counts.

1. The breed has already been recognised in the Smooth Fox Terrier and the Wire-haired Fox Terrier.

Whilst it is undoubtedly true that these two breeds are descended from fox terriers of the type bred in the nineteenth century, they have changed considerably since that time. The Parson Jack Russell Terrier is the *original* version of these breeds. The recognition of the original many years after a breed has been recognised in its later form is not without a precedent – *vide* the Cavalier King Charles Spaniel.

2.   Some supporters of the breed do not wish for recognition.

This argument has little validity, since those using it are not, in fact, breeders of Parson Jack Russell Terriers. They have a vested interest in the various types of so-called 'Jack Russell' terriers and see official recognition of the Parson Jack Russell Terrier as a serious threat to their own credibility.

3.   The Parson Jack Russell Terrier is not sufficiently established as a pure breed.

The PJRTC keeps careful records, and only admits to its Foundation Register Parson Jack Russell Terriers of the correct type, and of known breeding over the last three generations. Exceptionally terriers of true type but unknown pedigree are admitted to the Foundation Register but only after they have proved their worth through their progeny. We submit that this is at least as valid as the present registration system for the Lancashire Heeler, which after eight years of KC registration still allows for dogs of completely unknown pedigree to be registered, without asking for the safeguard of progeny assessment.

Recognition would acknowledge the debt owed by the canine world to the work of the Revd John Russell ('the father of the Fox Terrier' according to Hugh Dalziel); it would enable a group of breeders, who are at present denied access to the Kennel Club's facilities to become part of the mainstream canine world; conversely, it would require of those breeders the same standards of behaviour and ethics that are expected of others bound by Kennel Club regulations; it would give a numerical boost to the Terrier Group at Kennel Club shows; finally it would give guidance, by the publication of the officially accepted Breed Standard, to overseas Kennel Clubs who are themselves very close to recognition of the most English of terriers.

In view of the above, the Parson Jack Russell Terriers Club asks that the Kennel Club should consider favourably their request for recognition of the Parson Jack Russell Terrier as a pedigree breed.

Appendix 3

Breed Standard

In 1989 the Kennel Club finally gave official approval to the Parson Jack Russell Terrier. An interim Breed Standard, which differs only slightly from that submitted by the Parson Jack Russell Terrier Club, was approved at the same time. This Standard will remain in force until such times as entries at championship shows rise to and are sustained at the level at which Challenge Certificates can be allocated to the breed. Any changes which may seem to be desirable will be considered at that time.

Parson Jack Russell Terrier
Interim Breed Standard

(Reproduced by courtesy of the Kennel Club).

General Appearance Workmanlike, active and agile; built for speed and endurance. Scars and injuries resulting from work or accident are acceptable unless working ability is impaired.

Characteristics Essentially a working terrier with ability and conformation to go to ground and run with hounds.

Temperament Bold and friendly.

Head and Skull Flat, moderately broad, gradually narrowing to the eyes. Shallow stop. Length from nose to stop slightly shorter than from stop to occiput. Nose black.

Eyes Almond shaped, fairly deep-set, dark, keen expression.

Ears   Small V-shaped, dropping forward, carried close to head and fold not to appear above top of skull.

Mouth   Jaws strong, muscular. Teeth with a perfect, regular and complete scissor bite, i.e. upper teeth closely overlapping the lower teeth and set square to the jaws.

Neck   Clean, muscular, of good length, gradually widening to shoulders.

Forequarters   Shoulders long and sloping, well laid back, cleanly cut at withers. Legs strong, must be straight with joints turning neither in nor out. Elbows close to body, working free of the sides.

Body   Chest of moderate depth, capable of being spanned behind the shoulders by average sized hands. Back strong and straight. The loin slightly arched. Well balanced, length of back from withers to root of tail to be equal to height from withers to ground.

Hindquarters   Strong, muscular with good angulation and bend of stifle. Hocks short and parallel giving plenty of drive.

Feet   Compact with firm pads, turning neither in nor out.

Tail   Strong, straight, set high. Customarily docked with length complimenting the body while providing a good handhold.

Gait/Movement   Free, lively, well co-ordinated; straight action front and behind.

Coat   Naturally harsh, close and dense, whether rough or smooth. Belly and undersides coated. Skin must be thick and loose.

Colour   Entirely white or with tan, lemon or black markings, preferably confined to the head and/or root of tail.

Size   Height ideally 35–36cms (14in) at withers for dogs and 33cms (13in) for bitches, but none should deviate more than 1in from these heights.

Faults Any departure from the foregoing points should be considered a fault and the seriousness with which the fault should be regarded should be in exact proportion to its degree.

Note Male animals should have two apparently normal testicles fully descended into the scrotum.

Further Reading

Cavill, David, *All About Mating, Whelping and Weaning* (Pelham Books).
Chapters by several reliable authorities cover most aspects of breeding in a practical and thoughtful manner.

Davies, E. W. L. *Memoir of The Rev. John Russell and his Outdoor Life* (Chatto and Windus)
First published in 1902, this is the first and still by far the best biography of Parson Jack Russell. The book is now difficult to find and is likely to become increasingly expensive but it is one which most owners would love to have on their shelves.

Edney, Andrew, *Dog and Cat Nutrition* (Pergamon)
No better book is available for those who want to know more about canine nutrition.

Evans, Jim and White, Kay, *The Book of the Bitch* (Henston)
A useful book with a wealth of information about all things pertaining to bitches. A very useful source of reference.
  The Doglopedia (Henston)
Ignore the excruciating title; this is an encyclopedic little book with a mass of valuable information. Well worth having on your bookshelf.

Fiennes, Richard and Alice, *The Natural History of the Dog* (Weidenfeld and Nicolson)
Domestic dogs have their origins in the wild which this book explores in a way which will interest all thoughtful owners.

Hobson, J. C. Jeremy, *Working Terriers, Management and Training* (Crowood Press)
An excellent and practical manual for all who are interested in any aspect of working terriers.

Horner, Tom, *Take the Round Please* (David and Charles)
In a class of its own, this book should be required reading for
everyone who aspires to judge.
  Terriers of the World (Faber)
Excellent on all the officially recognised terrier breeds but less good
on those which remained outside the official pale. The piece about
the Jack Russell, especially the illustration, is to be savoured!

Jackson, Jean and Frank, *The Making of the Parson Jack Russell Terrier*,
  (Boydell and Brewer)
Recognised as the definitive history of the breed.

Lucas, Jocelyn, *Hunt and Working Terriers* (Tideline)
First published in 1931 and recently reprinted, this book combines a
glimpse of a world which has now disappeared, with advice and
comments which remain relevant.

McKay, James, *The Ferret and Ferreting Handbook* (The Crowood Press)
An excellent manual which serves as an introduction to a very
enjoyable sport but which has also got plenty to interest those who
have already made a start.

Morris, Desmond, *Dog Watching* (Jonathan Cape)
Desmond Morris is as well known as a zoologist as he is as a TV
performer. This book answers a lot of the questions which puzzle
dog owners as well as a number they never thought to ask.

O'Farrell, Valerie, *Manual of Canine Behaviour* (British Small Animal
  Veterinary Association)
A book which offers an opportunity to know about and understand
the behaviour of dogs.

Plummer, Brian, *The Working Terrier* (Boydell and Brewer)
The author takes a very catholic but practical and interesting look at
working terriers.

Robinson, Roy, *Genetics for Dog Breeders* (Pergamon Press)
An introduction to a complex subject written from a practical
viewpoint.

Sandys-Winsch, Godfrey, *Your Dog and the Law* (Shaw and Sons)
A practical guide for all dog owners and especially for those who may accept responsibility for the care of other dogs.

Serpel, James, *In the Company of Animals* (Blackwood)
A thought-provoking book by one of the new breed of animal behaviourists.

Silvernail, Evelyn L., *The New Complete Fox Terrier* (Howell)
Covers the recent history of the Parson Jack Russell's two cousins and, though there is a concentration on American experience, provides food for thought.

Sutton, Catherine, *Dog Shows and Show Dogs* (K & R)
An encyclopedia which covers the world of Kennel Club shows from A to Z and back again.

Index